Alison,

I'm sorry I couldn't be there
for your birthday, but I'll see
you at your 60th! May this be
your best, most transformative
decade yet. And remember — live
light, travel light, and be the
light.   w/love,

Jim Shuella

3/5/19
San Miguel de Allende,
MX

A Curious Year in the Great Vivarium Experiment

Tim Shields

Halo
PUBLISHING
INTERNATIONAL

ISBN: 978-1-61244-623-3
Library of Congress Control Number: 2018904093

Printed in the United States of America

Halo Publishing International
1100 NW Loop 410
Suite 700 - 176
San Antonio, Texas 78213
Toll Free 1-877-705-9647
www.halopublishing.com
E-mail: contact@halopublishing.com

Author's Note: If I had my druthers, I'd call this "sensationalized nonfiction." While it is based on an external journey I took after my mother passed away, the "truer" part of this tale is the internal journey. I say "truer" because this too has at times been fictionalized to serve the story. That said, make no mistake—this book is a work of fiction, as are the characters depicted. The last thing I need is a public lashing like the one Oprah gave James Frey.

Now that we've gotten that out of the way and before we get started, I want to leave you with a question: What happens between sunset and sunrise?

Table of Contents

Dedication

For Therese M. Morrisroe and John B. Shields, for without the union of your love, this labor of love would never have existed. And for my friend and first mentor, Joe Whalen. I wish you were all still among us so I could properly celebrate with you your influences.

***

vi•var•i•um [vahy-**vair**-ee-*uh* m, vi-]
a place, such as a laboratory, where live animals or
plants are kept under conditions simulating their
natural environment, as for research.

***

Spirit brought me into the world.
The body carried me through the world.
And the mind sent me in search of the world.

~ *Thomas Furey*

PROLOGUE: SUNSET

Every time I walked into the Sunset Nursing Home, the smell of disinfectant awakened my olfactory sense to the reality before me. It reminded me of being a child at my grandmother's nursing home and the Catholic nuns who took care of her—an association I made to life in its final stage.

Like its inhabitants, the visitor's lounge at the Sunset had suffered the effects of time, turning once vibrant walls into an institutional shade of blue. In the corner of the room beside a box of tissue, a bouquet of plastic peonies poked its head out of a kitsch vase, and beneath my feet the industrial carpet wore the steps of time. Flowery prints in cheap plastic frames adorned the walls, and on a round table in the center of the room, beside another box of tissue, was a bowl of plastic fruit. It was late morning on a sunny day in mid-May.

Throughout the building, Caucasian nurses and Latino attendants pushed the fragile minds and worn-out bodies of men and women in wheelchairs while others shuffled about the hallways with empty, parking-lot eyes. The ones fortunate enough to ambulate announced their approach with shuffling, slippered feet. Others used walkers to make their way through the long corridors, and those who were unable to lift the walkers slid them across the floor on cut-out tennis balls affixed to the front supports.

Some of the healthier residents who still inhabited their consciousness beamed smiles at me in passing. One elderly woman who clearly still possessed her facilities said, "Aren't you a handsome young man." I smiled cordially in agreement.

"It's so nice you came to see your grandma," she added, ruining the sentiment. From the time I was a child, people were always mistaking my parents for my grandparents.

Each time I came to visit my mother, there were a few residents who scowled at me. They glared at me as if I was the thief who for years, night after night, returned to the scene of the crime, stealing such small amounts of their mind and health that they hardly noticed anything was missing until it was too late.

My sister, the main caretaker of my mother after my father passed away, tried to prepare me for what I would see. Her big heart—and even bigger emotional states—tended to lean toward the dramatic, but when my mother was wheeled into the room, it was far worse than I imagined.

"You must be Thomas. I've heard so much about you from your sister. You're the one from Seattle, right?" said a gentle nurse with an aura of compassion.

"Oh hi. Yeah...yes," I said, trying to pull my gaze off the withered figure in the wheelchair.

"I just want you to know, I've known your mother since she first arrived here. Some of the people at this home are the most miserable people in the world, but your mom always had a smile on her face, and up until she could no longer speak, she was always laughing and joking with the staff, always asking us about our families."

"That definitely sounds like her."

"It may not seem like she's there, but she is. Just talk to her how you normally would and tell her what you need to tell her. She can hear you. She's there, Thomas. Trust me."

There was nothing more I wanted to do than run out of the room and never look back, to forget this episode, to forget the last decade that witnessed her complete mental and physical deterioration, but instead I mustered the bravest face possible.

"Hi, Mom! It's so good to see you," I said, walking toward her, kissing her on her cheek, and giving her a gentle hug.

I could have broken her if I squeezed too hard. She weighed no more than eighty-three pounds, her head was supported by an extension of the wheelchair, and her clothes hung from her slight frame like a late-November scarecrow. The faint scent of urine told me her diaper had not been changed, and her gaunt face was covered in lesions, scabs, and dry, flaking skin. Her lip—purple, grotesquely swollen, and infected—was the result of a seizure she suffered three days prior when a medication mix-up caused her to bite through her lower lip. If ten years prior I had been transported to this moment in the future, I might not have even recognized her. She was not even a shadow of the mother who raised me.

I looked into her eyes and reached for her small, withered appendage, my hand enveloping hers like some giant from a fairy tale, only in this story I possessed no magical powers to make things right. As long as I live, I don't think I'll ever forget what her hand looked like—how frail, bony, and lifeless it was, the constellations of age spots, the large blue vein that ran down the middle of her hand and forked like a river, her yellowed fingernails long and unkempt. The only thing hinting at a familiar past was her wedding ring that rotated loosely between her knuckle and the rest of her hand.

Because her head was propped up by a support, it seemed as if she was staring through the ceiling. Whatever was behind her eyes was far away. I wanted to believe there was consciousness and recognition, that there was something behind the lifelessness and seeming absence of spirit, and that she wasn't in pain. I wanted to believe she was looking in supplication toward the heavens just as Saint Sebastian had for centuries in the Uffizi Gallery.

Then something miraculous happened. Her eyes came down from the ceiling and met mine. In that moment, for the first time in the last several years that I had been visiting her at the home, she lit up, and I recognized something familiar.

"Uuuuhhhhh…mmmmhhhhhh…fffgggggghhhhh…"

"It's okay, Mom. It's okay. It's me—Thomas, your baby," I said, leaping to attention while trying to hold back the tears. "I'm here. You don't need to speak. It's good to see you. It's really good to see you."

And I meant it this time.

For the past seven years, every time I flew across the country to see my mother, a little bit more of her was gone, and each time I came to visit her, it was not out of need or want but out of duty. Throughout my twenties and thirties, while my friends were vacationing in exotic places, I spent my vacations at assisted living facilities and nursing homes in New Jersey.

Since I was a child, my mother had written me beautiful cards for my birthday and holidays, always stating how proud of me she was, and when I went away to college, we began a letter correspondence. Like her outward appearance once was, she had beautiful, elegant handwriting. About midway through my college career, however, I started to notice how the words began to fall off the page like wooden barrels cascading over waterfalls. But I didn't think much more of it.

After college, we spoke on the phone several times a week, but at some point it turned into several times a month. Then once a month. Then she could no longer communicate. After my father passed away, she went to live in an assisted living home, and when they could no longer meet her growing needs, she was transferred to a nursing home. Sometimes I saw her twice a year, sometimes only once, but the leaps of mental and physical deterioration in between those visits were more than I could handle.

Sitting before me, as the silence of those years stretched out between us, a fountain of guilt came over me and I began apologizing for every way I may have ever wronged her in our thirty-six years together on earth—for moving away, for not coming to visit her enough, for taking her for granted, for not calling, for not writing, and so on.

She tried to speak.

I apologized.

She tried to speak again.

I apologized for not being able to understand her.

I swallowed over the lump in my throat, and in an attempt to keep the one-way conversation going, I said, "Hey Mom, check this out. Before I left home I found this letter you wrote me in October 1995. I was a sophomore in college."

Dearest Thomas,

I just wanted to drop you a line because you've been on my mind all day. I wanted to thank you again for calling me on my birthday. Talking to you for two hours was better than any gift I could have received, although I wish you could open up to me without the lubrication of alcohol or marijuana. You have such an active mind, sometimes too active. I really wish you wouldn't smoke that stuff. You may think it's not a big deal, but like anything you rely on as a crutch, it can become an addiction. Just know that fears about the future are natural. I pray every day that you stop worrying about the future and just enjoy your time in college. If I may give you some unsolicited advice, don't be in such a rush for the future. It comes all too soon and takes care of itself. You'll see.

I stopped reading, leaned in, and looked into her eyes, noticing for the first time in years the familiar yellow stars around her irises. Again I took her hand in mine.

"I know you're holding on for us, Mom, but it's okay to go. I know you're worried about us, especially me, but you don't have to worry anymore. Things are going really good for me. Sorry—really well. You see? Your grammar lessons paid off," I said, trying to bring levity to gravity.

"I know you know this, but I just want you to hear it from me. Just because you're moving on doesn't mean our connection is going to be lost. We're always going to be together. It's okay for you to go home. It's okay. I'm fine. Really. We're all fine."

It was the first lie of the day I told. Things, in fact, were not going good for me. They weren't even going well.

I continued reading.

I mentioned we went to Mass yesterday at a Franciscan Church. The priest was talking about depression and how people get overwhelmed with sorrow, etc. He wanted to reiterate that God never promised everything would go smoothly, that we would have no pain, or that the road would always be clearly marked, but He did promise He would always be there for us. I really and truly believe this, even though sometimes I too get overwhelmed and forget it for a time. You have a friend in God so try not to forget it. He gets you through the toughest times.

Love, Mom

By the time I reached the end of the letter, my facade had crumbled and I could no longer be the man I was trying to be. The lines about God echoed from innocent times past, times when I wasn't so lost, when I had direction, when I had faith, even if it wasn't necessarily the Catholic brand of faith she subscribed to.

The thought of those times when things were easier—when I didn't have to make decisions, when I didn't have to make a living, when the woman before me was healthy, when I could call her for advice or just to share good news—finally broke me, and I bawled hysterically.

"I'm so sorry you had to go through this, Mom. I'm so sorry," I said, my breath becoming shallow and short.

"It's so hard to see you like this. I can't handle it. I can't fucking handle it. I would've done anything to prevent you from having to go through this. I just don't know what to do. I want our time back. I want you back. I want to hear your voice. I want to hear you tell me it's going to be okay," I said, my face collapsing in my hands, tears streaming down my cheeks like rain on a windowpane.

Her eyes began to water as she desperately tried to speak. In that moment, I flashed back to being a six-year-old boy. I was with my mother at her mother's nursing home, and the same scene was unfolding. I remembered my gaunt grandmother in a wheelchair. As she fixated on a corner of the room, I looked on with a mixture of fear, curiosity, and compassion, all the while wondering what she was thinking about. I remembered her trying to speak, my mother holding her mother's hand and crying as I looked on with my Kermit the Frog doll in my arms. And I remembered how each time my mother and I visited my grandmother, my mother was in tears the entire ride home.

Despite my mother's condition, for the first time in years—as far as I could tell—she was present and we were connected, so I continued holding her hand for fear that if I let it go the circuit would be severed.

When I cried it all out, I wiped the tears from my eyes and reached for a tissue. Attempting to collapse the void that time and disease had placed between us, I began telling her about my life—what I was doing for a living and how I hadn't met the woman of my dreams yet, though I was praying for her to show up. I asked my mom to pray for me when she got to heaven and to keep an eye out for me. And then I told her how I went to church every Sunday, which was the second lie of the afternoon.

In total, I spent about three hours with her that day recounting the best memories of my youth—holidays, birthdays, vacations, how funny my father was, how much he loved her, and how devoted he was to her up until the end of his life. For once, I was the one doing all the talking.

While I couldn't wait to get out of the nursing home, I also didn't want to leave because I knew it was going to be the last time I was ever going to see her. I didn't want to forget her, but I didn't want to remember her this way either. I wanted to remember the healthy mom, but her disease clouded my memory of who she was when she was healthy—whenever that was—because it took years for us to accept the fact that she was slipping. *Oh, that's just Mom. She's just forgetful and sometimes she repeats herself,* we would say. There were clear signs though, the waterfall letters being the first. Then the shaking and the tremors.

During my soliloquy on my present-day life, what I hoped the future held for me, and how I was going to make her proud, the connection between us slowly faded like the radio station in a car being driven out of range. First static, then nothing. No other station to turn to.

With the minute hand inching toward 2pm, I pushed her wheelchair down a long corridor and into a room where other residents were being spoon-fed a porridge-like concoction. I parked her wheelchair in a line of withered people who were once healthy mothers, fathers, and grandparents, and once again I told her how much I loved her. In the far corner of the room, the drama of a daytime soap opera played out on a mounted television screen.

When our eyes met again, I felt her confusion. She gazed through me like I was a stranger hovering over her. I kissed her on her forehead, hugged her tiny frame, then kissed her on the top of her head. Swallowing over the lump still in my throat, I whispered in her ear, "It's okay, Mom. It's okay to go home. I love you and always will."

At the far end of the hall, the brilliance of the spring sun cast the glass exit doors aglow. I felt like a dead man walking. Upon reaching the exit and walking out into the sunlight, my eyes began to burn. But maybe that was just the feeling of walking away from what I knew would be the last time I would ever see my mother.

When I opened the door and turned the ignition in my sister's Subaru, Bob Dylan's "Bucket of Rain" began playing:

> Buckets of rain, buckets of tears,
> Got all them buckets comin' out of my ears,
> Buckets of moonbeams in my hand.
> You got all the love honey baby I can stand.

It was a surprisingly warm spring day, so I turned the air condition dial to high, placed my hands on the steering wheel at ten and two, and collapsed.

I'm not sure how long I was in that parking lot. The last time I cried that hard was six years prior, the morning I arrived in New Jersey from Seattle after my father passed away. Even though I knew he was gone, I kept expecting him to come out of his bedroom and say in his nasal, Bronx-Irish accent, "Good morning, Thomas. Can I start the bacon and eggs for you?"

What I remember most about that morning was how it seemed like someone hit pause on his life. His glasses remained on the piano, his Fordham Rams baseball cap was on the kitchen table, a bookmark in the Stephen Ambrose book he was reading denoted his progress, and an empty coffee mug on the sun porch bore a stained ring from the last cup of coffee he ever drank. It's so strange how life can be there one moment and gone the next, and all that remains is a picture frozen in time of one's pedestrian acts on the last day of their life.

After surveying the scene of his absence, I walked down the hallway and found my mother lying in bed beneath a statue of the Virgin Mary. There was a rosary draped over Mary's hands, and a dried, braided palm wreath from an Easter past surrounded the statue like a halo. My mother had barely moved in the two days since my father passed and was still wearing the nightgown she had on in the ambulance when he breathed his last breath.

As she sat in bed staring out the window, holding a mug of hot water in her hands, her face was expressionless— no hint of loss, joy, sadness, or suffering. When she turned to look at me, she smiled warmly and said, "Thomas, it's so good to see you."

I climbed into bed and into her arms. I wanted to comfort her, but instead—like she had so many times before when I was a child and my feelings were hurt or my knees skinned—she comforted me.

We cried together at what we had both lost.

Part I. Spirit

The seeker is he who is in search of himself. Give up all questions except one: 'Who am I?' After all, the only fact you are sure of is that you are. The 'I am' is certain. The 'I am this' is not.

I Am That – Sri Nasarga

Chapter 1. Cause and Introductions

Since we're going to be spending all this time together, and since you're going to be learning more about me than I'm even comfortable with, I suppose I should introduce myself. My name is Thomas. Thomas Furey. I was born with an enormous need for affection and a terrible need to give it. That's a beautiful line, isn't it? I wish I wrote it, but Audrey Hepburn said it. Nonetheless, if I had to write one line that's been the driving force of my life, that would probably be the one.

Thomas Furey, aka me (I don't normally introduce myself in the third person, but since we're just getting to know one another) is many things to many people, but in my relationship to myself I am an investigative reporter, and the story I've been trying to uncover is the story of my life. When my father passed away and my mother started to fade away, I began losing my most important trail of clues. When she died, the trail ran cold, so I decided I needed to take the investigation in a new direction. After all, you can only go down a dead-end street so many times.

Why must I take this story in a new direction? I suppose one could argue that the decision started when I woke up on the morning of my thirty-sixth birthday. On this fateful bright summer morning, I awoke jobless, full of anxiety, and without a committed relationship, or for that matter, any of the other accoutrements that I was "supposed to have" at that point in my life (or that all my friends seemed to have).

It didn't help that I had spent the previous two weeks in New Jersey for my mother's memorial service, dealing with all the facets connected to the finality of such a singular life event. I said goodbye to her in May, and not long afterward she stopped eating, spending her final weeks in hospice. As May gave way to June, on the other side of the country in Seattle, Washington, I busied myself, waiting for closure. June was especially long, and she finally passed away at the end of the month.

You see, I've spent the better part of the last decade watching my parents wither away—my father physically from the effects of radiation and lung cancer, and my mother mentally and physically from a long, protracted battle with Parkinson's disease, which you may or may not know sometimes comes with a side order of dementia. She was originally diagnosed with Alzheimer's, but at this point the details are irrelevant. Let's just say it wasn't pretty at the end, and for everyone involved—including her—the end was a slow, drawn-out, painful process.

The truth is, I'm a self-admitted mama's boy, and despite the fact that my mother had essentially been mentally gone for years, no matter how much you think you're prepared for a sick parent's death, you never are. When a parent dies, it's like a tornado or tsunami sweeps through your life, destroying your home and rearranging the landscape. Even if you try to rebuild, something intangible is lost forever.

During the two weeks I was home for the funeral, I felt as lost as I ever have been. It was the longest time I had spent in my hometown since I was eighteen, which means it was the most time I had spent there in just as many years. When I wasn't eating the prepared foods from friends or welcoming the distraction of visitors, I wondered what the fuck I was going to do with my life. To pass the time during those lost two weeks, I lounged during the day at the pool of a childhood friend.

"What's next?" Aileen asked, tipping a Corona to her lips.

"I've always felt I have this story in me that wants to get out."

"So, what's stopping you?"

"To begin with, I don't have any money, I don't have a job, and I don't know what the story is."

"You've got no responsibilities, and you no longer have to spend your vacations visiting sick parents. If you want to write, then find a way to do it."

"You make it sound so simple," I said. "There's this little problem you seem to keep overlooking. I'm broke and I don't have a job."

"If this story needs to come out and you believe in yourself, take out a personal loan to do it. Just go someplace cheap to live and write, like India. I heard Dharamsala is a great place for artists, creatives, and expats to do their thing."

"Where's that?" I said as I popped the cap off a perspiring beer.

"It's in the Himalayas. It's where the Dalai Lama and the Tibetan government are in exile."

India had never been in my consciousness as a destination, yet once the idea was presented to me, it began showing up everywhere—television shows, magazines, passing comments from people I'd meet, and even conversations with strangers, including taxi drivers.

I usually become paralyzed by life's smallest decisions, like what to order from a menu or where to spend my Friday night, but for some reason the biggest life decisions I make are impulsive. Because of my conversation with Aileen, I decided I was going to write a book. But what would the story be? *I know! I'll just take off and find it.*

Even if I needed to take out a loan, and even if the book never came to fruition, I was going to look at it as earning my M.L.E.—Master of Life Experiences. It was a completely irrational decision, but I was tired—tired of fighting and tired of the resistance.

My desire to write didn't stem from a need to share my pain with others or to seek fame and wealth. You don't become a writer to get rich. You do it because you have to. I needed to write because somewhere along the way it became my process, the way in which I tasted and engaged with the world. I needed to write because I sensed that in the midst of this creative process there was something inside of me waiting to be born. It was only through this exploration that I believed I could uncover the source of what I had come to know as my "soul ache."

I sensed that if I could get to the source of this ache, I could uncover a truth central to my life. Even more than a sense, there was a voice. Occasionally, in moments of stillness, it whispered to me, *If you can just pass through this and stop running from it, you will know freedom.* Unfortunately, those little whispers are easy to ignore, especially if the voice in your head is always yelling.

The soul ache I speak of felt like an otherworldly loneliness deeper than the Marianas Trench. It was a black hole that had its own gravitational mass. It was like standing outside a house party, watching the guests inside go about their night without a care in the world. All the while you're left wondering why you can't walk through the door. That's the short of it at least.

While I am aware that everyone suffers from bouts of loneliness, what I'm describing is not your everyday, run-of-the-mill, generic loneliness. I'm talking high-end, designer, haute-couture loneliness. And I can tell you this: It's been with me since my first moment of awareness when I found myself standing in my crib, screaming out into the void, wanting so desperately to be heard.

If I could have properly expressed myself in that tragic moment, I would have said, *I'm alone in this world and I've got a pile of shit in my diaper. Someday I'm going to have to deal with this shit myself.*

As my thirty-sixth birthday drew near, I was scared—scared that the loneliness, this soul ache, was going to consume me. Although I knew not the source of the loneliness, and although at times I thought I had outrun it, I was still aware of its presence. I sensed that it lingered just beyond the "veil."

What all of this added up to was that I needed to find out who I was again. Who was I in the wake of my parents' death? Was I a man or just a man-child? And what did it mean to be a man? And how did one shed the weight of an unknowable, unnameable, seemingly sourceless sadness? Somewhere along the line I lost my way, and I needed to correct my course.

On the morning of my thirty-sixth birthday, I realized I was fighting something. It dawned on me that my life—

this ship I'd been attempting to steer—was more ship than I could handle. The more I fought to control it, the more my navigational skills were rendered useless by elements beyond me, and the greater the push and pull became, the more painful the course correction. Whether I liked it or not, this ship had a mind of its own. However, it wasn't the ship that took me places; the ship was simply a vessel. The wind and the currents facilitated my journey, and I needed to learn how to navigate them.

Since I no longer had the strength to fight, bolstered by acute awareness and implicit faith, I let go of the helm, surrendered to the winds and tides, and bought a one-way ticket to India to explore my truth.

***　　***　　***

I am so grateful for:

1. Having had such loving, selfless, and devoted parents; for the seeds of faith they gave me; and how fortunate I am for all the years I was able to spend with them.

2. The clarity to know I must travel to create the change I need in my life.

3. All the great things that I will learn, the experiences I will have, the people I will meet, and the adventures I will go on.

4. The blessings of my friends, who have supported me so that I may undertake this endeavor.

5. My future self—the person I will be when I get home from this journey.

Today I intend and create:

1. To be of service while traveling.

2. A windfall of money and a new MacBook Air.

3. A quiet mind and a peaceful heart.

4. The right people to show up to get me where I need to go.

5. To surrender fear, move into trust, and see beyond the veil.

Chapter 2. If you focus on nothing, it is nothing you will receive.

I'm alone in the front row of a small theater. Before me, from both sides of the stage, a curtain is drawn. I walk up to the stage and stand before it, but as I have been here many times before, I know it's more than a curtain. It's a veil, and I am terrified of whatever is behind it. I don't know if it's a thing, an energy, or a monster, but the thought of it has haunted me for as long as I can remember.

My instincts tell me it's dark and ominous back there. I want to scream, but I know it will only be audible to me. I want to run, but there's nowhere to hide. I'm terrified to discover what's behind the curtain, yet I'm drawn to it. But I'm going to do it this time. I need to know what's on the other side because whatever it is, it holds me prisoner.

I move slowly toward the curtain. My heart races with every inch of ground, and I wonder if it's going to burst out of my chest. My stomach is in knots and I feel nauseous. But I climb up onto the stage anyway. I take a deep breath and reach out to touch it...

***

Damn it.

I thought it was going to happen this time, that I was finally going to discover what lurks behind the curtain. Then again, I always think that. The mystery has haunted my dreams for as long as I can remember. Whether passing from high school to college, losing an important relationship, or getting fired from a job, I had come to know the dream as a signpost from my subconscious that I was going through a period of extreme transition, and this was no exception.

"Good evening," the woman said with a nod, a smile, and an Indian accent.

"Good evening," I replied. "I didn't expect to fall asleep so fast. I guess I was more exhausted than I thought. How long have we been in the air?"

"About twenty minutes."

The first thing I noticed about her was her smile. I guessed she was in her mid-fifties, but she had a much younger countenance. It cast an aura of peaceful wisdom, the kind that pulls you in and makes you want to know more. Despite this, I was hoping she wasn't a talker. I simply wasn't in the mood. I was leaving the United States and had no idea when I was going to return…if I ever did.

She wore a traditional Indian sari and on her face, modern, stylish glasses framed her calm brown eyes. From each arm dangled bangles that chimed with her every move. The bracelets stretched from her delicate wrists to the middle of her forearms, and her hair, dark and thick, was woven into an elegant braid.

From the moment I awoke at 6am that morning until I left for the airport, I was running errands, saying goodbyes, canceling my cable and phone services, and checking off items from a never-ending to-do list. It had been an intense day, and my head was spinning from the emotional adrenalin. I spent the last year thinking about the journey and the last three months attempting, rather unsuccessfully, to plan it. It was time to begin the great experiment.

When the drink service began on the nonstop flight from New York's JFK International Airport to New Delhi, I ordered a glass of wine, pulled out my journal, and began writing. With the exception of the recurring dream, I rarely remembered my dreams, yet all week they were as vivid as they were arresting. Three stood out in particular.

In the first dream I am caught in a tsunami in present-day Seattle, trapped in a houseboat with my friend. Water rushes in and fills up the room. We wait until the waterline rises nearly to the ceiling. When we can no longer breathe, we take a final breath and swim underwater toward the front door. All the while I push dead bodies out of the way.

In the second dream I am in an old farmhouse. It belongs to my friend from high school who committed suicide. In the dream, I am pulled toward a door that leads to a wing of his house. I know it's haunted but I can't control myself. As soon as I get through the door, the hair on the back of my neck stands up, and I feel an unsettling presence. I flee down a long corridor, but I am drawn back to that wing of the house again and again, as if I'm going to discover something different.

In the third dream I am out in the countryside of New Jersey in the town where I grew up. In the distance, a mushroom cloud rises up from New York City. I am with my earliest childhood friend.

Although we are more than sixty miles from the point of impact, debris falls all around us and people flee for their lives. I run, but when I turn back to look at the New York skyline in the distance, a plane engulfed in flames crashes toward me. I have no time to get out of the way, so I surrender.

I turn toward the plane, close my eyes, and outstretch my arms as if Christ on the Cross, but the plane misses me. Amazed I am still alive, I turn in the opposite direction and continue moving away from the destruction.

"So are you coming or going?" the Indian woman asked, startling me out of my thoughts. I was writing so furiously I was unaware that dinner service had begun.

"Excuse me?"

"Are you going home or leaving home?"

"I'm leaving."

"Vacation? Business? Pleasure?"

"I'm not exactly sure. A combo of all the above, I guess. I basically sold most of my possessions, put the rest in storage, gave up my apartment, and dropped off my car on the way to the airport. And...I'm not really sure what I'm going to do or where I'm going when I land in India. Jeez. That sounds even crazier when I say it out loud. I have a hotel in Delhi for a few days, and then I'm going to Dharamsala. I'm just kind of hoping the plan will reveal itself. I guess that's kind of naïve of me."

"Ah yes, the hero's journey," she said.

"Excuse me?"

"You are leaving home, setting out on a quest for something. Do you know what it is you are seeking?"

It was such a simple question, but I never considered it. Coming from a stranger the effect was arresting. *What was it I was seeking?*

"I don't know exactly. Maybe freedom. Maybe healing. To volunteer. To try to find out what I'm supposed to be doing with my life. Why does anyone travel?"

"It is for all of these reasons and more," she said. "Sometimes you don't need to know what you're looking for. In fact, I think that's the best place to be. When you boil it down, it's very simple. Pave your road with intention, surrender expectations, stay awake, and let the path take you where it will." It did sound simple when she put it that way.

"I've been trying. I just get impatient and tired. I exhaust myself sometimes."

"And what is it you do for a living?"

"I'm a writer. Well, a copywriter. I mean, I do marketing and advertising, but I'm hoping to find my story while I'm traveling. I'm also hoping to make some money along the way, or maybe volunteer. Whatever it takes to travel for as long as I can."

"Writing is a noble profession. The world changes through two things: story and consciousness."

"What do you do?" I asked.

"I was in academia for years but left it behind to do healing and massage."

"Why is that?"

"I reached a point where I knew the ivory towers of academia were no longer serving my highest good. I always felt a calling to the healing arts, and when the call was louder than I could bear, I answered it."

"What kind of healing?"

"Massage, energy work, Reiki, that sort of thing."

"Funny you say that. I unexpectedly had a massage today, and I don't know if I've ever experienced anything like it. It brought up a lot of emotions I didn't know were there, and I wasn't quite ready for them. I'm still a little rattled."

"It can do that. Plus, you are setting out and creating new dimensions of self, moving into an idea that is bigger than you. Just by making the decision to undertake this journey you are entering a state of expansion and growth, and both of these aspects of self are not always easy. By the way, my name is Preetika."

"I'm Thomas. Thomas Furey."

Preetika and I spent the next two hours talking easily as if we had known each other for years. I went on to tell her about my morning, how one minute I was having coffee with a friend, complaining about how tight my neck and back felt, and the next thing I knew I was lying on her friend's massage table.

The therapist "listened" to my body, applying pressure where she said my body requested it. She asked me about the feelings and emotions that percolated up through my pressure points, telling me how the body speaks to us through images, sounds, and colors. Heavy, deep-seated emotions of anger and sadness unexpectedly welled up within me.

Two images came to mind. The first is of me as a young child, crying at the foot of my mother's bed. It's morning in late June, and I feel summer asserting its dominance over spring. I hear the electric buzz of male cicadas as the frequency amplifies and compresses in crests and troughs of sound waves. I smell the freshly cut grass outside my window and hear the hum of the pool filter and the whirring white noise of the air conditioner.

There are piles of financial statements and papers covering most of the surfaces in my parents' room. On the floor are mounds of clothes burying the Electrolux vacuum (the carpet could certainly use its services). The Virgin Mary stands watch over the bed, and in the corner of the room there's an old thirteen-inch television with a dial that displays channels U through 13.

I see my reflection in the bureau's mirror. I'm inconsolable because my mother has just told me that in the fall I will be repeating second grade. She wants me to be older and more mature in school. In my mind, not only am I not good enough or smart enough, but I will lose all my friends since I will now be going to a small Catholic school. I am paying for the mistakes she made with my older siblings.

I watch this scene from the third person. Moments later, another image.

Perhaps I am older, perhaps around the same time. My mother is fascinated by a priest who performs handwriting analysis, and she is urging me to give her a writing sample to the point where I'm so scared I'm hysterically crying.

Finally she tells me it's okay, that I don't have to do it if I don't want to, although she doesn't understand why. She asks me, "Why are you so upset? You don't have to if you don't want to. The only reason I wanted you to do it is because I find it so fascinating."

What my mother doesn't know is that I am secretly haunted by *Leaves*, a Catholic monthly magazine she subscribes to. All I am interested in are the pictures, mystical pictures such as the ones where an unsuspecting photographer captures a dove, an angel, or the Virgin Mary appearing on a cloud above an altar. I'm equally fascinated by the mystery of the Shroud of Turin and people like Padre Pio who bear the wounds of the stigmata, and I wonder if I'll ever get the stigmata.

I know enough about Catholicism to know that Jesus is aware of my darkest sins. He knows I looked at the nudie magazines underneath my brother's bed, stole money from my mom's wallet, and stole candy from my town's general store. Jesus is going to punish me. I am particularly scared to go into our basement because I think He's probably down there. What would I do if Jesus confronted me? But what's worst of all—and what Jesus certainly already knows and what the priest is sure to find out through my handwriting— is how sad I am. I don't want to put that pain on my mother because I sense she has enough to worry about in her own life, even though I can't figure out why. While I am a mirror of her sadness, I am also a sponge.

Preetika continued. "Those feelings you felt in the massage, they are the feelings of a very young child, a child who was afraid to express the fact that he was afraid. It's okay to be scared, and it's okay to be sad. Fear and flight are the instincts that have allowed human beings to thrive and survive. But that doesn't mean you have to live by them."

I told Preetika how when my sister pulled out of her driveway that afternoon to drive me to the airport, I didn't feel anything in particular. Driving on the country roads to the highway, I felt more like a tired puppy that could barely hold its head up, but by the time we reached the highway, something inside of me popped.

The body worker must have uncorked the dormant sadness that had been lying in wait in my muscles, cells, and tissues. Like the good, repressed Irish Catholic I was raised to be, I pushed down any uncomfortable feelings that neared the surface. Most recently, I also pushed down questions about what I was actually doing. *Why am I traveling? Why am I leaving a good life behind in Seattle? What am I going to do when I get there? Where is there? What am I trying to prove and to whom?* With my twelve-year-old niece in the back seat, I lost all control of my emotions and they poured out of me in waves of heaving sobs.

"It didn't occur to me until almost the Long Island Expressway that I was in mourning," I told Preetika.

"Mourning what?"

"I don't know. The loss of my mother? My childhood? What my family used to be? Who knows. Maybe even the loss of my life in Seattle. I no longer have house keys or a cell phone contract, and whatever I didn't sell is boxed up in a storage unit. It's all so crazy."

"Not crazy. Liberating. You're just looking at it the wrong way. I'm going to tell you something very simple, Thomas. There is a light within you, the same light that is within all of us, and if you serve that light you can't go wrong. Just use your feelings as a guidance system. Move toward that which brings you joy and expansion, and leave behind that which causes you friction and contraction.

"You see, Thomas, there are inside all of us equal parts darkness and light, and whichever one you choose to serve becomes the dominant force in your life. And I'm not speaking of darkness as an outside force, like the devil or something religious dogma warns us of. The darkness I speak of lurks in the corner of our thoughts as doubt, fear, unworthiness, and shame. When you serve these thoughts, they become actions, which become character, which becomes modes of expression and ways of being. Eventually, these ways of being become addictions to feeling bad or feeling doubtful of your gifts or whatever it is that holds you back from experiencing your true self.

"I believe there is something inside all of us that wants to be born anew, that wants to come forth from the darkness into the light. It is the law of nature that light consumes darkness. Serve the light within you. Have no fear, Thomas. Morning always comes; some nights are just longer than others."

The sentiment landed on me as if it had come directly from my mother. If disease had not overtaken her body for the past decade, she might have uttered very similar words. As exhaustion overcame my mind, body, and spirit, this lovely thought carried me into slumber from my seat perched high above the earth.

When I awoke from a fitful sleep several hours later, "Clair de Lune" by Debussy enveloped me through my Beats by Dre headphones. It was my mother's favorite song and the one she most often played on her piano when I was a child. Preetika was already awake.

"Good morning, or should I say good evening?" she said with a smile. "Did you sleep with abundance?"

"I slept about as well as I could on a plane, which isn't very well."

She smiled.

"I was thinking about you while you slept and wondered how I can help you on your journey. You had mentioned volunteering. I know someone who has an eco-ashram. Would that be of interest to you?"

"I have no idea what that means, but sure. I'd be totally open to it."

"I am not sure of his needs, but he is a beautiful man. You would have to meet him and see if you two were agreeable, but I can't imagine it not being a match. He is actually in Dharamsala at the moment. This is where you will be relocating yourself to, is it not?"

"As far as a plan in India, it's the only thing I'm sure of."

"Surrender the fear, Thomas, and all will be well. You'll see."

"My mother used to say that."

"She sounds like a wise woman."

"She was indeed."

"If I may give you one more bit of unsolicited advice, remember that if you focus on nothing, it is nothing you will receive. Pave your path with intention and gratitude. Then get out of the way and let goodness happen."

"I've been doing that in my daily writing exercise for close to a year now. You know, my mother used to give me a lot of unsolicited advice," I said. We both chuckled.

The announcement was made that we were to lock our tray tables and put our seats in the upright position. Preetika and I exchanged email addresses, and she told me she would be in touch.

***   ***   ***

I am so grateful for:

1. Having sat next to Preetika on the flight and the wisdom she imparted to me.
2. The friends I will make on this journey.
3. The moments of revelation and insight I've had over the past few weeks.
4. All the serendipitous happenings that lined up to enable me to travel.

5. The teachers I have had and the teachers I will encounter.

I intend and create:

1. To meet new friends in Dharamsala.

2. For the path to reveal itself.

3. To have a serendipitous occurrence/meeting.

4. To move into the fear, surrender it, and trust that what I need will be provided to me.

5. To find a mentor.

Chapter 3. Learning Curve

The breadth of information I was armed with when I walked off the plane in New Delhi included, and was pretty much limited to the following: don't drink the water; if you want ice in your drink, make sure you ask for mineral ice; don't eat salads or the skin of fruits; and be prepared to get sick. I didn't even have a *Lonely Planet: India* guidebook. Instead I had *Lonely Planet: Nepal*, which I can assure you offers nothing worthwhile when landing blindly in the center of a city inhabited by twenty-two million people.

By the time I passed through customs, took out some rupees from an ATM, and flagged a taxi to take me to the Jorbagh 47 guesthouse, it was 10pm. As if preparing to jump from a plane during a foreign invasion, I braced myself for the chaos that would descend upon me when I stepped through the airport doors—the touts trying to get me to their hotels, the hordes of people in transit, and the hustlers trying to sell me fruit, enlightenment, or children.

It was, of course, nothing like I imagined. Instead, I walked through the departure doors and into a scene of order and civility. Like most large airports anywhere in the world, I found the queue for the taxis and patiently awaited my escort into the first night of my journey.

***

Outside the perimeter of the airport, the first thing one notices about India is the lawlessness of the roads. Horns trump blinkers and are the primary means by which drivers communicate. Painted lanes on highways are more suggestions than hard-and-fast rules. Motorcycles speed down highways with families on the back, and only the driver—the father—is wearing a helmet. At stoplights you see destitute beggars who—trapped in a caste system—have been maimed by their parents so they will be more valuable in the hierarchy of begging and poverty. For a Westerner, the result is an uncomfortable combination of guilt brought on by privilege, gratitude for privilege, and outrage at the system.

The gratuitous use of horns on Indian roadways would surely evoke deadly encounters of road rage in other parts of the world, yet when you pass cars in India, even though your driver has been leaning on the horn, the other driver is completely nonplussed. With more than twelve million cars on New Delhi's streets, it's hard to imagine that more deaths don't occur, but there's order to the chaos.

At stoplights, acceleration and hard braking make you feel as if you're in an arcade game, only the stakes are much higher. Drivers swerve to avoid trucks and pedestrians or lock the brakes to avoid rear-ending the three-wheeled electric rickshaw that comes to a screeching halt in front of them for no apparent reason. Lanes abruptly end without warning, and you slide in between cars at a high velocity with less than inches to spare. You may even find your driver making a sudden left turn across three lanes of oncoming traffic, nearly going up on two wheels. Or, if your driver is really impatient, he may drive head-on into traffic to get around a stoplight.

And this was just my first thirty minutes in India.

After a harrowing, white-knuckle-inducing drive, my driver dropped me off at the Jorbagh 47 guesthouse, which did not appear to be the same hotel as the one I booked online. For one, I would never call the room "elegantly" appointed. My bathroom had no delineation between the toilet and the showerhead, and the towels, coarse and pilling, told a story of many years' worth of use. Still, I tried with little success to find rest.

In the warm, crisp air of morning, much to my surprise I discovered the courtyard did match the photo on their website. So well-groomed and manicured was this lawn it could have easily passed for the eighteenth green at Augusta. Around the small courtyard, giant ficus trees splintered and diffused soft morning light on the flora. I sat down to breakfast and thought, *This is actually nice.* And then, in a jet-lagged daze, I mistook sugar for salt and ruined my first meal in India.

After a shower, which left me feeling less than clean, I went to the front desk to find a map of the city.

"Could you please tell me some of the things I might want to see?" I asked the man behind the counter.

"Oh, yes sir. There are many things to see in our great city. There is Qutb Minar here, the India Gate, Humayun's Tomb over here, the Red Fort," he said, continuing to circle sites on the map.

"I think I'll take in these two sites today. What's the best way to walk there?"

"Sir, those are both at least fourteen kilometers away." Indian maps clearly lacked scale.

"Thank you. I'll be back in a little bit. I'm just going to grab some things from my room."

I returned to my room feeling alone, overwhelmed, and terrified, which was exacerbated by jet lag. With the exception of a few fitful hours of sleep, I had been up for nearly thirty-six hours. *What the fuck have I gotten myself into? What am I doing here? Where am I going to go? Do I have even enough money? What if a taxi driver kidnaps me and holds me for ransom? How could I have been so stupid as to buy a one-way ticket to the second-most populous country on earth where I know not a soul?*

All I could think of were the countless conversations I had had with friends and the people I met in bars during the months leading up to my departure.

"You're doing what?"

"I'm buying a one-way ticket to India."

"When are you coming back?"

"I'm not sure."

"That's fucking ballsy as hell," the men would reply.

"You're so brave and adventurous," the women would respond.

"What are you going to do over there?" they all asked.

"I don't know. I'll figure it out. I'm pretty resourceful," stated I with confidence and bravado.

It was much easier to utter such words in the familiarity and routine of my daily life, not to mention it gave me an air of intrigue and adventure, but now that I was in it, I was finding the unknown very uncomfortable.

While I had heard great things about India, the only stories I could remember in my sleep-deprived state were those of tourists getting drugged on trains, pick-pockets stealing passports and wallets, crooked taxi drivers running up fares, and touts trying to take advantage of you. I imagined every person in India had it out for me. I knew they were going to see right through me, too, that I was a scared little kid posing as a grown-up.

With my mind and heart racing, I lay down, turned on the air conditioner, and fell asleep. When I woke hours later, possessed by the need to connect with someone familiar, I was crestfallen that the Internet was down. I paced the room for some time, trying desperately to think myself out of the situation, but lacking any ideas, I fell back into another deep sleep.

The following morning, I was up at dawn. *I need to get out of this room,* I thought, and so I set out in small, exploratory circles around the hotel.

Only a few blocks away I found Lodhi Gardens. It was a beautiful, warm, early morning, and once I made it deeper into the womb of the park, the sounds of nature drowned out the sounds of cars and buses. The sun hadn't yet risen above the tree line, and everywhere I looked people were exercising, meditating, or practicing yoga. In the courtyards of temples, kids played cricket while smiling, retired couples walked hand in hand through gardens and dogs lounged like Roman emperors.

The morning sun, still low on the horizon, cast its light upon ancient temples built by plotting architects. As the light rose on the temples, they appeared to be illuminated from within. All around the grounds were fountains and reflecting pools surrounded by dahlias and daisies, and parakeets, kingfishers, babblers, and drongos sang their morning songs.

This isn't that scary. In fact, it's kind of exhilarating. It's amazing.

Chapter 4. A Good Omen

When I returned to my hotel room from Lodhi Gardens, the Internet was working, and much to my delight there was an email awaiting me from Preetika. She had written her friend, the owner of the eco-ashram, and he had already responded, saying he would love to meet me. He asked if I could meet him in Dharamsala in three days as he was on a tight schedule and only had a small window of time. I didn't have to think twice. At least now I had someone in India to talk to and a direction to pursue.

The train was the more affordable option to get to Dharamsala, but it would take twelve hours, followed by a three-hour taxi ride. Flush with money, I decided to take the easy, efficient, and less adventurous route, so I booked a flight. When I hit "purchase" on the computer screen, I sat back on my bed and marveled at the good fortune of sitting next to Preetika. For the first time since I had arrived in India, the constriction in my chest surrendered to a deep, calming breath.

Below the email from Preetika, another email awaited me. It was from a college friend to whom I had not spoken in years. She had caught wind that I was heading to India and wanted me to meet a friend of hers who lived in New Delhi. She cc'd him on the email, and he had already replied.

Dude,

I'm having a party tonight. It should be really

cool. You should come. Drop me a line for details if you're interested.

– Abhay

I gave the driver Abhay's address. It was in the Chattarpur Farms neighborhood of New Delhi. In my experience of growing up in western New Jersey, any address with "Farms" at the end of it was either a wealthy family or a family trying to create the illusion of wealth. I imagined he might have a nice condo or something, but then my driver found the gated community, and it was much more than a condo complex.

Immediately inside the security checkpoint, twelve-foot high walls cordoned off large plots of land, each house with its own iron gates and armed guards at the entrance. When we found Abhay's house, we were met by a security detail that showed me in.

Is this a house? A hotel? Abhay's house? I was confused.

As it turned out, it was his parents' house (his mother owned a large ad agency in New Delhi).

Abhay's home looked like the grounds of a fancy hotel in Los Angeles. Corinthian columns and plush, white, sectional couches surrounded an infinity pool, around which was an impeccably manicured lawn. At each end of the pool was a bar serving top-shelf liquor. Accent lighting in the gardens and spotlights shining up through palm trees cast a warm, soft glow upon the grounds. Attentive waiters in white gloves and dinner jackets circled patrons while passing out champagne, hors d'oeuvres, and a whiskey cocktail created for the evening. Behind an endless table serving international cuisine there must have been fifteen chefs dressed in white with *toques blanches* upon their heads.

I had only seen Abhay on Facebook, so I didn't exactly know who I was looking for. The fashionable partygoers blended into one another, everyone dressed in pressed shirts you'd find at Nordstrom or Barneys New York. Being the only white guy at the party and wearing a plaid, short-sleeved, Billabong shirt (plaid being the ubiquitous uniform found throughout Seattle music venues), it was safe to say Abhay would find me before I found him.

When Abhay did spot me, he left the people he was talking to, grabbed me a cocktail off a tray, and gave me a welcoming hug. He introduced me to several of his friends, each one more warm and welcoming than the next. Much to my surprise, most of the people I met had an intimate knowledge of the United States, either by travel or by attending university. One man I was introduced to had gone to Notre Dame and another, Stanford.

"Wait, you bought a one-way ticket to India and this is your third day? No way!" one of them said, sending a high five my way.

"That's awesome! Welcome brother," another said.

Over the course of the next several hours, the music became louder, the women swayed their hips, and each drink went down more easily than the last.

"Hey man, you smoke weed?" Abhay asked.

"Does a bear shit in the woods?" I replied.

"What if the bear is in a wooded zoo? Seems like a technicality. In the meantime, follow me. Let's go burn one."

The interior of the house was light and airy, accentuated by an open floor plan and balanced with an artful mix of glass, iron, colorful paintings, statuesque sculptures, and designer lighting. I followed Abhay through several rooms, each one a contender for *Architectural Digest*. When we finally made it to the billiards room, he went straight to the bar. Designer sound from ceiling speakers made the groovy lounge music perfectly full, yet not too loud where we had to yell over each other.

"What's this music?"

"Cheb i Sabbah. He's an Algerian deejay who used to live in Paris and now lives in San Francisco. His name means 'young of the morning.' It's good, right?"

"I love it. I need to write his name down."

"What do you drink?"

"You got any bourbon?"

"Is Jim Beam okay? It's hard to get the really good American bourbons over here, but at least this is a twelve-year," he said, walking behind the bar and pulling out two Waterford Crystal rocks glasses.

"Rocks? Neat?"

"Rocks is good. The ice is filtered water, right?" The moment I said it, I knew it was a silly question. Abhay just smiled.

As I bellied up to the bar, he placed a circular ball of ice in each glass and poured us drinks.

"Welcome to India, my friend. Cheers!"

From one of the drawers behind the bar, he pulled out a latched box with a stone inlay. In it was a glass-blown water pipe, rolling papers, and several medicine bottles with handwritten labels on them.

"Mind if I choose the strain?"

"You kidding me? This is incredible. I feel like I never left Seattle."

He opened a medicine bottle, poured some weed onto the table, and broke up the buds.

"You're going to find that weed is really hard to get in India, good weed at least. Luckily, I got a solid hookup. Mostly though, you're going to see hash—Kashmiri and Afghani Gold being the best. Since you're my guest from America and I'm welcoming you to India, we're going to go with a sativa strain called Aloha. I'm going to throw a taste of Kashmiri in as well, which if you head north is most likely what you're going to get."

"Aloha? For real? Where did you get this?"

"I told you, man. I got a hookup. If you ever get migraines, this is the plant medicine you need," he said, smiling.

"Damn. When I was in my hotel room yesterday, you know, practically crying in the fetal position, wanting to go home and on the verge of a breakdown, I never could have imagined this is where I would be twenty-four hours later."

"Ha! I love it. Isn't that the beauty of travel?"

"Shit, if this is what travel is all about, I could get used to it."

He finished rolling a nearly perfect joint—not too loose but not too tight. Then from inside the box he pulled out a Zippo lighter, similar to one my dad always used when he lit his Winston Lights.

As Abhay lit the joint, we watched the front of the rolling paper curl up in the flame. When the flame reached the bud, he took a slow pull, held the large hit in his lungs, and exhaled easiness from his body in a long, exaggerated breath.

"Oh, that's good," he said, passing me the joint. "So what's going on, man? What are you doing here? What's your plan? How can I help you?"

"Well, I just got to India three days ago and today I booked a ticket to Dharamsala. I met a woman on the plane who set me up with someone I might volunteer for."

"Far out, man!" he said, lacking any hint of an Indian accent.

I took a drag and passed him the joint.

"No, no, no," Abhay said. "Hold onto it. Take a couple hits. So what will you be doing for him?"

"I have no idea. It doesn't matter much to me. It just gives me an excuse to organize my time, and it gives me some purpose while I'm traveling. I've basically been holed up in my hotel for two days freaking out. Some traveler I am, huh?"

"Oh, it's not you, man. Trust me. I've spent a lot of my life outside this country. I've lived in London and New York and went to school in L.A. Every time I come back here, I'm completely freaked out for a few days. But then, when you let go," he said, opening his arms, "then the magic happens. I'm telling you, India is an intense place. You're going to see some crazy shit. Some things will blow your mind, some will expand your soul and make you a better human being, and some will make you drop to your knees and curse the utter cruelty of humanity. But if you like the mystical, this is the place."

"I guess that's part of the reason I took off, right? Life experience. Shit, I just can't tell you how grateful I am to you for inviting me, a total stranger, to your party."

"You're not a stranger. A friend of Susanne is a friend of mine."

"This is the first time I feel like myself since I arrived. Actually, I think it's the first time I've had a real conversation with someone."

The mixture Abhay rolled was the perfect high for the moment. For days I had been a teapot whistling on the stove. With a few pulls of the joint, however, it was as if a valve opened and the pressure that had been building up within me—the profound weight of my unconscious anxiety—was let out in one great release. My body's chemistry found the mixture agreeable, leaving me energized and talkative in the midst of evaporated inhibitions.

"You know, this is crazy to say, but I already feel like my life is opening up. I don't know how to explain it. I just...I just feel it, you know? Granted, I am really fucking high right now—in the best possible way, of course—but still."

Abhay slapped his knee and let out a soulful laugh.

"No, no. That's great, man. I always seem to meet people at these inflection points where their lives are taking off. It's not the weed. It's real and it's happening, and it's going to be rad. India is a wild place. You just have to remember not to fight it. Things work differently here, real different. I mean, it's like an alternate fucking universe for Christ's sake. I'm talking time, space...hell, sometimes I think the laws of physics aren't even the same. It can be a cruel place, but underneath the dirt and shit is a love and redemption that elevates the soul to new heights. You just have to remember to keep your house clean, you know what I mean? I tell you what. If you're open to where the road takes you, you're going to have experiences that'll change your life. I'm excited for you, man."

"Well, meeting you here and now seems like a good omen."

"Seriously, I'm telling you it's real. There's an invisible field around all of us, and I can feel expansion happening in yours. It's what I tune into and the type of people I attract. We all have these electromagnetic fields of information around us, and electrons are constantly jumping in and out of each other's fields. I've just become really skilled at dialing into that vibe."

"It's good to know it's not my imagination."

"It's definitely not your imagination. Life's just a dream, and we can either awaken to it or stay asleep. The good news is that more and more people are waking up. Personally, I think we're on the brink of a major shift in human evolution that will come about through the evolution of consciousness."

"How's that?"

"Our bodies are just bags of matter that house consciousness, and consciousness is everything. It's what unites all of us, and every day more and more people are awakening to that truth—meditation, plant medicine, mindfulness. People I never thought would be open to these things are starting to ask me about them. It's exciting. People are finally waking up to the fact that the answers to life are not outside of us and that consumption doesn't make us feel better. Everything we need to know is already inside of us. We just have to connect to it. Our bodies are instruments of consciousness, and when we learn how to use them right, they are like antennas that allow us to tune into our higher selves. Atman is Brahman and Brahman is Atman, you dig? Are you familiar with that?"

"I don't think so."

"It's Hindu philosophy found in the Upanishads, which are ancient Sanskrit texts. The body is not our real essence. Atman is our real essence. Atman is the soul, the true essence of each living thing. Brahman is the world, or cosmic soul. You and I, we're both Atman *and* Brahman. It's like this. Imagine you and I are molecules of water in the ocean. For a moment, as waves crash together, we splash through the air. That moment is our life here on earth. But then that molecule returns to the whole, the ocean, to Brahman."

"I love that," I said, pausing to take it in. "So what do you do for work?"

"It's a long story. I've done a lot of different things. I started on Wall Street but hated the business. The sheer, unchecked greed and selfishness it produces is a cancerous trap for the unaware. There were definitely some good people but most...eh, I wasn't impressed. Then for a New York minute I went into advertising, but I hated having to sell my soul to some misguided soul who was trying to climb a ladder, protect their position, or get that corner office. As if that wasn't bad enough, I had to convince people that if they didn't buy the product I was peddling, they would never find happiness. That kind of bullshit just pushes people away from the truth, you know?"

Abhay paused to take a sip of his drink before he continued.

"What I was most interested in at the time was film, so I moved to L.A. and got into film production. After that, I came back to India to spend more time with my family. That time and distance gave me perspective, and that's when I realized I hated the way all these businesses felt like prisons. They didn't inspire and uplift. They beat you down and sucked every ounce of good out of you in the name of the almighty dollar. So, I started a business to transform companies from the inside out through green and spiritual practices."

"No way! That sounds amazing."

"Yeah, I love it. It wasn't always easy, and it was certainly filled with a lot of doubt, but I stayed true to myself, because if you're not true to yourself, then you're just lying to everyone else. It's like this. We have to work, right? Work is just the adult version of the sandbox. Some of us get pushed over, some of us push people over, some of us never learn to play by the rules, and some don't think the rules apply to them at all. You mind if I smoke?"

"Of course not. It's your place."

He turned on a fan and paused to light a cigarette. He took a drag, then through a strained voice said, "But it's all in the mind, bro."

When he exhaled, smoke billowed, barreled, and danced beneath the light of the stained-glass fixture that hung above the billiards table.

"You see, most of us are locked into one story of our lives. Maybe it's a story we learned on the playground or from our parents, but if we can't transcend that story, we get stuck. When we realize that the story doesn't characterize our lifestyles or our adult selves, we're free, free to be the architects of our own lives, using our thoughts as the building blocks of our external experiences. But the powers that be try to mold and brainwash those thoughts into conformity. It's bullshit."

"Which powers that be?"

"There are the gatekeepers, or the people who control the media. They'll do anything to maintain their grip on power and consolidate it. Then there's the puppet masters, the people who control money, power, and energy resources, the people who want us to remain slaves to their system of debt and not awaken to our truth, which is that there's a field of infinite possibilities around us, and all we have to do is tune into it. The more you move toward that truth, the more whole you feel, and the more whole you feel, the more you want to give back. When you tune into your truth, you become the vortex and it comes to you naturally," he said, drawing a circle around his body with his outstretched arms. He took another drag of his cigarette.

"What does that have to do with your work?" I said.

"Let's just say that what I do for a living is get systems unstuck. Whether it's a doctor working with cells, a healer working with energy, or a CEO working with a collection of disparate organizations and dysfunctional people, I give people the tools to get unstuck, to tune into the field of possibilities. I show them how to use their imagination to create new stories. This creation comes from within and radiates outward, bringing coherence to an organization as people move rhythmically and with positive energy, which they then bring home and share with their family and friends. And then you know the rest. We all live happily-fucking-ever-after, right?" he said, laughing.

"Wouldn't that be nice?"

"And oh boy, once you get someone to change their story, then you introduce them to meditation and mindful practices, and eventually, they learn that they can create anything they want."

"What about me?"

"Well," he began, giving me a once-over. "You're clearly stuck in your story, but you're a creator. You're going to have some crazy highs and some really hard lows on your journey, but you're lucky. You know why?"

"Why's that?"

"Because I can tell you've got three things going for you. One, someone's looking out for you. Two, you're protected by naïveté, and three, you connect easily with people. This whole thing of arriving in India without a plan or a guidebook might be the best choice you could have made. I sense these things. I could tell from your email that you're open and enthusiastic, and now that I've met you, I can see you're really personable. India's going to align you, and you're going to find a new story. But that'll be just one story. The key is to keep creating stories and living into them."

"Sounds great. Except I'm pretty sure I have no idea how to do that."

"Your consciousness will create the story and send out the signal. Your feelings will be like an antenna that pulls a story toward you, and your body will carry you to that new reality. Then one day, after you've been putting that thought into the field over and over, new realities will show up in ways you never could have imagined. And you say to yourself, 'Holy shit! I'm not just the writer of my life, I'm the motherfucking action hero!'"

With that, an uncontrollable laughter welled up from the cores of our beings, cementing a new friendship. Whether this connection was meant solely for that moment or was the foundation for some future encounter, only time would reveal. But if there actually was this field of information around us with atoms jumping between each other's fields, we were entrained to each other—at least for the moment—and I was carrying within me the energy of the ideas he had shared.

***

On the ride home, feeling drunk, joyful, and high on life, I rolled down the window. I began, as I sometimes do, having a conversation with my parents, telling them how happy and grateful I was feeling. I thanked them for looking out for me and apologized for momentarily losing faith in their guidance.

When I realized this conversation was occurring audibly and not in my head, I was relieved to see the driver's rearview mirror was missing. I rolled down the window to welcome New Delhi's morning air on my face and continued speaking aloud to whoever was listening.

***   ***   ***

I am so grateful for:

1. How quickly my experience in India is turning around.

2. The unexpected surprise of getting invited to Abhay's party and all of the new things he got me thinking about.

3. The beautiful, soulfully restorative morning I had in Lodhi Gardens.

4. The magic that's about to unfold before me.

5. Starting to relax and feel like myself again after several stressful weeks.

Today I intend and create:

1. To have new, enriching experiences, even if they are uncomfortable.

2. To have a great meeting with Preetika's friend in Dharamsala.

3. To feel awe and wonder and to have powerful experiences with nature.

4. To be surprised by a serendipitous meeting in Dharamsala.

5. To fall in love and lay with this person on a beach beneath a blanket of stars.

Chapter 5. An Auspicious Meeting

On our final approach from New Delhi to the Kangra Airport, located in the Indian state of Himachal Pradesh, I looked out the window of seat 12A and fixed my gaze upon the snowcapped Himalayas. There was no way not to be filled with awe and wonder.

At baggage claim, I met a girl from Turkey, and we agreed to split a ride into town. Up narrow, perilous mountain roads we climbed in a rickety old van. Blind turns, single-lane switchbacks, hundred-foot drops with no guardrails, and trucks and buses barreling down on us were just a few of the hazards we negotiated while dodging goats, monkeys, dogs, chickens, and donkeys.

Dharamsala, India was home to the Dalai Lama and the Tibetan government in exile, but unbeknownst to me, I was actually heading to McLeod Ganj, a town eight kilometers above Dharamsala (if I'd had *Lonely Planet: India*, I would have known this).

McLeod Ganj, often referred to as Upper Dharamsala, was a lively and well-traveled town that attracted Europeans, South Americans, Israelis, and seekers from all over the world on the hunt for drugs, enlightenment, and the wisdom of the Dalai Lama.

Backed by the dramatic peaks of the Himalayas, McLeod Ganj consisted of six roads that fed into a main square where taxi drivers, tour operators, touts, hotel owners, and beggars competed for your attention while old men sipped chai tea and orange-clad monks walked about town in Nikes as they talked and texted on their cell phones. Cars, hippies, artists, Indians, Tibetans, yoga and meditation students, and trucks avoided each other by millimeters on the well-worn cobblestone streets against the incessant noise of car horns and motorcycle engines. There was a palpable excitement in the air of motion, transit, and adventure.

Once I arrived at the taxi stand in the square, I asked a few people where Bhagsunag Road was and headed toward my guesthouse. After settling in and orienting myself to the town, I texted Preetika's friend, JD Chaudhary. He was staying on the other side of town and suggested we meet at his guesthouse.

I didn't know what to expect from JD. All I knew about him was that he was a lawyer and had an eco-ashram, all of which I garnered from his website. His photo showed that of an older, gray-haired man with a beard, a kind smile, and gentle eyes.

When I finally found him, I knocked on his door and introduced myself.

"It's a pleasure to meet you, Mr. Chaudhary."

"My father was Mr. Chaudhary. Please, call me JD," he said with a thick Indian accent. I was late to our meeting, which only made me more nervous, but much to my relief, his grounded energy and offering of tea and cookies immediately put me at ease.

"How are you liking India so far?"

"It's been a bit overwhelming, but I wound up having a great night in New Delhi. I met some really nice people, made some new friends, and had some interesting conversations, but I really love being up here in the mountains. The air is so fresh, and the views are breathtaking. Is this where you're from?"

"That is why I love to visit here. It is good for the mind and soul to be closer to the heavens, but I am actually from the Indian state of Jammu and Kashmir. Today it is a place of much unrest despite that it is truly God's country," he said. "The beauty of my home state juxtaposed against the environmental degradation of Delhi called me into social justice. It was not my plan to fight for the environment and the people of India, but when I journeyed from my state to Delhi and saw how we were destroying our natural resources, habitats, water sources, and food chains with the shortsightedness of industry, I could no longer stand idle."

JD was an environmental attorney who, for much of his professional life, fought big business and the Indian government. His most famous case was defending the Taj Mahal from "marble cancer," as he called it.

Throughout his career, he received several death threats when he challenged the mafia and polluting industries. Seeing how greed, corruption, and big business were polluting and destroying the environment, he started the JD Chaudhary Foundation, its mission being to protect the environment, the rights of people to clean water and air, the promotion of sustainable development, and the protection of the cultural heritage of India.

"What would you do if your mother was in danger? Would you not protect her?"

"Of course," I replied.

"Well, Thomas, Mother Earth is in grave danger, and we cannot afford to stand on the sidelines anymore. The time to act is now, or it is going to be too late. We are fast approaching a tipping point where we may do irreparable damage to her."

"I get it."

"My critics have tried to slander me and call me an alarmist. There have been people who have spent hundreds of thousands of dollars to disparage me and drag my name through the mud. But the science is all there. This is not just about melting icecaps and rising temperatures. It is about the security threats that will occur as huge migrations of people escape environmental disasters and search for water. When they do not have clean air, water, livelihoods, or purpose, trouble begins.

"In the next decade, I fear we are going to see some of the biggest refugee camps the world has ever seen. Do not believe those in the media, government, or business who try to tell you otherwise. Those who deny climate change are the same ones who stand to make big financial gains in doing so, and they will do anything to take down the people who oppose them. In defending the victims of these perpetrations, I have had direct experience in seeing how serious it is becoming. My country is dying from a Western way of life. The people who stand to make these gains, they are fixated on money, power, greed, and wealth. So, they buy the opinions of scientists. We cannot fight them in the traditional ways. What we need is a movement, a movement of peaceful warriors who are willing to stand up for the earth."

He didn't need to say another word. The words from his heart went straight to my own. I was already committed to whatever he needed me to do.

"Unregulated chemical and polluting industries are ruining the environment. At one point in my career, my cases against these polluters became so voluminous that the Indian Supreme Court held special courts for me every Friday, but that can only do so much.

"Apart from my court actions, I began grassroots organizing. I took my first green march in 1989 and walked three hundred kilometers. We walked for fifteen days. These green marches became a milestone for creating environmental awareness. My goal was to make people conscious of their responsibilities toward the protection of the environment and fight against pollution at all levels. Today I have walked more than three thousand kilometers.

"That first walk started with no more than thirty-five people. Along the way, hundreds and hundreds joined us from all cross sections of society—teachers, engineers, doctors, street cleaners, lawyers, leaders from communities and NGOs, and of course the students. People from all walks of life fell into the fold. We became a force. We fought against environmental pollution and the unjust actions of the government." He paused to take a drink of water and collect his thoughts.

"Students are very important to the cause because they have youth and passion on their side. I was very active during my student days. I was involved in social movements, but as far as the environment was concerned, I was naïve. I did not know much about it. When you have so much beauty and abundance of nature around you as I did in my home state, you don't have value for it. When you are in the lap of it, you do not say, 'Oh, I have to protect the environment.' Jammu and Kashmir is a beautiful, almost pure state.

"At the time, I was not aware that environmental pollution, degradation, and unjust actions at the hands of humans were destroying livelihoods and health. Environmental law was never taught in the universities in India. It was a new field that I had accidentally stumbled upon elsewhere." True to his humility, only later would I find out that he not only stumbled upon it, but he was also the founder of environmental law in India.

After an hour or so of talking about his mission and sharing our life stories, I finally asked, "JD, you've seen my resume and called me here, so how can I be of service to you?"

"Everything in the cosmos is God," he said. "God is a word people have become afraid of. It has been hijacked and misused by individuals, religions, and nation states. But God simply is. It is the energy and source that we are all connected to, that which gives us life. I am sixty-five now. I have maybe fifteen to twenty-five years left, and nothing I have done in the past matters to me. The past is the past. I want to make the next fifteen to twenty-five years the most important years of my life. The earth can last without us, but we cannot last without the earth."

I leaned in.

"I have many ideas, but I am only one man, and I cannot execute all of them. I need a team to help me. I do not know much about computers, and I do not have time to write grants and do all the other things that need to be done."

And he wants me to help him? Is this a joke? I had been expecting to be tasked with some sort of menial job, not the responsibility of saving the earth.

At the end of our two-hour meeting, JD told me to email him if I was interested in volunteering for him.

Later that night when I returned to my guesthouse, I decided to do some more research on him. What I discovered astonished me. In more than 120 cases, he had never lost. Not once. He was the only lawyer to successfully sue the Indian government and win, and his cases were studied in law schools throughout the world.

Most recently, he had created an eco-ashram in a small village not far from Rishikesh and the shores of the Ganges River. It served as a retreat center for lawyers, thinkers, scientists, and influencers from all over the world. It was there that he spread the gospel of environmentalism and sent people back to their countries to become agents of change. JD lectured all over the world and was the guest of dignitaries, presidents, and world leaders.

And then there was me—a kid from New Jersey, a backpacker from Seattle without a plan. I not only got to spend the afternoon with JD, but he asked me to help him with his cause.

I was inspired. I didn't need much time to think about the opportunity; after all, what else was I going to do in India? Volunteering for JD at least gave me purpose and direction while I oriented myself to the country. It would also immerse me in Indian culture, not to mention give me the opportunity to orbit an extraordinary human being.

The following morning, I set out to look for an Internet café so I could email JD and let him know I would love to volunteer for him. On the street below my guesthouse, I found a coffee shop called Moon Temple. I peered inside, and it was crowded and lively. Every table was occupied by travelers researching the next leg of their journey or Skyping with friends and family back home.

I was tempted to search for a less crowded coffee shop when a beautiful woman sitting at a table by herself caught my eye. I walked past the coffee shop two times, trying to get up the nerve to go in and sit down with her, but I failed. On the third pass, she caught me looking at her and waved me in.

Who, me? I pointed to myself through the glass. Then I looked left and looked right, assuming she must be pointing to someone else. But she smiled and waved to me again, so I walked in.

"You're welcome to share my table," she said.

"Thank you. I really appreciate it."

"You're from the States?"

"Is it that obvious?"

"You have an REI backpack."

"Oh right. Color me impressed by your observational skills. I'm Thomas. Thomas Furey," I said, extending my hand.

"Cassandra," she replied, taking my hand in hers.

As you do when you enter your thirties, the first thing I did was check to see if she wore a wedding ring. Much to my dismay, she did. Regardless, I was happy to meet a friendly face in a foreign land.

Part Indian and part American, Cassandra lived with her husband in San Francisco. One of the first things I noticed about her was how her Lulu Lemon yoga pants revealed strong, shapely legs. Her eyes were big and brown, her skin flawless and mocha, and her breasts full and hypnotic. She was exactly my type of woman, but as fate would have it, she was off limits. Despite my past, a married woman was a line I vowed to never cross.

Cassandra had been traveling throughout India for six weeks and spent the previous two weeks in McLeod Ganj relaxing and studying Ashtanga yoga. Despite having visited family in India many times, it was the first time she had ever traveled the country alone.

We chatted and exchanged our traveler's tales, the two-minute elevator pitch you give someone when you meet on the road for the first time. I would tell this tale hundreds, if not thousands of times over the course of the next year. While you vary the presentation according to the audience, it essentially consists of:

- Where you're from;
- When you arrived in the country;
- Where you've been;
- How long you've been traveling;
- How long you plan to travel;
- And sometimes, why you're traveling (e.g., divorce, career change, running away from—or running toward—something).

Upon completing my traveler's tale, the man behind me leaned in and said, "Excuse me, but are you Scott?"

"No," I said. "Sorry."

"Oh, okay. You sound like a guy I heard about from Seattle."

I turned back around and began talking with Cassandra again.

"Oh wait, you're Thomas! Thomas Furey! I'm Sam, Sam Dixon!"

I nearly fell out of my chair. *Am I on* Candid Camera? *What the hell is going on?* My jaw went slack with surprise.

As it turned out, our mutual friend, John Riley, had put us together on Facebook a few months prior. When I last corresponded with Sam, we left it at, "Perhaps our paths will cross," but with all the excitement of leaving the States and landing in India, I had completely forgotten about him. The last thing I expected was to almost literally bump into him in a coffee shop in McLeod Ganj.

Above me, through the speakers, the album *Boxer* by The National was playing through the sound system, and when I asked for the password to the Wi-Fi, it was "Noble Beast," the name of an Andrew Bird album I was currently obsessed with. It just so happened these were two of my favorite bands, both of which provided vital soundtracks to my life during the previous decade. For a moment, I pondered the possibility that my future self had left these clues for me in Dharamsala to let my present self know I was on the right path.

To make matters even more interesting, Sam was traveling with his buddy, Jake, who happened to work with a good friend of mine in Seattle. I might as well have been in a coffee shop in Phinney Ridge. For two hours, the four of us remained at the coffee shop, chatting with wide grins on our faces.

At some point, distant thunderheads overtook the sun, casting the sky in dark and ominous light. With the impending downpour fast approaching, we all exchanged contact information and agreed to meet up the following day. I was the last to leave, and as I was packing up, I noticed that Cassandra had left her phone charger behind.

"Cassandra, wait! You forgot this," I yelled, chasing her down the street.

"Oh my God! Thank you so much," she said. "I would have been so upset to lose that. Where are you staying?"

"At the end of this road on the right. The Dharamkot Inn," I said.

"My guesthouse is the one right before that."

"Can I walk you there?"

"I would love that. What are you doing for dinner?"

"Haven't really thought about it, but the restaurant in my hotel has a great view. Plus, if this storm actually hits, it's going to be a quite a show. You want to have dinner at my hotel?"

The distant thunderheads rolled toward us, and the air instantly became charged. A flash of lightning and a giant clap of thunder seemed to burst right above us, causing Cassandra to nearly jump into my arms.

"Holy shit!" we said in unison, followed by laughter and an all-out sprint to my hotel. Large raindrops began falling from the sky.

We found a cozy table by a window that looked out over the plains that rose to meet us. After ordering a bottle of wine, the conversation flowed as we kept discovering similarities: Our current favorite band was The National, we both came from the East Coast, we were the youngest from a family of four, we did time in Catholic schools, and that was just the start.

Perched on the side of a hill carved into the foothills of the Himalayas, for several hours we shared our lives and watched the storm. Lightning bolts struck the earth, thunder rattled the window frames, rain and hail pelted them, and the wind howled through every nook and cranny it could find. It seemed inevitable that the power would go out, and when it did, the room was transformed by candlelight.

Through it all, the twinkle on her ring finger left me distracted. Seeing as it was the most romantic night in as long as I could remember, had I been living in a work of my own fiction, Cassandra would be single. *Two Americans with parallel backgrounds meet in a coffee shop in a foreign country...*

Like the smoke of a locomotive, the stormy night spread out and consumed everything in its wake while the rain relentlessly pounded the window at our table. A bottle of wine each into the night, we were completely unaware of how much time had passed when the restaurant announced last call.

"Why don't we grab a couple beers and head down to my room? I'm sure the restaurant will let us borrow some candles. You ever play Yahtzee?"

"I love Yahtzee," she replied.

"Great! We can play Yahtzee and listen to The National."

The restaurant gave us some candles for our room. We stayed up talking, rolling dice, and playing music. Around 2:30am the rain let up, so I gave her my headlamp. We hugged in a slightly longer than normal embrace, and into the Himalayan night she ventured.

***

Cassandra and I spent the next four days together, along with the duo from Seattle. When I was with her, it was as if the past melted away and only the present moment existed. The fact that I had left home without a plan and knew not where I was headed didn't seem to matter anymore.

While Sam and Jake hiked during the day, Cassandra and I walked about town, browsing shops and sampling local foods like yak cheesecake and street momos. On the third day we went for a hike in the mountains.

"I was twenty-three when I got married, and we've been together for ten years, married for eight. Would I do things the same if I could do it all over again? I don't know," she admitted. It was the first indication that things were not all peaches and cream in her marriage; she was, after all, traveling alone in India.

That evening, she coaxed me into playing guitar at an open mic night in a small restaurant. Although I once fronted a band in Seattle, in her presence I felt shy. However, always being one to rise to the occasion when onstage, I quickly won the crowd over. Granted, there were only ten or twelve people in the restaurant, but as I strummed and sang, Cassandra might as well have been the only person there. With my eyes closed I could feel her gaze, and when I looked up and our eyes met, I knew she was thinking the same thing.

Over the course of our days together, the sexual tension between us grew to a measurable degree. We flirted relentlessly with playful touches, and through a smile or a roll of the eyes we could speak volumes to one another across a room of strangers.

On our second to last night, we went to a traditional Tibetan restaurant, got drunk on bad whiskey and Kingfisher beers, and had a nightcap at a bar not far from our accommodations. On an empty dance floor, we found ourselves moving to Patsy Cline. While the rest of the bar looked on, our bodies swayed, entwined, and became entangled in familiarity.

Eventually the bar thinned out, and it was time to go home. When we reached her guesthouse, like awkward teenagers trying to figure out how to end a second date, we hugged each other long and tight. With her arms still around me, she leaned back, surveyed my face, looked into my eyes, and leaned in to kiss me. I have no idea how long we kissed, but I didn't want it to end.

The following morning was Cassandra's last full day in town before heading to Chennai to meet up with her sister and family.

"I need to go shopping for my family. You don't have to come if you don't want to. We can just meet up later when I'm done."

"You think I'm going to let you walk around a dangerous town like this all by yourself? You can't trust these orange-clad monks. No way. I'll be escorting you all day."

"That was the right answer," she said.

Since we had crossed a line the night before, we walked around town all day as if we were in a relationship. At the Moon Temple, she massaged the back of my head while we drank coffee. I held her hand. She held my arm while walking. I put my hand on her leg while we ate. She kissed my forehead and leaned into my shoulder.

After dinner we found ourselves back in my room, reenacting the first night. We listened to music, drank wine on the balcony, kissed, and moved to the bed as our articles of clothing fell to the floor. It didn't take long before her bra was off and we were both in our underwear.

"We can't do this," I said.

"I know, I know. It just feels so good and right."

"I know, but we can't. You're married. I can't do it." It didn't matter how much I wanted to. It didn't matter that she had talked about divorce. I couldn't do it. I couldn't let myself cross that line.

We lay in bed kissing, fondling, groping, and caressing, but mostly we just held each other and looked into each other's eyes. For at least one night, both of us managed to keep our own privately labeled brand of loneliness at bay, both of us amazed at how good something so unexpected could feel. We were reminded in our own way how long it had been since either of us had felt something so extraordinary and divinely orchestrated.

Around 4am we finally fell asleep. Her alarm went off at 6:30am so she could finish packing and make it down the mountain to catch her flight. I slept for another hour and then went to her room to see her off. When she had finished packing, unpacking, and wrestling her suitcase closed, we ate breakfast in our restaurant while skirting around the topic of what the hell had just happened over the last four days and whether or not it was real or had any bearing on the future.

"Well, this is it I guess," I said to her when we returned to her room. "It just doesn't seem fair that I had to travel to the other side of the world to meet you, and on top of that you're married. It's been so long since I've felt this way that I didn't even know it was still possible. So thank you for letting me know it actually is."

"Me too," she said, sniffling, her eyes welling up with tears. "Me too. Let's keep in touch, babe. I want to know all about where your adventures take you. I don't know where or when, but I have a feeling our paths will cross again."

Cassandra and I kissed and held each other until her taxi arrived, and just as quickly and unexpectedly as she had entered my life, so too was she exiting it.

Chapter 6. Sometimes you're the bumper, and sometimes you're the ball.

In my unexpected encounter with Cassandra, a life lesson I had received many times before was repackaged and wrapped in a new language: Life is like a pinball machine; sometimes you're the bumper, and sometimes you're the ball. And sometimes these brief and intense encounters come together with the impact of a high-speed collision, and the velocity and direction in which you thought you were heading cannot help but be altered. This happens every day, on every street corner, and in every bar and café in every city around the world. But when you're traveling, become open to possibility, and you surrender your human instinct to manufacture and control your experiences, these types of encounters are magnified.

And so it was in the course of two days that I had become a bumper, not the ball. Cassandra, Sam, and Jake had bounced off me—Cassandra to Chennai in southern India and Sam and Jake to Manali, a dreamy Himalayan hill town six hours east of Dharamsala. I was once again alone on the other side of the world.

The morning Cassandra left, I busied myself by packing up my belongings. Since she had vacated her room at the guesthouse, and because it was considerably less expensive than mine, I took over her room. What seemed like a good and cost-effective idea at the time only served to feed the loneliness and longing I felt in her absence.

As if her sudden appearance and subsequent absence weren't making me feel low enough, a few hours after I switched rooms, something sinister rumbled within my being. For the next three days, I moved no farther than my bed to the bathroom and back, and in that short journey, my ass and throat became very sore.

Momos. Street momos. Tiny, delicious, bacteria-laden dumplings. In our jaunts through town, Cassandra and I broke the golden rule for Westerners visiting India: Don't eat food from street vendors. It's akin to playing Russian roulette with your bowels. I was so enamored by her, I forgot the golden rule. I was simply following her lead.

In my sickened state, I had lost track of the days, and it was not until Sunday at 6pm that I began to feel better. It was then that I also realized that back home and in many countries around the world it was Easter Sunday. I opened the blinds for the first time in three days to let light in, and I gazed out upon the plains that were aglow from the setting sun. I was thousands of miles from home and what felt like light-years from my past, but my mind sought solace in the memories of my many Easters past.

A potpourri of feelings welled up in my heart—longing for what was, gratitude for what is, hope for what would be, and pride in the fact that something inside of me gave me the strength and courage to set out on this journey, despite the fact that for the better part of my life an unknown fear consumed me.

***

Despite the punishing artillery and air campaign the small but fierce army of bacteria waged in my bowels, I was rolling on a lucky streak in my travels thus far. There had been setbacks back home before traveling that more than once threw the inevitability of the trip into uncertainty, but I kept moving forward, telling myself, *Despite x, something better will come along.* And it always did.

As I sat looking out the window, sitting on the corner of what only a few days ago was Cassandra's bed, my mind drifted to a conversation we had several days prior.

"What's your secret?" Cassandra asked at breakfast three days after we met. The previous morning, I decided I needed to get *Lonely Planet: India.* I told her the book I sought was going to find me before the day was over, but as soon as I said it, I forgot about it. Sure enough, on the way home from breakfast—on the same route we took several times a day—we spotted a bookstore that neither of us had noticed before. Upon entering the store, directly in front of me was a discounted copy of *Lonely Planet: India.*

"It's not really a secret as much as it is an experiment," I said as I slathered jam on my toast, "but here it is."

My experiment in gratitude and intention began one afternoon a few weeks after my mother passed away. It was a warm day in August, and I was sitting outside a coffee shop in my Phinney Ridge neighborhood of Seattle, catching up on an old issue of *Rolling Stone* while half-heartedly searching for a job. Feeling dejected and lost, I looked up from my magazine. A block away I eyed a woman walking toward me, but I paid no more attention to her than that. She was dressed in bohemian garb and was probably in her early sixties. I put my head back down into the magazine when all of a sudden she was upon me. She walked right up to me and said, "Have you read the cover story yet?"

I had not. We began talking innocently enough about the article, the neighborhood, and the weather when she abruptly said, "I'm sorry to be so direct, but I sense a real heaviness about you. What is that?"

She had my attention.

"Jesus, is it that obvious? Yeah, it's been a really challenging summer."

"Why is that?"

"My mother passed away a few weeks back, and I haven't worked since late May."

"I'm sorry. That must have been awful."

"It wasn't ideal." I always said this when making light of unfortunate circumstances. "For the entire month of June she was wasting away in hospice care, waiting to die, and I was back here, unemployed, just watching the clock and killing time, waiting for her to pass on."

"I'm so sorry."

"Thank you."

"What was that like for you?"

"It's weird when you know someone is going to die. You wonder what it's going to be like, what it will feel like to cry and mourn them, what that absence will feel like in your life, what the sympathy from others will feel like. But no matter what you imagine, it's not even close to what you feel."

"I can sympathize. I lost my mother after a long battle with cancer. It's an ugly, ravishing disease. What do you do for a living?" she asked.

"Nothing now. I was a touring musician for a little while but couldn't really make a living at it. Now I work in advertising. I'm a writer. I was freelancing at an ad agency for five months. It was supposed to last until Christmas, but by the time I returned from saying goodbye to my mother for the last time, either the budget for my project had dried up or they replaced me. I don't know which. It doesn't matter really. I went back East to say goodbye, and here I am three months later, still out of work."

"I'm so sorry about your mother. As far as work, the right thing just hasn't shown up yet. My name is Claire."

"Nice to meet you, Claire. My name is Thomas," I replied, extending my hand.

"May I?" she asked, pointing to the empty chair at my table.

"Please," I said.

We sat in silence for a moment, looking west toward Green Lake Park and the snowcapped Cascade Mountains that loomed in the distance.

"If you could do anything, Thomas, what would it be?"

"I've been thinking about this a lot lately. I've always wanted to just take off and leave everything behind. I think I'm finally going to do it. I just don't know how yet. It doesn't feel like there's anything here for me right now. I don't have a career, a girlfriend, or a mortgage. I've got nothing holding me anywhere. Of course, I don't have any money either, so there's that. I guess I just want to find the right job for right now, the one that will get me to where I need to be."

"What does that mean exactly? What does it look like?"

"I'd like to find a six-month contract where I have some autonomy, a great boss, a fun team, and maybe even some room to be creative."

She paused before responding. "This may sound strange, but I'm very sensitive to people's energy. Sometimes

I'll be walking down the street and just hear a voice instructing me to talk to a person I see. Something told me that I needed to talk to you. I didn't know why, but I think I do now. I just had an idea. Are you open to trying something new and different?"

"I'll try anything at this point."

"It might sound silly, but I promise you it's powerful and will provide you with clarity. Ready? It's very simple. I want you to go buy a small notebook, and in it I want you to write down five things you're grateful for and five things you want to create and bring into your life. Do it every day. Be specific, be playful, be creative, and have no attachment to what you write. Simply write it down, close your notebook, then keep your eyes open as you go about your day. This exercise is going to land you in new places you could never have otherwise dreamed. There's a certain power to writing out your intentions."

"You want me to literally do that?"

"Literally," she said. "Literally write 'today I am so grateful for' and 'today I intend and create.' You're a writer, so just look at it as a daily writing exercise," she said. "You're going to find that the things you want to create are going to become the things you're grateful for in the future. Remember—and this is the most important part—surrender the how. If you try to predict how your intentions will come to fruition, you're limiting the creative power of the universe. You're not making room for the unknown. Just create and get out of the way. Let the greater intelligence organize it in a way that's best for you."

There was no way to know in that moment that eight months later I would be on my way to India, sitting next to a woman who would set my adventure in motion, launching me on a trajectory of surrender, healing, discovery, and faith. There was no way to predict the hundreds, perhaps thousands, of coincidences and synchronicities that would lead me to a coffee shop in Dharamsala, India where I would sit next to a beautiful woman from California and two people from Seattle. There was no way to predict how the money to fund my trip would magically appear and how it would keep appearing along the way.

Had I met this stranger on the street several years earlier, I would not have thought much more of our interaction, but considering I was feeling so lost and aimless, I took her suggestions to heart. When you lose a parent, or even both, you can't help but lose your sense of direction.

It first dawned on me one night in 2008 that my mother was gone and not coming back, even though her life force remained in her body for two more years. The realization was blinding, crippling, and anxiety-inducing, so I sought out anything to take the pain away. I started with my doctor and an antidepressant and then moved on to a therapist. Then I talked to a psychic. Then I got naked with a bunch of lesbians at an American Indian sweat lodge on an island off the coast of Seattle. I saw an acupuncturist, an energy healer, an astrologer, a naturopath, and a hypnotherapist. I took Reiki classes and tried yoga and meditation. All the while, however, I was medicating with pills, booze, and women. In my journal, I asked to be released from the pain, from the soul ache, but there was emptiness in my heart and it had a voracious appetite. I had to keep feeding it so I didn't have to feel the emptiness of hunger, loss, and the longing for the fruition of my dreams.

Every day in my mind it felt like I was standing on a side street at the World Trade Center that fateful blue September morning. This cloud came over me, and for a time I was lost in the darkness of ash and soot just waiting... waiting...waiting for the dust to settle while I wondered if I was actually alive or dead.

With my sharp edges dulled by Zoloft and Xanax, I lost everything I thought I knew and believed in, including my faith. Human beings have an innate connection to hope. Hope is a derivative of faith. I lost that connection to hope and faith, so I lost my way.

A writing exercise seemed harmless enough.

Claire told me she worked at the zoo and walked past the coffee shop every day at lunchtime. I had spent many of my unemployed days at the coffee shop, yet I had never seen her. I was also there many days after our encounter and never saw her again. But when she said goodbye that afternoon, I finished my latte and went straight to the closest Bartell drugstore to purchase a $2.69 notebook. A small investment with big dividends.

My first task was to create the perfect job for this moment in my life. I surrendered pay and all other personal creative requirements. Lo and behold, within a week the perfect job showed up. While it didn't pay what I normally made, it paid enough, and there were other perks involved. As long as I got my work done, my manager didn't care how or where I did it, and in time we became good friends. I supported him while he was going through a divorce, and I helped him move out of the house he had lived in with his wife for seven years.

To exorcise his anxiety and nerves, he exercised excessively. When that stopped being effective, I gave him a few Xanax to take the edge off. I was doing nothing more than being a friend, but a week later he told me to start billing him for forty hours a week, no matter how much I worked. Months later, when I told him I would be leaving in April to travel, he posed the question, "Would you be interested in still working for us while you're in India, maybe ten to twenty hours a week?" And just like that I was earning an income while traveling. I had been planning on buying a used MacBook Air to travel with, but coincidentally, work provided me with a brand-new one.

Thus began my personal experiment in surrender, trust, gratitude, and intention.

Once I started seeing results from the morning exercise, I started calling it "conscious creation." Most mornings, I simply asked for happiness and joy or to be an instrument of peace or light unto others. Those types of asks, more than physical or monetary ones, seemed to produce the most interesting and unexpected results.

Day by day, something told me that—beyond my other attempts at self-development—it was through the channels of gratitude, intention, and the present moment that I would one day find peace.

***

In total, the food poisoning knocked me out of commission for almost a week. When I was strong enough to go for a hike, I decided I needed to get out of town, so I set out looking for the Dharamkot Falls, a dramatic series of waterfalls whose source began high in the Himalayas. Carved out millennia ago by glaciers, between two towering mountains the waterfalls made their way down the valley, filling up wading pools, overflowing, and continuing down to the next pool like a bottle of bubbly poured into the top a champagne tower.

When I finally found a flat rock, I stripped down to my boxers and laid out my belongings around me. I settled in for a few hours of sunning, reading, writing, and relaxing. I felt a new sense of gratitude and expanding joy unlike anything I had ever experienced. It was physical in sensation and spiritual in connection. I could literally feel the joy and gratitude radiating out of my heart. I thought, *Okay, so many amazing things have already happened in such a short expanse of time. Now is the time to surrender even more.*

I imagined myself falling more deeply into the protective folds of the great mystery so that when either the grandest or most mundane ideas took form, I would be equally amazed and surprised. I focused my attention on opening my heart to let more possibility, gratitude, and love seep into my being. It meant surrendering any fear that stood in the way of having an extraordinary life. I needed to start thinking bigger, creating bigger, and removing all fear-based limitations—the requirements to truly test my experiment in surrender and creation.

Sitting on the mountain, it occurred to me that traveling was a lot like writing. When you sit down to write, you have no idea where you'll be when you get to the end. Sometimes the journey is joyful, sometimes it's terrifying, and sometimes it reduces you to tears of gratitude or despair. And sometimes the most fantastic, serendipitous events get you to the next chapter when you simply do the work, stay open to ideas, and follow where they lead you.

With these thoughts filling my soul, I watched a large, noble bird with great, expansive wings circle me. It circled for some time, making its way out into the valley and back again. Then, with no warning, it dive-bombed me.

It happened again and again, and each time it ascended it let out a shrill squawk. I gathered my things close to me, making sure I didn't turn my back on the bird. Clearly its intent was to torment me. As it became increasingly aggressive, the thought finally entered my mind that it probably had a nest nearby and was protecting its young. I decided to surrender my position to the elegant beast.

"Okay," I said aloud without taking my eyes off it. "You win. I'm leaving."

The moment I did look away to pack up my belongings, I felt its shadow descend upon me at lightning speed. Before I had a chance to react, it dropped a turd on my shoulders and neck that was equal to, if not greater than, its size.

When it hit me, I screamed at the pitch of a schoolgirl and nearly leapt off the rock into the water. I quickly put my hand to my neck and shoulders, revealing whatever the bird had been digesting.

I was in awe of this incredible act of instinct and nature. The mystery certainly had a good sense of humor.

***   ***   ***

I am so grateful for:

1. The reminder of how powerful and intelligent nature is.

2. The downloads of insight I seem to be experiencing.

3. My encounter with the woman who encouraged and challenged me to start my gratitude-intention journal.

4. The opening and unfolding that is occurring within me.

5. The time I got to spend with Cassandra and how she opened my heart to the possibility of love.

Today I intend and create:

1. Direction as to whether to wait for JD or move on.

2. To meet inspiring people who can teach me new things.

3. To surrender and trust even further and to feel gratitude and joy more deeply.

4. To experience more connections that cause my heart and/or understanding of the world to expand.

5. To receive a sign from my mother that she is looking out for me and is with me.

Chapter 7. The Waiting Game

It had been almost two weeks since I emailed JD to tell him I would love to offer my services to his cause. Since I had not heard back from him, I assumed he wasn't as excited about our meeting as I had been. I passed the time in wait by hiking, exploring the mountains, and looking for opportunities to meet new people, but in each day's passing the possibility of volunteering for JD seemed more remote. I was getting antsy waiting for his decision, so I decided it was time to move on.

In talking with fellow travelers, it sounded like Rishikesh was the next best stop. Should JD still want to work with me, it was not far from the eco-ashram. If I did not hear from him after a week in Rishikesh, I would assume he wasn't interested and head to Nepal to rendezvous with a new friend I had met a few days prior. As it turned out, when I arrived in Rishikesh, there was an email waiting for me.

Thomas,

My apologies for my tardy response. My wife has been sick and other preoccupations have kept me busy. I am also not very good on the computer. If you are still interested in working with me, I could be ready for you in a week.

Best Regards, JD.

***

After an unexpectedly eventful week, on my final evening in Rishikesh I found myself sitting on the banks of the Ganges River. As dusk settled upon the holy city, a haze of heat hung over the river valley, muting the sun's intensity and softening the sharp edges that otherwise gave form to the river, the mountains, and the horizon. The air, humid and dense, hinted at an approaching storm.

It was the hour when Indians gathered on the banks of the Ganges as they had for centuries, coming to wash, coming to pray, coming to lay offerings, and coming to be in community. A grand set of stairs led them to the water's edge where tourists, locals, and seekers of enlightenment waded knee deep in the mighty river. Some bathed, some washed their clothes, while others sought quiet spaces of stillness.

In reverent acts of *puja*, people both joyful and solemn placed *diyas* upon the water's surface as ancient prayers and distant chants echoed down the valley.

Filled with offerings and supplications, people in need, people in pain, people in joy, and people in wholeness released their *diyas* into the river. From there the *diyas* began their passage beneath the narrow Ram Jhula Bridge and traveled onward toward the holy city of Haridwar. From there they continued on into the northern plains, eventually emptying into the Bay of Bengal. Had the *diyas* been released from the river's source high in the Himalayas, the journey would have spanned 1,569 miles.

In the velvety glow of twilight, crepuscular insects came for a drink of life, only to find their own consumed by something greater beneath the water's surface. As if held in place by the strings of a diorama, a fingernail of a moon hung directly above the city. All the while, the *prana* of

India's mother river, the great Ganges, inhaled and exhaled its timeless breath into the denizens of its shores. And there I sat, in awe and wonder, soaking it all in.

For the first time since I arrived in Rishikesh, I was truly alone. I thought I knew what gratitude was, but since I had made the decision ten months prior to walk away from everything familiar, a cascade of serendipity flowed toward me. As one good fortune after another plotted a course, I could not help but feel like I was being led by some divine GPS system; after all, I was in a country whose national motto was "Truth alone triumphs."

At my first breakfast in Rishikesh, I met Silvia. We were staying in the same guesthouse and began talking over breakfast. Breakfast turned into lunch, and since then, we had been inseparable. I found myself alone on the banks of the Ganges because I was waiting for her. It was to be our last night together. The following day she was heading home and I would be meeting up with JD at his eco-ashram.

Silvia was a thirty-four-year-old Argentinian woman who was studying to be a yoga teacher. She was drop-dead gorgeous. All I could think of was how many hearts she must have broken and how mine could easily be one of them. What made her even more attractive was that she didn't know how beautiful she was, nor did she take herself too seriously. There was a childlike innocence about her, which—beyond beautiful eyes—had always been the nectar that attracted me to someone like a bee to the pistil.

"I had an undeniable calling to come to India," she told me our first morning together. "I stand to inherit a winery at home. My parents are not happy with my choice, but I said fuck it, you only live once. So, I came here to learn to be a yoga teacher and to work on my photography. The family business is always going to be there. I'll pick grapes in the future if I have to, but life is too short to live under someone else's pretenses."

All this before we had even finished our coffee and fresh pineapple. I also discovered that her mother was suffering from Parkinson's disease. She had only recently been diagnosed. Intellectually, Silvia knew what the fate of her mother would be. I knew, however, that intellect was no match for the reality of experience. When Silvia articulated the love and fear her mother's diagnosis engendered, she began to cry.

"Just so you know," she said in her Argentinian accent, her eyes twitching from contacts and tears, "I don't usually tell strangers these things. At least not before lunch," she added, trying to make light of the situation.

"It's okay," I said, reaching across the table, taking hold of her hand instinctively. "We're not strangers anymore."

I couldn't name it, but I knew in a smile and a touch we had shared something familial.

One of the things you don't know you'll learn while watching your parents decay over the course of a decade is compassion. When you see someone walking a path that you know will end in pain, you want to protect them. You wish you could absorb or deflect the pain like the Buddhist monks who practice *Tonglen*. But you know there are truths they must traverse, so all you can do is be with them in the present moment in love and solidarity.

After breakfast turned into lunch that first morning, we walked into town. Eventually Silvia brought me to a sandy beach just north of the Lakshman Jhula Bridge where, under her tutelage, I took my first dip in the Ganges River.

Neither of us had a bathing suit, so I stripped down to my boxers and she to her underwear. She wrapped a sarong around her top, which perfectly outlined her breasts. Despite trying my best not to stare, they beckoned my curious eyes.

"*Normalmente* I would go topless, but the Indian men around here, they are very creepy," she giggled.

"Damn creepy Indian men," I replied.

"At this bend in the river, you don't want to go farther out than where you can stand. You see where the current is breaking? My first day here I saw the body of a dead man dressed in a suit floating down the river. Perhaps he slipped and fell in and couldn't swim."

"In a suit? I suppose that's one way to frame it."

"Regardless, you must respect the Ganges, for as much as it gives life, it can also take it."

She waded knee-deep into the river.

"The Ganges is supposed to purify you with its waters, so when you immerse yourself, you are supposed to make an intention of what you want to be purified of."

We both closed our eyes and took a moment to set an intention. Then we took each other's hand and slipped beneath the surface of the Ganges. My intention was that when I emerged, I would be cleansed of the mental and emotional clutter that no longer served me.

We spent the next few days walking about Rishikesh getting to know each other. We went white-water rafting down the Ganges. We visited temples. We ate, talked, and ate some more. It was a dry city, so instead of going out for a beer we drank *limonanas*, a frozen drink made of lemon, ice, and muddled mint. Surprisingly, the absence of alcohol provided a refreshing way to get to know one another.

One day Silvia asked if I would like to join her at a nearby ashram for *satsang*, daily prayers and chanting that occur at sunrise and sundown. That evening, with the sun falling behind the mountains and the light draining from the sky, we sat in the back of the small temple, she on the women's side and me on the men's side. The participants smiled and rocked on their floor cushions, emanating into the room energies of joy and gratitude that I imagined floated out the windows and down the river valley. We sat for an hour listening, meditating, and soaking in the love.

Afterward we went to dinner, and Silvia told me that she knew of a holy man in town considered a living saint. She was meditating outside his room one afternoon when someone brought her inside to meet him, and she received a mantra. The man was very old and bedridden, and it was said that most of his organs no longer worked. She asked me if I wanted to meditate there the next morning.

We sat in meditation outside the door of the holy man at 7:30am. I tried to stay focused, but my untrained mind drifted, imagining what the old man inside looked like, thinking about what we were going to do afterward, and how hungry I was. Eventually my thoughts were absorbed into blackness. Once in that space of nothingness, as if illuminated by the switch of a light, I was back in New Jersey saying goodbye to my mother. A slideshow of images from those last moments flickered through my mind as tears of longing streamed down my face. I missed her comfort, security, guidance, and companionship. It had been exactly a year since I said goodbye.

After an hour or so of sitting outside the holy man's door, devotees began showing up, and a select few, including us, were escorted into the room one by one. The man stared off into the distance as if in a trance. We were encouraged to kneel in his presence, touch his foot over a blanket, and ask in our hearts for his blessing. Just like my mom had a year prior, he stared through the ceiling, motionless.

***

After an afternoon of wandering, which included taking in the ashram where the Beatles sought enlightenment, Silvia and I returned to our guesthouse and sat on her balcony, eyeing a storm over the nearby mountains. Distant thunder gave way to lightning and wind as we watched sheets of rain move toward us through the mountains. Even though we could feel the electricity in the air, we were determined to remain on the balcony as long as we could.

When the storm shifted into high gear, despite the fact that we were beneath an awning, the wind blew the rain sideways. As the rain soaked us, lightning seemed to strike a building near us, followed by a tremendous crash.

"Holy shit!" we both yelled, leaping from our seats and running into her room.

With all its might, the storm tried to follow us in, but Silvia won the battle, leaning into the door and sliding the deadbolt into place. "This is to keep the storm out. I know this doesn't look good, but don't worry! I won't bite, and if I do, I promise I won't break skin…unless that's your thing, but I can't promise I'll enjoy it," she said, laughing.

As the storm rained down, Sylvia complained about an ache in her neck and asked if I would massage it. She lay down on her bed, and I began massaging her neck and back.

"Hold on," she said, taking off her shirt and bra, revealing a back of flawless skin. *This is interesting. Am I reading this wrong?*

We spent the night tangled in a mass of lips and limbs beneath the thunder and rain. We awoke to a crisp, bright morning, but it was time for me to move on. If our lives had crossed at a different time and place, I could have fallen hard for her, but I was moving on to work for JD, and after more than three months in India, she would soon be returning to Argentina.

This time I was the ball and *she* was the bumper.

Chapter 8. The Eco-Ashram

The next morning, I set out to meet JD. What should have taken thirty minutes took nearly two hours. When I sensed I had been taken advantage of by my driver, the latent New Jerseyite in me said, "Go fuck yourself," to which he replied, "Get out." It was 118 degrees Fahrenheit, and I was in the middle of nowhere.

After finding some shade and collecting myself, I realized I lost my transportation over approximately seventy-five cents. It was a lesson about travel I would learn over and over: Sometimes, if your skin is a different color, you have the wrong accent, or your garb is different, well sometimes you just have to nut up and pay a right-of-passage tax. In the end, it's all about the experience anyway.

When I finally did make it to the bus depot, JD was waiting patiently with his driver.

"I'm so sorry I'm late," I said with rings of sweat around my arms and neck and my brow dripping as if I had just stepped out of the shower. "I had a driver that was not very cooperative."

"Welcome to India," he chuckled.

When we arrived at the Dhyana Eco-Ashram a half hour later, I finally understood what eco-ashram meant— minimal amenities and back to nature. *For fuck's sake, what am I getting myself into?*

JD showed me to my room at the back of the property. It was a simple stucco building with a slate roof. There were two twin beds beneath mosquito nets, a writing desk, two chairs around a table, and a toilet. What it lacked (besides décor) was hot water and reliable electricity. There was a shower, but the only thing that came out of it was bone-chillingly cold water that I could not tolerate, so my hygiene depended on bucket baths. The electricity I relied on for lighting and electronics was subject to a fickle power grid. JD made a point of leaving several candles for me. "You may need these from time to time," he said.

We returned to the front of the property where he showed me the eating quarters, which was another small stucco building with a tiny kitchen, a refrigerator, a table, and four chairs.

"Thomas, I would like to introduce you to Miranda, my assistant. If you two will excuse me, I need to get home to my wife. She is still not well."

Miranda was an Ayurvedic doctor from Mexico who had come to India to help JD get the ashram started. We came to know each other over a simple dinner of rice, dhal, and roti, which at the time I did not realize would be my meal almost every night. On the rare occasion when I got a ride into the closest town, from a small roadside shack I loaded up on Pringles, Kit Kats, Snickers, soda, peanut butter to dress the roti, and anything else that would break up the culinary monotony.

The ashram was situated on the edge of a national park where leopards and elephants roamed freely. Beneath a moonless night, in the shadows of darkness, lurked the unknown. It was for this reason that JD advised me to stay in my room after sundown. It was approximately the length of a football field from the kitchen to my room, but under the blanket of night it felt like I was running along a conveyor belt going the opposite direction. Each evening that I didn't make it back to my room before nightfall, I scurried from the kitchen to my quarters, beaming my headlamp into the woods, hoping I wouldn't see a set of hungry eyes gleaming back at me.

Quickly I learned I had roommates—ants, lizards, and even the occasional wandering frog. And those were just the things I could see. One night I spotted a spider in the rafters larger than my outstretched hand. I had no choice but to live in harmony with it. The way I saw it, it was either sleep with the spiders or sleep with the leopards.

"Okay, I'm going to do my human thing, you all do your creature thing, and we can all just live in peace, okay?" This was my nightly negotiation with them. So far they had abided by the rules.

On the night of my arrival, I spread the belongings of my backpack on one bed and climbed into the other. Once I was safely under the mosquito net, I tucked it below the mattress so no creepy critters could crawl up and surprise me in the middle of the night. Exhausted from the day's journey, I pulled out my notebook to write. Then with my headlamp on, I read *The Autobiography of a Yogi* until just past midnight. No sooner had I turned off the light and put my head on the pillow than a crosswind ripped through the room. As if possessed by ghosts, the curtains fluttered and the papers inside the mosquito net opposite my bed were blowing about.

I got up to close the windows and noticed the silhouette of the nearby hills appearing in purple flashes. The sounds of distant bowling alleys grew steadily closer. In a matter of a minute, the storm broke open above the property. In its exhalation, the tempest ripped at the rafters and hail pelted the slate roof, echoing the sound of thousands of marbles bouncing relentlessly.

Moments later, the storm blew open my door. I released a litany of profanities while trying to untangle myself from the mosquito netting. I leapt from the bed to force the door shut. No sooner had I closed the door than the roof began dripping on my bed. In a panic, I moved the bed a few feet to the right, noticing that my bare feet were sloshing through rainwater on the floor.

And then I waited.

And waited.

And waited through a long night. When the storm finally let up around 3:30am, I was not only wired, but I was also completely freaked out. I took a Xanax in the hopes of fading into oblivion. Then I fell into a deep sleep.

When I awoke the next day, much to my surprise the sun was well into its afternoon arch. I surveyed my tiny little piece of property. *This must have been what Gilligan's Island looked like the morning after the wreck.*

***

JD's home was in Dehradun, the capital of the Indian state of Uttarakhand. It was about twenty minutes from the ashram. When not at home, he spent his time between the ashram and the Indian Supreme Court in New Delhi. He was a very busy man.

Over the course of the next few weeks, I tried to grab time with him when I could, but he was constantly fielding calls, appearing in television debates, educating the public about the destruction of ecosystems, or being summoned to New Delhi or Rishikesh to protest unfair labor practices. He was the voice of the people, and when the powers that be were working to build a dam at the mouth of the Ganges River that would cut off water downstream and destroy the source of livelihood for millions, the people asked JD to defend them.

In the meantime, I was entering a new phase of my trip where I was living in a single location instead of traveling around. I didn't mind that the pace was slowing down; I was too fascinated by JD and felt incredibly blessed to get to know the man behind the legendary career.

"Thomas, the world is sick and not enough people are paying attention. The signs are all around, but most people have their blinders on. We live in a 'me' world, but if we are going to survive as a species, we are going to have to switch the paradigm to a 'we' world. We are going to have to wake up and act as one with swiftness, or things are going to get very unpleasant.

"It begins with finding peace within one's mental and spiritual world. Then we must bring that peace to the physical world by curbing the tides of climate change before we hit a tipping point. Mankind is wiping out entire ecosystems, forests, and jungles. I am certain the answers to cancer and many other illnesses can be found in the medicinal plants and herbs in these forests and jungles, but every day we continue to decimate them. Nature is perfectly balanced. For every sickness there is a cure. We just have not found it yet. I do not want our grandkids to say, 'Why didn't they do anything when they could?'

"The reason why I have enlisted your help is because I have a grand vision for creating an international climate change center, and I want you to help me write two grants—one for the center and one to study cancer in India."

"Whatever you need to me to do, I'm here to help. What's the cancer study?"

"As recently as thirty to forty years ago, India was an agrarian culture and cancer was all but nonexistent. As India moved from a developing country to a developed one, mass migrations of people moved out of the country and into cities, and the life spans for men and women improved. This is a good thing.

"But what also happened was that the Indian diet changed drastically, and greedy industrialists began polluting the environment, rivers, and the water table. With the introduction of lethal insecticides and pesticides, they were essentially poisoning the food chain and slowly killing people. We Indians have made the mistake of copying a western model that does not work for India. The same companies that were once poisoning your people are now moving to developing countries because there are no restrictions or laws in place to protect the people there. These industrialists are not interested in fixing problems, only increasing profits."

"Why are they still using these insecticides and pesticides?"

"Because Indian laws are antiquated and promote business over protecting the farmer and the consumer. You can't begin to comprehend how corrupt the entire system in India is and how widespread mafia control is."

"Why don't the police and government just come in and put a stop to all of it?" I asked.

"Ahh. That's cute," he said with a big grin. "Because these mafia-controlled entities have so much money that anyone who can impede their progress is put on the payroll."

"Maybe India and the U.S. aren't so different. We just call them corporations and Congress. Politicians put their hands out, and the corporations fill them. Everyone knows it, but no one does anything about it."

"Exactly. Most people do not understand the gravity of what climate change is going to create and do not think it is going to affect them. It is going to cause mass migrations of people, which will cause huge security problems for countries all over the world, and still people try to deny it. If you cannot have objectivity in science, what is left?"

***

While most days I tried to stay focused on what JD wanted me to accomplish, inevitably I couldn't help but wonder about his personal journey.

"Can I ask you a question?"

"Certainly."

"You've had such a successful career already. Most people would want to retire, but you say this is the most important time of your life. Why?"

JD changed his body language from open to contemplative by bringing both hands together over his lips, each fingertip touching its counterpart on the other hand.

"Thomas, when I first began my career, I did not know this was what I was going to be doing. I never desired to do this. When I came out of law school, I did grassroots organizing, and it was only by fate that my public career began."

"How?"

"One evening, I was attending a community gathering. I had just finished speaking when a man stood up. He not only personally insulted me, but he lambasted all lawyers, saying they were criminals. 'Lawyers used to be important, productive members of society during the freedom movement,' he protested. 'Now they represent nothing but greed!' So I asked the man, 'What is your problem?' He was visibly upset. 'It is the Taj Mahal,' he said. 'It is everyone's problem, but no one is paying attention. It is suffering from marble cancer! The polluting industries around it are literally pitting the marble and making it turn yellow! India's greatest monument of cultural heritage is being ruined, and no one is paying attention!'

"He was visibly upset, so after the meeting I asked him to send me more information about the Taj. When I returned home that night, I couldn't sleep. A week later, I received the materials, but he didn't leave his name or a return address. Almost forty years later, I still don't know who that man was, but he launched my career. Because of him, I filed my first case in the Supreme Court against the State of India, claiming the cultural heritage of India was not worth the short-term gains of industry.

"What ensued was a twenty-year legal battle. The win resulted in the creation of a green belt around the Taj, and all the offending factories were forced to shut down, change location, or upgrade to clean fuel and energy. In total, this included more than twelve hundred industries."

"Did you just say twelve hundred?" I asked for clarity.

"Twelve hundred. In the process, I saw the harm these industries were doing to the poor and voiceless. I could not in good conscience turn my back on them and still live a life I could be proud of."

"That would never pass in the U.S. Our government is too broken, divided, and bought," I said in awe.

For a man to take on the Indian government and all those mafia-run industries took balls the size of Jupiter, and I wanted to know what it was like to have them swinging between your legs.

***

"I was supported by two things in my career—my faith and my vision," JD said to me one day. "A vision is not born, it is created. Vision is a choice. Everyone has a vision, but not everyone has the courage to see it through. Fear is a ferocious impediment. Just as Gandhi and his followers threw their clothes in the fire and had nothing but their faith and their will, I too am supported by both. It only takes one person with courage, a voice, and a vision to create a movement. I will tell you this: People will call me old and out of touch, but modern India has forgotten its roots and lost its way."

I was in complete awe at the depth, wisdom, and down-to-earth nature of this man, not to mention how privileged I felt to have had one-on-one time with him. He was one of the teachers I had been seeking my entire adult life, and he spoke to me how I wished my own father could.

Chapter 9. The Indian Night

The days at the eco-ashram moved at a snail's pace. After two or three weeks, one evening I finally ventured into the courtyard outside my room (all twenty feet of it). I had taken to smoking one cigarette during the day and one at night, so I rolled a Drum, walked out to the courtyard, and lit it up. Above me, an endless lattice of sparkling stars peppered the belt of the Milky Way. Before me, the monochromatic night hinted at foothills and distant mountains.

For the first time in as long as I could remember, I felt a calm within me. There were hints of this peace like the night I sat on the banks of the Ganges in Rishikesh, but this was something deeper. Stillness. I had nowhere to go and nowhere to be. All I had to do was inhale and exhale. Breathe in and breathe out. Within my breath I sensed that I was shedding something. An effortless molting was taking place, nurtured and fed simply through intention and the breath of being.

On one of my regular nightly forays into the courtyard, I was smoking a Drum beneath a waxing moon when my thoughts drifted to a spring night in Baltimore. I was a senior in college. I had not thought about this night in years, and there was nothing special about it. In fact, it was a scene that had played itself out countless times in the past, from New York City to Portland, Oregon, and from Siena, Italy to Crete to the Rift Valley in Tanzania.

That night in Baltimore I was standing in front of the mirror. I remember standing there for some time looking at the reflection before me because I had no idea who the person staring back at me was. Who was this stranger, and what was going to become of him? Would I ever know him completely? Would he ever be able to shed the soul ache—that unnameable, unknowable inner sadness that seemed to have no source? Would he ever be able to shed the heavy weight of existence that was dense, physical, yet intangible?

Was that inner sadness something that was a product of his nature? Or was it something born of nurture, passed on to a highly sensitive kid through the DNA strands of his parents and ancestors? Perhaps the soul ache was engendered in that first moment of self-awareness, when consciousness determined it was separate from all that is. Would this person in the mirror ever know what was behind the curtain, the veil?

Like a nagging anxiety, the questions began when I started keeping a journal at seventeen, and they continued through my late twenties and into my early thirties. I suppose there is no other logical outcome when one is so intensely studying the self and cataloging the journey. The questions always felt like a dream from the night before, full of hazy, nonsensical images that were familiar but foreign, near yet distant, culminating in a maelstrom in my heart and soul. Sometimes I questioned my will to go on.

But as Preetika predicted, India was beginning to provide me with a new dimension of self. The difference between the person who was staring at me in that mirror and the person I was becoming was a growing inner strength, a trust in the self that can only be known with time, and for me, could only have been expanded and fortified by the self-reliance that solo travel afforded me.

During one of our afternoon sessions, I told JD I was reading *The Autobiography of a Yogi.*

"Thomas, Yogananda once said, 'One's values are profoundly changed when he is finally convinced that creation is only a vast motion picture and that not in it, but beyond it, lies his own reality.'"

"What does that mean to you?" I asked.

"Everything out here," he said, gesturing to the property, "and everything we see through here," he said, pointing to his eyes, "is an illusion. The only reality is right here," he said, pointing to his head and heart.

"The sooner you learn that the mind is a wild, unpredictable stallion that must be tamed, the sooner you can take control of it. When you control the mind, you are not affected by the illusions, by the noise of the motion picture. As a young man, for a very long time I fought an outward battle of pride and ambition, but with age I learned that finding harmony within one's self is the most important thing you can do with your life.

"Okay," I said. "But how?"

"You are a guitarist, no? It's like using an electric tuner for your guitar. You make adjustments until the needle, which operates on vibration and frequency, comes to center— not too flat, not too sharp. That is the place from which music, harmony, and rhythm become ordered into song. This internal vibration, or energy, is unique for everyone, like a fingerprint. It is the key to life. When you align your inner self to this energy, you are brought into alignment with your soul's purpose, and the universe organizes itself around you."

He paused, taking in the surroundings of the property. "Once you achieve this, all things are possible. It is how we change the paradigm of reality we understand as cause and effect to affecting the cause."

"That's very different from our Western way of thought, but I think I get it," I said. I was struck by the similarity between JD's words and the advice Abhay gave me in his billiards room in New Delhi.

"When I was a child, Thomas, my mother used to warn me to guard my thoughts. Naturally, in the arrogance of youth, I scoffed at her. But in her wisdom, she was onto something. Most of our thoughts are unconscious programs subject to the laws of attraction. Like attracts like. What we send out is returned to us in form and matter. The secret they don't teach you in school is that our thoughts are powerful forces that can at once be incredibly creative or destructive. This is why the ancient masters and saints said that developing the mind and controlling the ego should be our highest aims."

***

With not much more to do around the ashram than think, write, and ponder JD's teachings, I set out to tune my inner guitar. I opened myself up to the stillness and silence that the ashram afforded me. With every passing day, I came to a greater understanding of my relationship to energy and reality. I realized that I was an observer who was in fact not separate from all living things but rather an extension of a greater consciousness that was responsive to my thoughts, intentions, and energy. And it wasn't just hyperbole; my gratitude-intention journal was empirical proof.

It would have been easy to dismiss these creations as coincidence, but the more attention I paid to my inner world, the more I believed I was feeding it energy. I observed my thoughts as creations, and as I did, the more my subjective reality shaped my objective experiences. The more I tuned into this universal energy, the more I let it flow through me unobstructed, the more I believed it was making me magnetic. This function of the magnetism was to attract the experiences I wanted to create.

JD got me thinking about the story I was writing—the story that set me off on my journey—as if it were a film. If I were the director, how would I edit the film of my life? There is a structure and arc to each of our lives, including a rise and fall of action and climaxes that mark the beginning and end of certain acts.

In the midst of an increasingly mystical Indian night, I thought about the structure that held my story together. It was not an intellectual idea or a clever storytelling trick. The glue was the relationships in my life—my friends, family, mentors, lovers, and the people I bounced off of and the people that moved through me.

All of these individuals gave me the gift of their hearts. Even the ones who hurt me deeply had been my teachers. They shaped me, carried me, created me, and delivered me to this moment. They were part of a divine gossamer tapestry that was invisible to the human eye and unquantifiable to the objective mind, yet knowable through the feelings of the heart and the language of emotion.

In the darkness of the Indian night, I felt their light supporting me, holding me in perfect alignment to where I was supposed to be. I looked up at the stars, felt tears of joy welling up within me, and for an hour spoke aloud each one's name (at least as many as I could envision), offering them a prayer of gratitude and prosperity.

Without doing anything, by simply being open to possibility, I fell more deeply into the mystery. Unlike that young man who was burdened with questions so much larger than himself, who looked in that mirror in Baltimore and had no idea who he was, I was coming to know my place in the mystery through the experiential discoveries of the heart, not through the intellect. Living, being, loving...*that* was the mystery. I was not separate from the mystery but an indelible part of it. Whatever the mystery was, perhaps my role was to let it experience itself through me.

It is the law that all beings must go through periods of uncertainty and disorder to create space for transformation. It's inevitable that somewhere along the journey of life, everything we know shatters and we're forced to figure out how to put the pieces back together. If only someone had explicitly told me that it is the nature of nature to organize chaos and complex systems into order and balance. We only need to look at the Fibonacci sequence scattered throughout nature to see this truth in action.

If we can just hold on through the darkest periods of our life, eventually we'll see that life's most beautiful moments of becoming and delivery happened during the hardest parts of our journey when we thought we couldn't go on. In my lowest moments, if I could have just tuned my senses to a higher frequency, I could have avoided a lot of pain by realizing that the most challenging times of my life coincided with guidance toward a new path.

For the last several years it felt as if my world was breaking down. In the process, I retreated from my body into my mind. Only now was I beginning to settle back into my body again, putting the pieces back together to create a new form. India was awakening something dormant within me, and I felt like something greater than me was running the show. It would take care of things; I only needed to give it permission. My thoughts, feelings, and emotions were forming a new foundation of reality by dictating the strength, creative potential, and ultimately the response of an interactive universe.

With a head full of thoughts and a heart full of gratitude, I retreated from the courtyard and its night sky to my room where once again I began reading *The Autobiography of a Yogi*. In it, Sri Yukteswar, yogi and master to Paramahansa Yogananda, said, "There is a deeper astrology not dependent on the testimony of calendars and clocks. Each man is part of the Creator, or Cosmic Man; he has a heavenly body as well as one of the earth. The human eye sees the physical form, but the inner eye penetrates more profoundly, even to the universal pattern of which each man is an integral and individual part."

Beneath my mosquito net, I closed the book, rolled over, and fell into a deep, restorative sleep.

***　　***　　***

I am so grateful for:

1. The insights I am receiving in the stillness of nature, night, and my heart.

2. Being able to trust the metamorphosis/ transformation within me that is underway.

3. A mentor showing up in the form of JD and for all I have learned from him.

4. The incredible series of events that had to occur for me to be living my dream of traveling the world and writing about it.

5. Being on the most incredible journey of my life (so far).

Today I intend and create:

1. The wisdom of my mother and father spoken to me through others.

2. To have profound experiences that will help me see the truth.

3. To find a way to make money and keep traveling.

4. To have a serendipitous meeting that leads me to new and interesting people.

5. To find peace within me so I can be an instrument of peace and a light unto others.

Chapter 10. The Dinner Party

With approximately 750,000 people, Dehradun was a small town by India's standards, but it was just as overwhelming as the next Indian city. It was a snaking sprawl of cars, exhaust fumes, motorbikes, cows, pedestrians, litter, and of course, no Indian city would be complete without the constant soundtrack of car and motorcycle horns.

Not many tourists came through Dehradun, putting me on the receiving end of even more blank stares and photography requests than normal. Throughout India, people frequently came up to me and asked to take a photo with me. At first I thought it was funny because they were clearly mistaking me for a celebrity. Later I found out it was because the Indians just wanted a picture with a white guy, which I found hilarious.

"Can you imagine if I was in Harlem and went up to a black guy and asked him for a picture?" an American friend said to me one afternoon.

For me, Dehradun served as an outpost for an Internet connection and a place to do research for the grant proposals. After living in the conditions at the eco-ashram, it also served as luxurious retreat where I could hide out in an air-conditioned hotel room, order room service, catch up on a backlog of *60 Minutes* episodes, email friends, drink Carlsberg beers in bed, and eat Oreos in a hot bath.

I was originally supposed to spend three days in Dehradun, but JD was so busy that he had no time to fetch me. Thus, three days turned into a week, which was fine by me. I was enjoying taking hot baths and ordering daily room service. By day three, however, after uttering not a word to a soul, I felt despondent and lonely.

That Friday evening, I needed to email JD a draft of the proposal I had been working on. Since my Internet connection in the room was running slow, I went into the hotel's business center and plugged into the Ethernet. While there, a well-mannered Indian man around my age poked his head in and asked if I would like tea or a lime soda.

He returned with a cup of mint tea, and when I was finished with my work, I knocked on his office door to thank him. Upon his desk was a large Apple computer monitor.

"Nice computer," I said. "I love Apple."

"It's a beautiful machine. Please, come in and sit down."

Pranav introduced himself and began extolling the virtues of Apple products, telling me how although iPhones were not yet available in India, he had found a way to purchase enough for his entire family and several friends.

"Even my father, who can barely work a clock, is using it," he said.

As we chatted, I described how serendipity had intervened to connect me with JD and the eco-ashram.

"Don't get me wrong," I said. "I'm no Mother Teresa and not looking to take a vow of poverty or anything. I still like my iPod, my MacBook Pro, and the financial freedom to eat sushi when I feel the need."

"Oh? You like sushi, do you?" Pranav said, kicking back in his chair. "What are you doing tonight? Would you like to have dinner? I'm going to a friend's house and you should come along. I've been trying to have her make sushi for a long time. Maybe she will if it's not too late. If nothing else, there will be interesting people."

"I was just going to walk across the street and grab a bite, but your invite sounds much better. Thanks, I'd love to."

"What do you like to drink?" This was one of the best questions anyone had asked me in a long, long time.

"I'm pretty easy. Beer, wine, whiskey."

"Perfect. I was going to grab something from the hotel bar, but Minna should have all of that." *Minna, huh? Sounds exotic. Now we're talking.*

I returned to my room to shower and put on the most respectable outfit I could muster while Pranav grabbed some things from the hotel restaurant.

About four kilometers north of Dehradun, we arrived at Minna Abramovitz's house. I was imagining smooth, dark skin, a shapely figure, and mid-thirties, not a seventy-five-year-old Jewish woman from western Philadelphia's Main Line suburb. Nonetheless, I was intrigued. How was it that this small woman had come to live in India for more than twenty-five years?

***

Pranav was right; it was an interesting mix of people.

There were Pranav and Minna, of course. Pranav's family owned the hotel where I was staying, and Minna had studied and practiced the macrobiotic diet for years under the tutelage of George Ohsawa and the couple Michio and Aveline Kushi. Other guests included an architect who was also a tarot card reader and energy healer, a recently divorced Indian woman (which was taboo in Indian culture), a retired, high-ranking air force officer and his wife, and another older gentleman who looked like an Indian version of Ernest Hemingway. When I told the Hemingway lookalike about JD, I was shocked that he didn't know who JD was. I just assumed everyone in the country knew this national hero.

Instead he replied with condescension. "Ha. I didn't even know there was such a thing as environmental law. Tell me, what has this Mr. Chaudhary done?"

"You have not heard of JD Chaudhary?" the tarot-card-reading architect and energy healer chimed in. "He is a most impressive man. I have been following his work for years."

For a good part of the night, I stared across the table at Minna in bemusement, watching her chain-smoke Pall Mall menthols, never once thinking that the smoke might bother any of her guests. Each time she tried to light a menthol, her long, hot-pink fingernails challenged her resolve and dedication. But these traits, I would later learn, were the cornerstones of her life.

The air force officer held our rapt attention for some time, recounting tale after harrowing tale of his service, like when his helicopter suffered mechanical failure and dropped out of the sky from several thousand feet when he was just a year away from retirement.

"I thought it was my time," he said. "But miraculously I walked away with just a few cuts and broken bones. The real miracle was that I received something not a lot of people get—a second chance."

"How has that affected you?" the divorceé asked.

"I no longer take anything for granted. As the helicopter plunged to earth, I stayed focused on what I had to do. I had been well trained. At the same time, there was a part of me that was separate and outside of myself. I saw my life flash before me, and all I could do was think of my wife and children and how I wasn't ready to leave them. When you think you are living your last seconds, every moment you have after that is a blessing," he said, placing his hand on his wife's lap.

For three hours we cocktailed, ate, and chatted as young Indian men refilled our glasses and brought out plate after plate. When the evening ended, I hugged Minna and said, "It was great to meet you, Minna. I'd love to hear more of your story."

"My door is always open. You come back for tea, but I prefer whiskey."

"You're the boss," I said, giving her a hug and thanking her for her generosity.

I was feeling pretty warm on the ride home, my head swimming in a bit of vodka and wine. Serendipity had once again touched down in the form of a conversation about Apple products, but then again, I had written that morning in my journal that I wanted to have a serendipitous meeting.

"That man," Pranav said, "the one who challenged you, don't take offense. His is a very sad story. He was driving in the car that killed both of his children, and he alone survived. The year before the accident, his wife died of cancer. It sent him into several years of severe alcoholism. He doesn't drink, but he hasn't recovered. I fear he never will."

"Wow. I don't really know what to say."

"There is nothing to say, really. It's life. Beautiful, unpredictable, humbling, and tragic." After some silence, he continued. "If you don't have any plans tomorrow and since you haven't seen much of the area, would you like to head up to the hill town of Mussoorie and go for a hike?"

***

The next day, Pranav and I met in the hotel lobby at 1:30pm. Outside, his driver awaited us. Pranav had the hotel prepare us lunches and asked if I would mind making a quick stop at his home to pick up a few provisions. His home was actually a palatial residence where he lived with his parents, wife, son, servants, and security guards.

An hour later, we reached our destination and began our hike up the mountain. Another hour later we reached a small mountain temple. Pranav's first act was to pay his respects to the Hindu deity, Shiva. While he prayed, I found a seat on some rocks and admired the splintered sunbeams that reminded me of stage lights shining down on the endless amphitheater of the Himalayas. I took a moment to say my own prayer of gratitude.

When Pranav finished, he made his way back toward me and we sat in silence for a moment, both admiring the magnificently rugged beauty and jagged peaks.

"Can I ask you something, Pranav? What do you ask for when you pray?"

"Why would I ask for anything? I already have all I need, and whatever else I do want or need, Shiva already knows. So mostly I just say hello and ask how Shiva is doing. I really don't need to ask for anything because I know Shiva is working for my highest good. Instead I try to find tranquility within me because that is the place from where the voice speaks. All of life's answers can be found in the silence." *Just like JD's message of stillness.*

"I like that."

We sat in an easy silence until he continued. "Thomas, have you ever heard the story of the old woman who was knitting in her house and lost her needle?"

"I haven't."

"A man came by and saw her on the ground outside her house. He offered to help her find the needle, so they looked all over the grounds outside the house. Alas, it was nowhere to be found. 'Where did you lose it?' he finally asked her. 'In the house,' she replied. 'Well, then why are you searching for your needle out here?' he said. 'Because it's dark in my house and I'm scared.'"

Pranav paused as I looked on in curiosity. "You see, Thomas, the point of the story is that we all know where to look for the answers, but most of us are afraid to go there."

"That's what brought me to India," I told him.

"The search for self and the exploration into the self is the journey each of us should be undertaking. Life happens from here to here," he explained, pointing from his left temple to his right. "It all exists in the mind, then it is brought forth into existence through language. The world occurs to us through the marriage of language and images. Anyway, I want to hear more about this grateful intention journal you spoke of last night."

"It's an experiment in...well, in consciousness really. Consciousness, creation, and connection. And in trust and surrender, I guess. What it comes down to is I'm looking for my sewing needle, and after years of looking in all the wrong places, I've finally decided I need to look for it in the house, despite how scary and dark it is, and let me tell you, it's pretty scary in there sometimes."

"Yes, but you know, when you're in there long enough, your eyes adjust and you can see clearly in the darkness."

"The thing is, it's been so long since I've seen this needle that I don't even remember what it looks like. I'm just trusting I'll recognize it when I see it. All my life I've been writing in my journals about this search, the experience of the search, and hoping that within it I'll find a truth. Or at least find my story, the one no one else can tell. It's been a constant process of surrendering and creating, trusting and surrendering, surrendering and creating. I'm putting all of my faith into this act, trusting there's something greater guiding me."

"And how is that experience?"

"It's terrifying, exhilarating, and affirming."

"Just like life," he added.

"Yesterday morning I was feeling very lonely and wrote in my journal that I wanted a serendipitous meeting. Then in the afternoon I met you. It's hard to see the forces at play in the present, but I hope someday it will all make sense."

"What do your parents think of your search? Do they support it or do they have a different idea of who you should be and what you're doing with your life?"

"My mother passed away a little more than two years ago. The whole time leading up to it and the months afterward were really hard for me. I was filled with anxiety and self-doubt. Basically I felt like a loser. I was unemployed and more than three thousand miles away from where she was dying in hospice. And I couldn't do a goddamn thing about it. Without a job to occupy my day, I spent three weeks pacing the floor of my apartment, just waiting for the call."

After we sat in thoughtful contemplation for a few minutes, Pranav spoke. "Our parents made great sacrifices to provide us with bountiful lives, and as a result we have the time and luxury to think about what we actually want out of our lives. But nothing comes without a cost. Freedom can be paralyzing. It requires that we be responsible for the choices we make. Every generation has its own unique challenges to address. Our parents had theirs and we have ours."

"I suppose my kids, if I'm ever lucky enough to have them, will know about my challenges from my journals. I started journal writing when I was seventeen. I have more than forty of them."

"Do you ever go back and read them?"

"Very seldom."

"When you do, how does it make you feel, reading about your life?"

"I guess I have a lot of compassion for the kid who wrote them. But sometimes what I wrote ten or fifteen years ago is as fresh and painful as when it occurred. There's been a lot of sadness and longing in my life."

"What's that all about?"

"That's what I'm trying to find out. I guess like anyone I just want to know that my life means something, that I didn't just waste my time walking the earth searching for something or killing time."

"You'll find it. I'm confident. Life is the greatest free education you can get, but that's not to say it doesn't come at a cost. Unfortunately, we keep learning the same lessons until we get it right. Only then can we graduate to the next level. Every time we don't get the lesson, we repeat the grade, and every time we repeat the grade, learning the lesson gets that much harder. Eventually the lesson becomes so painful we have no choice but to get it. It sounds to me like you're always living in anticipation of the next thing, right?"

"Absolutely. It's not how I want to live, but it's how I've lived for the majority of my life. Maybe it's an American tendency."

"You should focus on being in the here and now. It's all that exists."

"I've been trying. I've had some success, and it's a lot of what this trip is about, but...I don't know," I said, trailing off.

"No, finish that thought. You need to hear it, more for yourself than for me. The sounds of these words need to resonate within you, like a bell."

I cleared my throat and inhaled.

"Well, this experience of travel has brought out some of the best parts of me that I've always known existed but have been afraid to admit to. And that's been incredible. I've had some really profound experiences and have come to know this inner joy like I've never known before. And I know that when I feel this way, I just attract more good stuff into my life. But how do you stay there?"

"You can't unless you reach enlightenment, which almost no one achieves. You know how you have compassion for that young boy you just spoke of? And you know how this experience of travel is bringing all these new revelations and expansions? Remember these joyful feelings and meditate on them when you are in your sad places. Meditate on them in silence as if you are searching for your sewing needle.

Move into those spaces of joy and liberation. And you have to forgive yourself for your mistakes and your feelings from when you were younger. A boy can never possess the knowledge of a man. It's a law of nature and time. You are here right now, right where you're supposed to be."

As we made our way down the mountain, the encroaching night began its final assault on the day. The wispy orange and magenta clouds in the distance mixed with storm clouds, causing them to glow as if a battle raged within. By the time we reached the car, the day had all but burned itself out, leaving only smoldering embers of tiger, crimson, and fuchsia in the western sky.

I stared out the car window for what felt like an endless drive.

Not far from the hotel, Pranav broke the silence. "You know, Thomas, we went on that beautiful hike today and we climbed to the top of a mountain, but we only spent about twenty minutes up there. It was an end point, a goal we reached, but that wasn't really the purpose of the trek. The trek really occurred during the journey, and that is the beauty of life."

How did I get so lucky? I thought.

Chapter 11. Whiskey and Pizza

As if on autopilot, the next morning I found my way to Minna's door.

"Hello? Anyone home? It's Thomas looking for Minna." I heard her shuffling toward the door before I saw her.

"What the hell are you doing out there, Thomas? Get your ass in here. You know my door is always open. What are you drinking?"

"Some chai would be perfect."

Minna yelled to one of her houseboys as we made our way to her sitting room. She tapped out a Pall Mall and fussed with the lighter.

After some small talk about the previous night and the oppressive heat, I finally asked, "So what's your story, Minna? How did you wind up in India?"

"There's so many places I could begin that story, but you have to start somewhere, right?" She took a drag before she continued.

"I was sick. Really sick. I was dying, but the macrobiotic diet healed me. I know, it sounds goddamn dramatic, but I kid you not. It saved my life. Most people come to the macrobiotic way of eating because they are sick, so the motto is 'one and ten thousand.' That means that you can take as much help as you need to heal, but once you're free of your illness, you must pay it back ten thousand times. It's what

I've been trying to do ever since my journey of healing began in my thirties. That's the short of it at least. How about you? How did you wind up in my parlor?"

"Two years ago my mother died. When she finally passed, it really shook my life to the core. When I looked at who, what, and where I was in my life, I didn't like what I saw, so I decided I needed to change course. At the time, I was working on a book proposal about this woman in Tanzania who started an orphanage. I spent some time there in 2006 after a relationship and a job ended in the same week. Anyway, I was shopping the book around to literary agents when I finally realized I didn't care about the story anymore. I had become a totally different person from when I started the process. That's when I threw everything in storage to search for the next story. So I bought a one-way ticket to India and here I am in your home."

"I'm going to tell you something, Thomas. You don't know why you walked in my door today, but I do." I kept waiting for her to tell me why, but the answer never came.

All day long we ate, drank tea, and shared stories. With the sun well into its afternoon arch, Minna had smoked nearly a pack and we were sipping on a quarter-bottle of whiskey.

The following day I was trying to find the Grand Bakery to do some work, but it appeared the tuk-tuk driver had no idea what I was talking about. Once I realized I was near Minna's house, I decided to stop by (something I would do several more times before I left Dehradun).

Minna was incredibly generous with her life, her experiences, her loves, her losses, and her regrets, all of which amounted to a reservoir of wisdom from which I drew. I just assumed this was her way of being until one afternoon she said, "You know, a lot of the things I've told you I've never told anybody."

My mother was only two years younger than Minna when she passed, but unlike my mother at the same age, Minna's mind was sharp and clear. What the two did share, however, was an immense faith.

Minna's story read much like a Hollywood script. At a young age she fell in love with a boy below her social status, but at the advice of her parents she married a person of means and class.

"He was a goddamn bastard," she said with vitriol, exhaling, coughing, and extinguishing her cigarette in one grand motion. She immediately reached for another Pall Mall, tapped it out of the box, and lit it.

"The son of a bitch beat the crap out of me regularly. Bruises, broken ribs, you name it, but he never hit me in the face because then other people would know what a bastard he was. The abuse didn't start until I married him.

"Not long after we married, we had a child. I was under immense stress from the marriage. I couldn't do anything right in his eyes. At one point my daughter, still under a year old, became very sick. I noticed she would only cry when my husband and I were in the same room, but when I was alone with her she was fine. Our relationship was so toxic that a child, a one-year-old, could sense it.

"One weekend two years into our relationship, my husband was away on work. Like a bat out of hell, I packed up my life without telling anyone and drove across the country. My husband called the FBI, and they put a warrant out for my arrest for kidnapping. The years of internal unhappiness and the stress of being a single mother on the run slowly destroyed my body, but through a series of auspicious events a friend introduced me to George Ohsawa and Michio Kushi, the founders of the macrobiotic movement. While I was recovering, I even lived with Michio and his wife, eventually becoming their student. I changed my lifestyle, my eating habits, and even my thought patterns. Eventually I was nursed back to health. That's the short of it anyway." She paused to extinguish her Pall Mall and light another.

"But now, hey, look at me. My life just works. It took seventy-five years, but it works. For most of my life I struggled. I fought anyone and anything that brushed up against me because I had all of this rage beneath the surface. But now, it's like I think about what I need and it just comes to me without effort. It just comes."

Minna told me how years later an astrologer told her there was something she needed to learn and people she needed to meet in Goa, India. When she found them, they would show her the way. So she traveled to Goa. After not finding what she was looking for, she surrendered the hope of meeting these guides and decided to return to the States. That was when she met an amiable group of travelers who were heading to Kashmir, and that's how her life in India began.

At one point in the 1980s, Minna was one of the only white people living in Kashmir. She befriended the Gujarats, an indigenous mountain population, and they looked out for her. In fact, they foiled three assassination attempts on her life.

"I already almost lost my life several times between my husband and my health, so I wasn't afraid of death, or any person for that matter. I wasn't going to let a bunch of goddamn inbred, radical, drug addicts bully me just because I'm living peacefully in their area and trying to improve the health of the community," she said, taking another drag on her Pall Mall.

"These fucking cocksuckers. They have no education and they're addicted to drugs. Well, one day the commander of the area and his rebels came to my house so high they could have floated through the doorway. They were there to kill me.

"An intense standoff occurred between the Gujarats and the commander. He grabbed me and held a gun to my head. He cocked the pistol and I thought, 'Oh well, I've had a good life.'

"As all of this was going down, the sky was turning blacker and blacker. Then the wind picked up. Then all hell broke loose. I kid you not, Thomas, a tornado practically touched down on the house. 'Open the windows! Open the windows!' I yelled to my guards. Meanwhile, the commander screamed, 'Don't anybody move!' I yelled, 'Why don't you just shut the fuck up already!'

"With that, the commander went running in terror and the house was saved. I think he thought I possessed some kind of black magic," she said with a chuckle that turned into a hack. "If anything it was white magic—the Light, God, Angels. Someone was looking out for me. There's no other way to explain it because it was the only place in the area where the tornado touched down. And you know what? No one in the area ever bothered me again."

For the last decade, Minna had been training chefs in macrobiotic cooking, many of whom went on to establish their own restaurants. She was writing a book about healthy eating—admittedly a work in progress—and she had started a Sunday farmer's market in Dehradun. She was not always as gracious to her staff, however.

"No! This spoon doesn't go with this dish. Are you stupid? Go! Get! Get away! Shoo!" she admonished, slapping the servant's hand.

"Minna," I said, "I love ya, but if I worked for you, I would kill you."

"No you wouldn't," she said. "You wouldn't take it and you'd walk away. If I was easy on these boys they wouldn't become the best."

Between Pranav and her other friends, Minna had a strong support system, and she was a support to many people in her community as well.

One night while I was at Minna's, a girl who had worked for her showed up battered and bloodied. Since Minna could no longer drive, she called another friend who took her to the hospital. The husband, an abusive alcoholic, had come home drunk and taken the day's disappointment out on her. He had done it before but never to this extent.

"I've had it with this motherfucker!" Minna loved to curse. "It's time for a little justice. I'm calling the police."

"No! Please, he will take it out on me," she pleaded.

"Don't worry, honey. This justice is not going to be carried out in the courtroom. I'm calling a friend from the police force. This is Indian justice, and it's going to be done in the woods or an alley. He's going to learn to never touch you again."

Minna was, without a doubt, one of the toughest, grittiest women I'd ever met.

***

The final evening of my stay in Dehradun before returning to the ashram also happened to be the anniversary of my mother's death. I had planned on having a quiet dinner by myself and then retreat to my hotel room to write, think, and reflect upon her life. Before I left for the evening, however, I dropped into Pranav's office to say hello.

"What are you doing tonight? Shall I call my kitchen at my home and have them make a pizza? Would you like a drink?" And so we had rum and Cokes, pizza, and beers.

Pranav, always finicky and accustomed to perfection, was dissatisfied with the way the kitchen reheated his pizza, so even though we ate almost the whole pie, he ordered Domino's.

As he prepared another rum and Coke, I said, "Tonight's kind of a big night for me."

"Oh?"

"It's the anniversary of my mother's death."

"Your mother's transition," he corrected.

"My mother's transition."

"What was that like?"

"To be honest, it was pretty surreal. I was on my way to meet a friend to go for a run when I got the call around three in the afternoon. Even though I had been waiting for that call for months, maybe years, I was in complete shock, and not knowing what else to do, I met my friend at a park near my house. When I met up with him, we made small talk for a bit. Then after some time I said, 'So something weird just happened. My mother just passed away.'

"After the run, I went home and composed an email to my friends and family announcing her death. That evening, a few friends took me out to dinner at a neighborhood restaurant. We ate Mexican, drank margaritas, and laughed as if nothing had changed, yet everything had. It was the beginning of my world being turned upside down. She was a pretty amazing woman, my mother. She was a mother not only to her kids, but to all of my friends who passed through our doors."

"Well then, Thomas, let us raise our glasses. To the love she created and her love that endures," he said.

It was as fine a toast as I had ever heard.

The next morning, before my ride picked me up, I purchased a small journal, wrapped it in a torn-out page from the *Times of India*, and slipped it under Pranav's door. I wrote him a note on the inside, thanking him for his generosity and friendship.

It was now his turn to create the life he wanted in his own gratitude-intention journal.

Chapter 12. The Teachers

As I was growing and changing, so too was the season. With increasing frequency, brief, late-afternoon cloudbursts announced the approaching monsoon season, offering a welcome respite from the relentless, punishing sun of April and May.

Drawing on the instinctual strength of nature, each day I observed flowers pushing their way through the earth's once arid crust, splashing a pallet of eye-popping colors across the ever-greening landscape. One afternoon I watched a massive swarm of dragonflies perform a complex mating dance. The next day it was mayflies. The following day the grass came to life, buzzing, crackling, and humming with grasshoppers.

Due to the remote location of the ashram, there was not much to do each day after putting some time in on the grants except read, go for walks, and watch the afternoons pass by, luxuries I realized I had not been afforded since childhood.

On one of these late afternoons, I came back to my room to see an entrained black cloud swarming in syncopation. I was used to sharing my space with winged and multi-legged insects, but certainly not with this many. *Motherfucker! I just want to lie down and relax.* Exasperated, I walked to the kitchen, ate dinner, and read. I couldn't be bothered to deal with it.

When I returned to my room two hours later, reconciled to the fact that I would be spending the night with hundreds, if not thousands, of buzzing flies, I opened the door to my room. The flies were nowhere to be seen. I was flummoxed. I couldn't figure out where they had disappeared to until I noticed a light film on the floor. Closer inspection revealed countless tiny wings, and upon the ceiling rested a handful of sluggish, satiated lizards. I thanked them for the good work, and from that point forward I greeted them each time I walked in the door.

***

While in Dehradun, I read the first chapter of the book JD had written. I didn't know much about his early career, but much like Minna's life, so too did JD's appear to be straight out of a Hollywood script. It gave me a thousand more questions for him.

When the book began, he was a lawyer fresh out of law school in his home state of Jammu and Kashmir. The political turmoil of the state was running at a feverish pitch, and JD was asked to lead an independence movement. He was bothered that his peers nominated him, but reluctantly he took the role.

One by one, those who supported him began disappearing, either because they needed to earn a living, tend to family needs, or the risk it involved was too great. It seemed JD was on his own when he began going door-to-door and village-to-village.

He eventually reinvigorated the movement. In the process he caught the attention of those in power and thus the attention of the police. Constantly on the move and with the authorities hot on his tail, JD sometimes was only hours ahead of them. In his wake, the police tortured his friends for information on his whereabouts, but the friends never gave him up. Sometimes JD would be on the move for days, barely eating.

With just ten rupees in his pocket, he staged a protest that drew twenty thousand people. Everyone came to hear JD speak, despite the fact that the police cordoned off the area, determined not to let him get on stage. It seemed all might be lost if he did not appear, so friends and supporters of the movement smuggled him through in disguise. When he did take the podium, he delivered a fiery speech that ignited the crowd.

The police dared not move in due to the possibility of an ensuing riot, but their intention, when things calmed down, was to arrest him.

After the speech, hats were passed around to collect money for the movement. In the chaos that ensued, supporters cloaked JD in a shawl and ushered him through a window where he climbed to the roof of the building.

Jumping from rooftop to rooftop, he found the location where a motorcycle awaited him. He paused, realizing the ground and the motorcycle were two stories below. He looked for another option to the street, but there was none. When he turned around, his eyes met those of a large monkey gnashing its teeth.

The monkey lunged, and JD—in a desperate act of self-preservation—leapt to the ground below, knocking himself unconscious in the process. When he finally came to, he was put on the back of the motorcycle and driven out of the city at breakneck speed.

When he wasn't engaged in phone conversations or preparing for a trial, JD would sit in contemplation outside his office on a concrete patio in a tattered chair, partially slumped with legs crossed, elbow resting on the right armrest, and chin resting on his hand. There was barely any foam left on the armrest where he propped his elbow. Had I met JD the public figure and known about his accomplishments before I met JD the man, I might not have felt so comfortable in his presence.

One afternoon, a law student came by to drop off some papers for him. The student tried to bend down to touch JD's feet, the ultimate sign of respect in Indian culture, but JD would not have it. Instead he was embarrassed by the gesture.

Later, when I asked the student about JD, he said, "Every landmark environmental case in India that has been brought to the court was filed by Mr. Chaudhary. Every environmental case we study in law school is JD Chaudhary versus the State of India or JD Chaudhary versus some polluting industry. He's the only one who has been able to beat the government."

What I found even more remarkable was that JD had not been paid in any of his cases against the government. His precedent-setting lawsuits against hazardous waste-producing industries were personal crusades funded by his private practice. He had fought more than one hundred cases in the Supreme Court of India and never lost. At one point, a special court was held every Friday to hear his cases.

In winning a landmark case against the State of India, five thousand factories along the Ganges River had been directed to install pollution control devices, twelve hundred were displaced, and three hundred were closed. He was also responsible for the order that made approximately two hundred fifty towns in the Ganges River Basin set up sewage treatment plants and for the order that made lead-free gasoline available in New Delhi.

JD also worked to ban intensive shrimp farming and other damaging activities along India's 7,000-kilometer coast. He was responsible for bringing environmental protection into India's constitutional framework and almost singlehandedly obtained some forty landmark judgments and orders from the Supreme Court against polluters, a record unequaled by any other environmental lawyer in the world. Countless corporate and government lawyers were getting paid hundreds of dollars an hour to fight him or outwit him, but he was an unbeatable, one-man legal brigade who sometimes had to worry about paying his bills.

Through all of this, he was a simple man of great faith. Every day that JD came to the ashram, the first thing he did was visit the temple on his property and pray. It spoke volumes about the man and from where he garnered his strength. Most people of his stature would rest on their laurels, bathing in their own self-importance, but JD was an honest and humble man, and unless prompted, rarely spoke about his past accomplishments. Instead, he focused on the future and all the work still to be done.

On top of all that, he was funny. Damn funny. Several times we laughed so hard we were both in tears. When I asked him about his cases, in recounting the details he would laugh hysterically and slap his knee as he described the surreal details of outwitting his "very cunning" opponents and using the press and media to his advantage. It was no wonder he was so greatly respected in India.

However, this was not always the case. The industries targeted by JD's wrath worked hard to disparage him, and the press did not help as they obfuscated facts and picked and chose their political angles to acquire financial gain.

"At one point in the 1990s," JD explained one afternoon, "twenty thousand industrial workers burned my image in effigy to protest the lawsuit I was bringing against their employer. They had no idea their company was causing the white marble of the Taj Mahal's exterior to turn yellow, nor did they care. What they could not see was that there was more worth in the long-term image of the Taj Mahal for India and the health of its citizens than the short-term profit for a handful of individuals.

"The factory owners did not have to close down their business, which is how the press portrayed it. All they had to do was convert to clean energy practices. Some did and some did not, and those that did not evolve their businesses are no more. In ten years, these industries did more damage to our national landmark than hundreds of years of war. I was offered payoffs to keep my mouth shut and disappear, and when I said no, that is when the death threats came."

"What did you do?"

"I had to have twenty-four-hour security for two years."

One time, JD was summoned to the prime minister's residence for a discussion about plans to develop dams along the Ganges River. The two sat outside, having tea while several peacocks, the national bird, ran around the grounds. Almost nothing had been said when a peacock came toward them. Always looking for the simplest way to drive home a point, JD said, "Can I kill that peacock?"

The prime minister's jaw dropped, and he nearly fell out of his chair. "What? What are you talking about? Of course you can't kill that bird! Are you mad?"

"Then how can you allow these dams to be built that will kill the Ganges River, our national river, the Great Mother of India?"

To hear him tell the story was hysterical.

"One thing you must always do as a lawyer and investigator is visit the environmental sites that are being destroyed. I have had to go in disguise several times," he continued.

"In one case, I was working to close down an industry that was contaminating the drinking water for the surrounding villages. The scene was apocalyptic. People were deathly ill, skins of animals were peeling off, clouds of smog and pollution blocked out the sun, trees withered away, and crops were burning up in the fields. As the courtroom drama played out, opposing lawyers worked furiously to denigrate me. They spoke for an hour to the court how I was out for publicity and my own self-interests. How could I be out for my own self-interests? The evidence was so clear. These people will do anything for a dollar, and they are very, very clever.

"But I waited patiently, and when it was time for me to speak, I pulled out a bottle from my bag. 'What is that, rum?' an opposing lawyer chided, bringing laughter to the court. I paused to add drama before I continued. 'This is contaminated drinking water from the site.' As soon as I said this, a hush fell over the court. 'If any of the opposing lawyers will drink this water, I will withdraw the case right now.'"

The opposing lawyers knew at once they had lost. The judge asked JD what he wanted, and he requested clean drinking water, medical relief, compensation for damages, and for the industry to be closed down. All were granted.

"I do not take a case unless I know I can win it," he said. "Sometimes I wait a long time until the conditions are favorable on the bench or until I have sufficient evidence. In my view, you are fighting for your principles. If you are speaking the truth, if you are guiding the court properly, respectfully, and presenting the facts, even the hardest judges become soft."

Like all great men and women, JD was driven by an inner vision that was both individual and universal. And like all great people who have left their mark on history, JD's legacy would not be built on the size of his palace but on the quality of his thoughts and what he had done for his fellow human beings. He was the rarest breed of men whose actions were truly in union with their words.

One evening I attended a lecture he gave to students at a nearby university. Afterward I met an American biologist who had also won the Goldman Prize (a prize JD had won), which is the equivalent to the Nobel Prize for grassroots environmentalism.

"JD is perhaps the most important barrister in India since Gandhi," the biologist said to me, "and almost no one outside India knows who he is. He's like a John Adams figure. He's that big in what he's doing."

I was humbled.

***

With my time in India coming to an end, I spent the next several weeks moving between Rishikesh, Dehradun, and working with JD at the ashram.

One afternoon back in Dehradun, Pranav took me to an ashram in the mountains to meet a "holy man." Earlier in his life, Pranav nearly went down the path of renouncing the world and joining a monastery, so he was interested in meeting the yogi.

We lasted thirty-five minutes before we were thrown out.

Pranav asked challenging questions, which clearly offended the yogi. I was the naïve Westerner looking for his words or presence to somehow enlighten me, but instead he threw us out of his ashram. I was shocked and disappointed but kept it inside.

As we walked out, Pranav said, "Don't worry, Thomas. I've seen a million of these guys throughout India, and many of them are charlatans. They renounce the world, their pride, and their ego, and yet they act superior to you because they have done this. A true yogi would not have taken offense. A true yogi lets each person find their own truth and their own path. They don't say there is but one way—his way. The real ones are simple and humble."

After my initial shock and disappointment of getting kicked out of a supposedly holy place, we laughed on the ride home and waxed philosophically about the essence of being.

The next morning I sat in the hotel lobby waiting for my ride. Pranav came out to say our final goodbye, and we exchanged a hug.

"It has been great to share time with you, Thomas. I wish you the best on your journey, and I hope you find what you're looking for. If I can leave you with something, remember this: All great, successful people have three things in common. One, they find time for themselves as a ritual. Two, they have a good core, whether it's from family, parents, a foundation in God, or a handful of key supports. And three, they always have a sense of purpose and a vision. They look within to define themselves instead of looking outside. I will pray that Shiva guides you to what you need to see on this journey and that you find your sewing needle and make beautiful things."

That same week, I also said goodbye to Minna. She too left me with some parting words of wisdom. In a short time I had grown to love Minna, and it felt as if I was saying goodbye to my mother for the second time, only in this version my mother would have been a salty, chain-smoking, whiskey-drinking, cuss-like-a-sailor Jewish lady from Philadelphia.

"I can tell you from experience and having lived a little that the key to a successful life is to have a huge dream. Everyone's dream is different, but it has to be big, damn it. Big enough that you want to go out and struggle to make it happen." The emphasis was on the word "struggle," and when she said it she leaned forward and slammed her fist on the table.

Minna sat back again. With her left hand she took a drag off her Pall Mall and with her right hand wet her lips with a glass a whiskey.

"Look at me, Thomas. I'm going to tell you right now what happiness is, so pay attention. Happiness has nothing to do with riches, wealth, or fame. Happiness is peace of mind. If you don't have peace of mind, everything else in your life is out of balance. Achieving our goals is great, but it's a lie, a dirty, filthy lie bought and sold to us through media. Speaking of which," she said, leaning over to grab some papers off the table, "I never finished my book about healthy eating. But I'm giving it to you to do with it what you will. Maybe you will do something with it, maybe you won't, but it doesn't matter. I learned what I needed to learn in the process." She handed me the stack of typewritten pages.

"Wow, thank you. I'm humbled, truly humbled. I will do the best I can," I said.

"The climbing, the going, the doing, the experiences, the struggle...all that in the name of making the dream happen, that's where true freedom exists. When you have a big dream, Thomas, somehow you never get tired because the dream is so big it keeps you going. That's where true happiness exists. In the pursuit. Because after you reach your goal you're just sitting on your ass again."

"I've been told I have a pretty good ass."

"It's not bad, Thomas. I may be old, and my eyes may be failing, but for God's sake I've still got eyes, and it's not bad. But don't let that go to your head."

She lit another cigarette and took a sip of whiskey.

"Now I have another form of peace," she went on. "Sitting here, letting it happen, letting go of the pursuit, letting go of everything. Now I have quiet time. It's very different than the pursuit, and now things come to me with grace and ease. For the first time in my life, what I need is coming to me. But I am tired, Thomas. I'm very tired. I'm not sure I'm going to make it another year. In the meantime, I'm going to trust and let nature take its course."

Chapter 13. A Cause for Celebration

During those three months in India, my life crawled to the slowest pace I had ever known. There were long afternoons and even longer nights where I had nothing to do but sit, stare, and think. In India's wild, open expanses of space and thought, without even realizing it I began feeding and nurturing a dormant seed within. When I stopped directing my attention outward—when I stopped searching, struggling, and fighting—a new potential was born. In the act of surrender and trust, what I needed to flourish appeared.

In JD, I found the advice and strength of a father.

In Minna, I found the compassion and guidance of a mother.

In Pranav, I found the companionship and connection of friendship.

In Cassandra, I felt the tenderness and intimacy of a lover.

And in my own heart, I felt something I had not felt in as long as I could remember: hope.

A new sprout had sprung, and this was cause for celebration.

***   ***   ***

I am so grateful for:

1. The incredible teachers I met in India and the many ways in which each one influenced me.

2. All the new experiences I have in my life's bag of tricks.

3. Being able to continue feeding this new thing that is arising within me.

4. Having a new, profound appreciation for the creative power of gratitude and intention.

5. For the adventure and laughter that awaits me.

Today I intend and create:

1. To let loose and find the party.

2. To find a way to make money.

3. To make new friends, laugh until my stomach hurts, and find myself in grand adventures.

4. To expand even further and gain an even deeper understanding of myself.

5. To experience romance and fall in love.

Part II. Body

I overcame myself, the sufferer;
I carried my own ashes to the mountains;
I invented a brighter flame for myself.
And behold, then this ghost fled from me.

Thus Spoke Zarathustra – Friedrich Nietzsche

Chapter 14. Wanted: Assistant to the (International) School Photographer

Had there been a job description for the position of Assistant to the International School Photographer, it may have read something like this:

> **Wanted**: An individual with minimal to moderate computer skills. Must possess an intuitive eye to capture the image, likeness, and adolescent awkwardness of international students, ages K-12, for all of eternity.

> **Duties Include**: Set up/break down of equipment/backdrop when arriving/leaving schools, as well as the ability to use a steamer to keep the backdrop looking pristine and wrinkle-free. Help with the white balance and focus, as well as ensure that flash bulbs are working.

> **Requirements Include:** Applicant should have an eye for detail and be able to handle occasionally stressful situations and/or workflows. Possess a curiosity to explore neighborhoods to procure a decent breakfast and lunch. Be willing to make multiple coffee runs a day in the pursuit of the perfect cup of *cà phê đá* when in Vietnam or 咖啡 when in China.

> **Compensation and Benefits Include:** Free travel, lodging, food, and booze during the

duration of each assignment, as well as $500/week.

International travel experience, an easygoing nature, an adventurous appetite, and a willingness to make a fool of yourself will put you at the front of the line. You think you have the chops? Apply now.

***

After three months of volunteering for JD, the plan was to head to Goa in southern India. After my somewhat monastic life, I was ready to sit on a beach, drink in the sun, and check out some scantily clad women.

On one of my trips to Dehradun, however, I received an email from a friend back home who asked me if I would be interested in doing some work with him while I traveled. I had left home with six thousand dollars. I had been earning an income in India from my previous freelance job in Seattle, so three months into my trip I was actually up two thousand dollars. However, I wanted to travel as long as I could and for that I needed money. The job seemed like a good idea.

Hey Tom,

So my assistant just quit and I need someone to help me with my photography business. It would basically be for two months in Vietnam and China. All of your expenses will be paid, including food, hotels, and booze. Interested? It's a pretty hard deal to beat, especially since you're already over there.

~ John

John was a photographer who had carved out a niche as a school photographer at international schools throughout the Middle East, Asia, and Australia. He had been doing it for ten years. Five months out of the year he would schlep his photography equipment from one school to the next, trying to make kids smile for the camera. The rest of the year he spent playing poker in Vegas and listening to poker podcasts.

Depending on the year, the photography business was his bread and butter. Other years, when he made a killing on the table, the business was an excuse to travel and organize his time (and his earnings were a nice supplement to his winnings). And so it was that instead of flying from New Delhi to Goa, I found myself on my way to Ho Chi Minh City, Vietnam.

***

It was about 9pm by the time my driver dropped me off at the Bong Sen Hotel in downtown Ho Chi Minh City. In India, I had been staying in fifteen-dollar-a-day guesthouses or sharing my room at the ashram with insects and rodents. In just an eight-hour plane ride, however, I had upgraded my status from backpacker to business traveler, and my lightly soiled sheets were replaced with fresh linens, mini bars, branded bath products, and card keys.

John had left instructions with reception for me to meet him at a bar around the corner, but first I showered, unpacked, and most importantly, climbed into the bed for a moment to remind myself of the feeling of high thread-count sheets.

I found John holding court at a table of several very attractive Vietnamese women at the bar of the Asian

Ruby Hotel. In front of him was a nearly empty bottle of Belvedere vodka.

"John!"

"Tommy! There he is!" John said, nearly knocking the table over as he leapt up to give me a hug. "Girls, I want you to meet my good friend, Tommy. Say hello, girls."

"Hi!" they said in unison. They smiled and giggled as they sized me up.

"Another American."

"Oh, so handsome."

"So big and strong."

It was a phenomenon I liked to call "cultural relativity."

"They love Americans over here. What can I say?" John laughed, leaning into me.

John was single, never married, and in his late thirties, but he could have easily passed for his mid-twenties. He had broad shoulders and stood six-foot-four, a hard man to miss in Vietnam. Every time I saw him, he sported different facial hair, and this time it happened to be a Frank Zappa mustache and soul patch. His commanding presence was accentuated by a head of hair that gave him the air of a mad scientist.

In a booth, we caught up over vodka and soda while the girls carried on in Vietnamese. Beside us sat three Australian men watching Arsenal play Liverpool. They patiently waited for the game to end and for the Aussie-rules football match to begin. The music was just loud enough so that when we communicated with the Vietnamese women who barely spoke English, it seemed almost normal.

Cake, Muse, and Smashing Pumpkins pumped through the bar while ceiling fans pushed about the heavy, humid air. On the walls hung pop art, including a painting of Bruce Lee in a karate pose holding a Coke can, the Mona Lisa listening to an iPod and wearing a Che Guevara shirt, the Buddha wearing a black and white checkered robe made by Vans, and a picture of Jason from *Friday the 13th*. In the painting, Jason wore his traditional hockey mask, and above him in the Google font and colors it read, "Google knows what you did last summer." Behind the bar hung a close-up painting that depicted Buddha bringing his hands to his mouth. Written on the painting in the font from the movie *Apocalypse Now* was, "I love the smell of my palm in the morning."

Several drinks later, "I Might Be Wrong" by Radiohead radiated through the speakers.

"Girls!" John yelled over the music to the girls on either side of me. "Tommy here, he's a writer. What's the name of your book? Go ahead, tell them!"

"Wow!" the girls replied.

"Handsome *and* smart!" the girl to the left of me said, rubbing her hand on my thigh.

"You very nice," the girl to my right said.

"Looks like they like you, Tommy. Welcome to Asia."

It was fortunate we had two days off before school started, because around 12:30am one of the girls procured a small, unmarked bottle from her purse and placed it on the table. Her friend went to the bar and grabbed several small glasses.

"Shots! Shots!" she said. "Don't smell. Just do."

We clinked our glasses and threw the shot back. It had an earthy taste that nearly made me spit it back up. I grabbed my vodka soda to wash it down.

"What the fuck was that? That may be the worst goddamn thing I've ever tasted."

"I'm not sure what it's called," said John. "It's kind of a Vietnamese equivalent to mushroom tea. It's strong but it doesn't last too long. Enjoy the ride!"

"Wait, what? Are you kidding me?"

"No. It's really fun."

"You think you could have maybe told me ahead of time?"

"It happened so fast I didn't even think of it. Just relax into it. Trust me. It's organic. You're going to thank me."

"Am I?"

It was yet another act of surrender and trust.

***

The night unfolded quickly. The girls led us to an industrial warehouse. Locals and expats danced inside while deejays spun hypnotic beats from a booth above the dance floor. Lasers ricocheted off the walls and disco balls splintered the light into particles.

When the mystery shot began to take its course, I felt ill.

And time slowed down.

And undulating waves of nausea and ecstasy rolled through my body.

I bounced my way off the crowd and the walls and made my way to the street. I scanned the scene and spotted a nearby alley. I ran toward it, found a spot behind a dumpster, and purged the magic mixture. It needed no prodding, and within seconds of exorcising the mystery potion, I entered another dimension. A wave of relief poured over me, like lying in a mountain stream at the height of summer.

I made my way to a park bench across from the club, sat down, and looked up at the skyscrapers that surrounded me. The ancient Egyptians thought we possessed 360 senses, and I was pretty sure I was using at least 147 of them. *That means that they could fully experience everything around them. Imagine that, a sense for every degree.*

Light fractured into fractals and geometric shapes. A web of dendrite-like filaments looking like neural pathways spread about the city and into infinity. Upon these pathways traveled telepathic information that I could tap into. I felt connected to everyone and everything.

I could hear every sound the city was manufacturing, from below the streets to high up in the sky. It bounced off the sides of buildings in waves and swirled around me in vortexes. I could listen in on the thoughts of people who walked past me and saw colors surrounding them.

Two cats came up to me and rubbed against my leg.

My parents visited me. I communicated with them. They told me how much they loved me and that they were looking out for me, that I had nothing to fear.

I wept at the universal truth of love. It was eternal and boundless, stretching beyond the outer limits of the multiverse and back.

I was no longer temporal but timeless and dimensional. My body was just a structure that housed my consciousness, a consciousness that was connected to a field of information, to which everyone and everything was connected. *If only people knew the truth,* kept ringing through my mind.

I looked down at the macadam beneath my feet and watched as it turned into a petri dish. It was not solid but in perpetual motion. Life at the atomic level is the movement of energy, and we are either conduits or impediments of that energy.

Two German girls walked past me and I said, "Excuse me, what's with purple? I see it all around you."

"What? How did you know that purple is my favorite color!" she said. She leaned in and kissed my cheek. Her lips were wet and electric and nearly knocked me over. I began giggling uncontrollably and they followed suit, the three of us falling into a hysterical laughing fit for no reason. They wished me well and moved on.

Angels surrounded me. My heart burst open in gratitude, and I felt a doorway open up within me. Feeling warm, loved, and protected, yet having no idea how much time had passed, I made my way back into the club.

It was packed wall to wall with people, but I floated through the crowd, guided by intuition. I didn't have to search for my friends; I just had to lock in on their energy. Led by their vibrations, I found them immediately, each of them wide-eyed and grinning.

"Buddy! I was worried about you. I'm so happy to see you. How do you feel?"

I grinned from ear to ear and gave him a thumbs-up.

John and the girls enfolded me as we moved and swayed in waves of elevated emotions.

***

The most important lesson I adopted in Vietnam (and quickly, might I add) was also the one most critical to survival. It was how to cross the street. This act required a bold fearlessness not found in the Pacific Northwest. If you hesitated when crossing the street, you risked causing an accident, or worse, your own death.

Traffic was relentless, a nearly impenetrable stream of bicycles, motorbikes, mopeds, taxis, and cars. The key was to wait for the smallest opening and then move into the stream with the blind leap of faith Kierkegaard spoke of. Cars were immovable forces in their line of forward motion, but you trusted motorcyclists to steer around you. It was like playing the original arcade game Frogger, but once you were off the sidewalk, there was no turning back.

We spent the next two days rantum-scooting through the city, walking for miles at a time. We moved from the modern center of Ho Chi Minh City to the outskirts where chickens, pig heads, and unidentifiable slabs of meat hung in shop windows. They were the types of shops where virtually nothing had changed in the last thirty years. The Bitexco Financial Tower, the newest iconic member of Ho Chi Minh City's evolving skyline, was our compass, and sometimes we were so far out in the districts we lost track of it. My heart felt expanded and full of gratitude, awe, and wonder at the life I was living.

On day two we went to the Vietnam War Remnants Museum, which held exactly what the name promised— remnants of the war America left behind when we made a hasty exit from the country. Tanks, heavy artillery, Chinook and attack helicopters, jets, and smaller aircraft lined the courtyard. Inside the museum were medals, clothing, and other artifacts that American G.I.'s donated or left behind. In one display was a G.I.'s uniform, and upon it was a note dated May 7, 1980. It read, "I was wrong. I am sorry."

Known in Vietnam as "The American War," the museum told the story from the Vietnamese perspective. In one room, pictures of protests from countries all over the world such as Palestine, Bolivia, New Zealand, and Zimbabwe told a different story of the war, the story you don't read about in American textbooks. Photography exhibits displayed the effects of napalm and different atrocities perpetrated by America.

Museumgoers stared at pictures as tears streamed down their faces, myself being one of them. The voice in my head kept repeating, *How could my country do this? Why does the world have to be this way?*

Chapter 15. Ho Chi Minh City

By the time school started on Monday morning, I was relieved to have a routine, not to mention I was finally starting to feel levelheaded after my unexpected psychedelic, consciousness-bending, dimension-expanding introduction to Vietnam.

Workdays began with a wake-up call at 6am followed by breakfast at 6:20am sharp in order to be ready for a 6:45am pickup. From there we made our way to the international school in District 2 of Ho Chi Minh City where we would photograph kids from 8am to 4pm depending on the workload and their agreeability to smile.

In between negotiating my way through an Excel spreadsheet of Vietnamese names consisting mostly of *Nguyễn*, *Trần*, and *Lê*, I had about ten seconds per student to choose the photo that would best immortalize the child for that year, if not longer.

We met our greatest resistance with the Korean kids and their sheer unwillingness to show joy. Those with braces attempted an equal level of stoicism, their lips bulging around skewered remoras clinging to their toothy hosts. Day in and day out, pimpled faces, poor postures, and noses disproportional to faces posed before the camera. In time they would learn a simple, healing truth of not just adolescence, but life: Like all growth processes, a time of uneasiness and pain is required for transformation.

Each time a kid walked up to be photographed, based on their body language I wrote the story of who they were and who they would become. There were the sensitive artists, who would turn into the soon-to-be tortured artists, and the athletes who would get any girl they wanted. There were girls who knew what to do in front of the camera and would use their sexuality to their advantage, maybe as a weapon. There were also the kids who were confused about their gender or sexuality. There were the curious, engaging kids who wanted to know everything about us, drawing on an extroverted curiosity that would propel them to explore the world, meet interesting people, and run businesses. There were the girls who were going to have unforeseen complications due to their beauty and the girls who had no idea how beautiful they were. There was the class clown who couldn't sit still, always trying to make others laugh. There was the child whose anger was going to hold them back from connection, the musician who was going to get hooked on heroin, the child who would be a prisoner of their shyness, and the child who—no matter how physically beautiful they became later in their life—would always see themselves as an ugly, awkward duckling.

I had befriended an art teacher named Janice at one of the Vietnamese schools. On our final night in Ho Chi Minh City, she met John and me at a restaurant downtown. It was filled with drunken Vietnamese men and even drunker, more boisterous Chinese businessmen who downed whiskey like their kids popped Pez from Hello Kitty dispensers.

John and I agreed that seeing live music would do us good, so Janice escorted us to the backpacker district. Organized around a promenade, the bustling area was filled with pedestrians, some with purpose, others with none.

Eventually we found a table outside a bar. Inside, a three-piece rock band was doing their thing. Above us, telephone wires crisscrossed the street, and where they intersected with telephone poles they became tangled messes, like the wires of earbuds after being in your backpack all day.

Christmas lights adorned the exterior and interior of seedy-looking bars. Outside on the sidewalks in plastic chairs, the effects of alcohol and drugs disarmed locals and tourists alike. Young women in short skirts hawked lighters and cigarettes while revving motorbikes competed with thumping music vibrating from every bar sporting a Jägermeister sign. Through the open windows of each dimly lit establishment, backlit liquor bottles were lined up behind the bar like awards in a trophy case. Vietnamese prostitutes cozied up to tourists and anything from sex to cocaine—and everything in between—was for purchase.

Janice brought along Chi, her son's best friend, who had left America for Vietnam a year before. Seven years prior, Chi had been a twenty-three-year-old aspiring filmmaker in Los Angeles. He wanted to make a film about Brazilian jujitsu fighters, and in the process he began to study it himself. Several years later, he was number two in the world for his weight class. He had the teeth and posture of a nutcracker and the skills to do just that.

"I devoted my life to the art of Brazilian jujitsu by training ten hours a day for weeks at a time," he told us over Tiger beers. "I was just following it because I loved it. I had no ambition, only passion, and I loved what it did for my mind and body and my confidence. But when I started winning the big ones and success started coming my way, it also came with all sorts of strings attached. I mean, I was living in the United States, I was almost thirty, I was making my living in a dangerous sport, and I didn't have any health insurance. If something really bad happened, I would have been fucked because the whole American healthcare system is fucked. I started to freak out because I watched as the sport began taking its toll on my body."

"Are you still practicing?" I asked.

"My last coach was a tremendous fighter, but he was a terrible coach and an even bigger prick. He didn't give a shit about me. He wanted me to win for his own reputation and for the gym's reputation. He pushed me to my limit, but not in a good way, you know? Not in the way a coach should. I had hair down to the middle of my back then. I hadn't cut it in years. It was part of my image. Well, one day I'm like, fuck this, fuck that, and fuck it all, so I cut off my ponytail, stuffed it in my gym bag, left the bag in his office, and bought a ticket to Vietnam."

"Wow. I pretty much did the same thing, minus the hair and the dramatic exit."

"Ha! At least for now the next chapter of my life is about getting to know my Vietnamese heritage so I can better understand my parents, who immigrated. They're getting older, and I want to bridge our connection. I'll figure the rest out later."

Since arriving in Vietnam, Chi had been teaching students English in addition to starting the first Brazilian jujitsu gym in Ho Chi Minh City. It was filled with people who wanted to learn to fight, but it wasn't fighting that Chi wanted to teach. He wanted to teach them the *art* of fighting, which not only required skill but discipline and improvisation.

"Like any art, you learn the foundation, and when you have mastered the forms, you throw away all the rules and make it your own," he said. "In my practice, I've learned inexpressible things about people. I can tell you everything you need to know about a person in one round. There are two types of people in this world—those who approach life aggressively and take risks and those who approach it defensively, always choosing the safe option. I don't even need to fight you to know you approach life aggressively."

"I wouldn't say I approach life aggressively, but I am certainly glad we don't have to fight."

"You wouldn't be sitting here and traveling the world by yourself if you weren't somewhat aggressive."

"I took off because I'm looking for my story."

"Well, you're not going to find it sitting on your ass in a desk job, right?"

"Point taken."

"You can also tell who's an asshole by the cheap shots they take or whether they are compassionate, perhaps by letting up on a choke hold moments before the final count."

As we sat on the street, Chi showed me a highlight reel of himself on his iPhone.

"I can't put this online. Otherwise my opponents will study it and use it against me," he said.

The first thing I noticed in watching Chi fight was his calm centeredness and steely focus. While his opponents made herky-jerky lunges at him, he remained centered and poised. He was like a coiled spring in a mousetrap, full of concentrated tension, waiting for release, waiting for his opponent to make the wrong step. He was a praying mantis waiting to strike. I could see in him not just a fierce warrior, but much like a writer, painter, or musician, an artist whose craft had become a way of life.

Each time one of us went to the bathroom, we played musical chairs. When I sat next to Janice, she too told me a fascinating life story of leaving home at an early age, a story of an outlaw love gained and lost that took her all over the world and through the hell of her partner's heroin addiction. She found her way eventually and learned that teaching art at an international high school was a lucrative job that enabled her to be a painter. It also gave her a way of giving back, a way to positively influence the course of her students' lives.

"One of the hardest things to do as an artist is to figure out how to make a living while you're trying to be an artist," Janice explained. "Teaching at international schools, it's a pretty good living. I mean, it's priceless in terms of the experience and cultural understanding. I've always had an inner vision, this feeling that I have to get it out of me and into existence on the canvas. If I don't get it out, it just eats me up and I sink into a depression. Fortunately, this job allows me to do that—make a living while I create—and I'm always learning something new from the kids. What I teach them pales in comparison to what I learn from them."

Janice and I talked for a long time, one artist to another, about process and the decisions that have to be made in creating art, from removing elements of a painting you may love to removing parts of a story that didn't fit the narrative. As Janice poetically declared, "If they don't serve the greater whole, you have to surrender them."

The life of an artist is not an easy one. This I always knew. But one thing became clear that night: Being an artist was not just a way of being; it was a way of action. You can't call yourself an artist if you're not actually practicing your art.

*** *** ***

I am so grateful for:

1. The dimensional and cosmic experience I had the first night in Vietnam and for trusting the course change of the journey.

2. The conversations I had with Janice and Chi that deepened my understanding of what it means to be an artist.

3. Getting paid to travel with John.

4. The countless ways this trip will transform me.

5. For the new friends I've made all over the world and for the ones I've yet to meet.

Today I intend and create:

1. To fall more deeply into the mystery.

2. To continue to surrender the parts of myself that no longer serve me.

3. To trust the creative process and to trust that when the time is right, the story will reveal itself.

4. To have spiritual experiences.

5. To feel the love, presence, and guidance of my parents.

Chapter 16. The Journey of a Thousand Kilometers

With work consuming most of the day and mornings coming all too early, a week in Ho Chi Minh City passed more quickly than I would have liked. Since John wasn't shooting photos that week, his only task was to process them. With our next gig in Beijing in two weeks, I was left without an agenda and a week of time to fill. For some reason, John thought it was in my best interest to fly to Beijing out of Hanoi, so he booked me a ticket without my consultation.

"Wait, what? Isn't that a thousand kilometers north?"

"Exactly."

"Why the fuck did you do that?"

"To force you to get out into the unknown. There's a lot to see in this beautiful country."

"Were you going to consult me?"

"Um, no. What fun would that be? Surprise!"

After a busy week of work (granted, I had essentially been unemployed for five months), my only goal was to spend a few days on a beach doing nothing.

To determine my direction, I set about informally polling the teachers at the international school. In an almost unanimous decision, the collective suggested I go to Hoi An, a UNESCO World Heritage site midway up the country's coastline. The second-most suggested trip was to Ha Long

Bay, one of Vietnam's greatest tourist attractions, not to mention one of the most impressive natural wonders of the world. The only logical decision was to squeeze in both. I'd go to Hoi An first and jet over to Ha Long Bay with only a few days to spare.

A short forty-dollar flight and a thirty-minute cab ride and I was in Hoi An. It was exactly what I was looking for—a sleepy, well-traveled town, charming and perfectly manicured with white-sand beaches only four kilometers away. For the equivalent of one dollar a day, I could rent a bike and take a leisurely ride through verdant rice paddies to a world-class beach. Swimming and reading during the day and Tiger beers and authentic Vietnamese food at night were all I wanted to think about. It was exactly what I needed.

By day three it was back to the airport and onward to Hanoi. Via a teacher's recommendation, I found a hotel in the old French Quarter, a frenetic hub of pedestrian and tourist activity.

On every corner locals hawked fruits and vegetables. Chickens and roosters ran freely through the street while teenagers and young men tried to sell you wallets, Zippo lighters, and knickknacks emblazoned with the yellow star of the Vietnamese flag. It was nearly impossible to walk fifty feet without a Vietnamese man on a motorcycle trying to offer his moto-taxi services. With seven million people living in Hanoi, three to four million of its inhabitants owned motorbikes, proving that crossing the street in Ho Chi Minh City was merely a warm-up for Hanoi.

I was surprised that there were not more restaurants and bars in the French Quarter, but as night fell upon the city, electric neon signs illuminated the inexpensive restaurants and dive bars that slept during the day. These establishments beckoned tourists and travelers into their lairs, which were low-lit dwellings offering anything from drinks to drugs to Vietnamese prostitutes, not to mention drinks and drugs with Vietnamese prostitutes. Red and blue miniature plastic tables and chairs—appropriate for schoolchildren but meant for adults—crowded the sidewalks. At the interdenominational sidewalk celebration, all were welcome to receive the sacraments of beers and mystery meat.

Being a solo traveler with unlimited time and without an itinerary, I didn't always know where I would find myself the following day. When I did decide on a direction, it was a rare event if I did any research about where I was going. This meant that each time I arrived in a new city, the same conversation went through my head: *Oh my God. What have I gotten myself into? What am I doing here?*

When I arrived in Hanoi, it was no different. All I wanted to do was camp out in my hotel room for two days and feel good about the decision, but inevitably the guilt of being on the other side of the world, compounded with the undeniable desire for connection, found me wandering the city's avenues, alleyways, promenades, and eateries.

The first night in Hanoi would be an early one. The next morning I was to board a bus at 6am to Ha Long Bay, a place considered to be one of the "New Seven Wonders of the World."

Located 175 kilometers east of Hanoi in the Gulf of Tonkin, Ha Long Bay contained 1,969 limestone islands that rose from sea level to towering heights, many of which contained hidden caves, grottos, and ancient lore. There were more than four thousand small islands to be explored between Ha Long and the two sister bays to which it connected.

As the legend goes, *Ha Long* literally means "descending dragons." When the country was newly formed, the Vietnamese had to defend it from northern invaders. As battles ensued, the mother dragon and her children suddenly appeared and incinerated the enemies with divine fire, jade, and emeralds. As the emeralds fell from the dragon's mouth, they formed a defensive wall that sunk the approaching ships of the invaders. After thousands of years, the wall of jade and emeralds turned into the many islands that were scattered about the sea. Attracted by the beauty it created, the dragon family decided to stay, and some fishermen living in Ha Long Bay still believe the dragons lurk beneath the waters.

***

On board the *Gypsea*, the junk boat that would be my home for the next twenty-four hours, there were ten of us. The brochure in the hotel lobby made the *Gypsea* look like a noble sailing vessel containing three masts. In person, however, it lacked the masts and appeared to be held together by duct tape. I couldn't help but question its seaworthiness, especially since only a year prior one of these boats went down in the bay, taking with it the lives of both tourists and crew.

Throughout the day, I made small talk with the other passengers while we sailed between the giant limestone karst outcroppings, many of which had taken 500 million years to form. When we dropped anchor, we swam in coves, visited the Thien Cung Grotto and Sung Sot Cave, and waved to locals in wooden kayaks as they tried to sell us M&M's, Ritz Crackers, and Marlboros. We smiled at inhabitants of the floating villages we passed. For centuries they had lived in peace on the water, and now, drunken tourists from all over the world made fools of themselves in their front yards every day.

Since we were some of these drunken tourists, we drank our Tiger beers in the sun with no inhibitions. The drinks continued through happy hour, into dinner, through a beautiful sunset, and well beyond. By sundown, a small group of us sat above deck while the rest sang karaoke below.

Hours passed in the bottom of empty beer cans. By the end of the night, it was myself, an Australian fellow who had arrived in Hanoi a few days prior to find a teaching job, an expat Indian couple living in Hanoi, and their daughter who busily played in our orbit. Mandy, a designer and design teacher, loved the expat lifestyle, but her husband, Taj, a journalist, was ready to go home to India.

They had just moved from Beijing to Hanoi, and seeing as I was on my way to Beijing, Mandy and I bonded over the Chinese capital. Their favorite bar in Beijing was the Irish Volunteer, and as fate would have it, it was directly across the street from the Lido Park Hotel where I would be staying upon my arrival there.

It was good fun until Taj drank one too many. In an instant, he went from fun and cordial to angry and bitter.

"So how old are you again?" I asked.

"Thirty, but I wrote my first book at twenty."

"Okay, first book at twenty," I said, feeling the warm glow of alcohol with a hint of jealousy. "How the hell did you get a book published at twenty?"

"Eh, it wasn't that big a deal," he said slowly with a slur. "My family is in the publishing industry in India and all it took was a phone call. It doesn't matter. I fucking hate the book anyway. It's a murder mystery. I fucking hate it, but I'm working on adapting it into a screenplay."

I told him about working with JD Chaudhary and what an impact JD had on his native country, to which he replied, "Yeah, there's one everywhere in India."

"A Chaudhary?"

"No, a bleeding-heart environmentalist."

"Oh?" I had just the right amount of alcohol in me to go from being Pacific Northwest Thomas to New Jersey Thomas. "So you don't care that the world is going to shit? Or that these companies are poisoning your water supply?"

"I don't."

"Yeah, it's nothing to worry about. As we speak we're mining planets for water and resources, so it's cool. I mean, water's an inexhaustible resource that can't be polluted or destroyed, right?"

"Hey, as long as it doesn't go to shit while I'm alive, what the fuck do I care? Why would I care what the world is like when I'm dead? What's in it for me?"

"You see that little girl running around over there? You know, the one you produced? Don't you want your daughter to live in a healthy world and not suffer?"

Every time he exercised the slightest bit of thought, he brought his hand to his head, paused for a moment, and wiped it across his face, as if the motion would somehow sober him up.

"Honestly? Nah. I just don't care, man. If it doesn't serve me, right here right now, why should I care? I don't give a fuck," he said, applying emphasis to the word "fuck."

Since I first eyed them, Taj and Mandy had been at each other's throats, occasionally making the situation awkward. It was hard to tell if it was a normal thing or if it was due to how drunk and confrontational Taj was being. Based on the intensity and vehemence they displayed, I suspected things were not going well. In the meantime, another couple from downstairs sat beside us, deflecting Taj's brutal assault on everything that contained an inkling of humanity. All the while, Taj and Mandy's three-year-old daughter danced and twirled, slightly intoxicated from the giant pulls she was taking from her parents' beers.

The Australian fellow said he would have one more at least five times. As he cracked open another beer, Taj pulled out a joint and passed it around. The moon tried to show its face behind the clouds, and from another junk boat in the bay the pulse of techno music came across the water.

The Aussie took a long, deep drag, paused on his inhale, and began to spin as he exhaled.

"I think I'm going to use the bathroom," he said. As he tried to get up, he fell backward, taking the table and several beers with him.

A moment of concern turned to hilarity, and I used the break in conversation as an excuse to retire for the evening. After all, I wanted to be up by 5:30am to catch the sunrise. Taj wasn't having it, however.

"One more. Come on. Don't be a pussy. I want to tell you a thing or two about Americans."

"Oh yeah? You think you know Americans, huh?"

"Yeah, I do."

"And what do you know about Americans?"

"I know you're all a bunch of arrogant assholes." Off to my right, I felt Mandy's anxiety surge.

"Cut the shit, Taj. You're being a fucking asshole. Just cut the shit. He didn't do anything," she said with authority.

"It's okay. This should be good. Let's hear it," I added.

"All you Americans," Taj started, as if those three little words were a declaration of their own. He took a deep breath and a pull off a whiskey bottle he produced from his bag. "You're a bunch of entitled, lazy fucks. You know why? You've had too many generations of easy living."

"You think so, huh? You think maybe that's just an image you're being sold on TV?"

"You're a society that's comfortable living in a state of unmet expectations. You're supposed to be leaders of the free world, and look how miserable you all are. Look how divided your politics and your country are. I bet the average educated Indian knows more about your country than you do," he said, pointing at my chest. "You have the wealthiest nation in the world, and instead of looking inward and taking care of your own people, you look outward to consume and conquer. You're a fucking virus that destroys everything in your path.

"Meanwhile, you're all hopped up on meds prescribed by doctors on pharma payrolls. And then they switch up your meds to make more money, and every time it happens, someone goes crazy, picks up a gun, and goes on a shooting spree, but they don't tell that part of the story. You think gun control would be a good idea? Nah. Some evolved society you are when a mentally ill person can get a gun as easy as a kid can get candy." With every word, his anger and vehemence intensified.

"You want to be guardians of the world but you can't take care of your own people because your politicians are bought and sold by fucking parasites. Greatest democracy in the world? Ha! To be a democracy you have to participate in democracy, but you're all a bunch of lazy fucks."

"Got it. You said that."

"You know what? I'd go so far as to say you're a fucking blight on the earth. Just get out of my face."

I said nothing. Instead I gave him a slow golf clap: 1-2-3-4.

"Bravo, my friend, bravo. Are you finished? You're really smart. Is that what you want everyone here to think? Or just that you're an angry prick? I want to have compassion for you, but really, you're just a miserable dick."

"I'm just getting started, actually."

"Great. But what I don't understand is how someone can smoke pot and become so aggressive. You made some valid points. There's some merit to what you said, but I'd also argue that at our best, Americans are some of the most generous people on the planet."

"When it's in your best interest."

"Fuck you, Taj!" Mandy interjected, throwing her empty beer can at him. "Sometimes I can't even believe you're the father of my child. You're such an arrogant asshole. You think you're better than everyone else, but you're just a piece of shit."

"It's okay," I said. "Mandy, I really enjoyed meeting you tonight. Taj, if you want to discuss this tomorrow when you're sober, I'd be happy to listen to your argument. You might want to think about channeling that anger or getting some therapy though."

"Go fuck yourself, American."

Mandy kept apologizing for Taj's behavior. "I'm so sorry, Thomas."

"It's not a big deal. I'm ready for bed anyway."

***

Whereas the previous evening's sunset was grandiose and heavenly, low cloud coverage the following morning made the sunrise unremarkable. By 7:30am, however, fault lines in the clouds began to reveal the morning sun. Through these cracks in the sky's crust, a bright blue sky told of the beautiful day to come.

When I got to breakfast, Taj and Mandy were nowhere to be found, and by the end of the meal, I'd had my fill of being social. I was distracted by the awe-inspiring scenery and didn't want to waste my time in conversation, so I took my iPod to the small deck above the captain's bridge and hit random on a playlist. Out of thousands of songs, my favorite song from my teenage years, "Eyes of the World" by the Grateful Dead, began to play.

There have been certain moments in my life when my external and internal environments have lined up to create a déjà vu of sorts, but the déjà vu feels more as if I am living in a hologram of my own mind. It's as if I—or some greater consciousness—lined up an internal feeling with an external environment to alter the timeline of my life, to change its direction, or to lighten my load. This overlay of the internal and external is called an epiphany.

When I heard the first few notes of "Eyes of the World," that's exactly what happened. A portal opened up and I was a seventeen-year-old kid driving to high school, a drive that each day took forty-five minutes one-way. The daily ninety-minute round-trip drive provided just enough time to listen to a ninety-minute Maxell tape in my car's cassette player. On each side of this tape I had recorded different versions of "Eyes of the World." I was obsessed. To me, Jerry Garcia's meandering, soulful melody yearned for something beyond the physical world, and that yearning opened up something in my heart. The song was a reflection of my internal world, and I would listen to "Eyes of the World" for days on end until I knew every note of each version on the tape.

As with most adolescents, at seventeen I was bored and ready for the next phase of my life—to have grown-up experiences, to love, to create, to fuck, to suffer, to lose, to travel, to conquer, to experience all things I needed to experience in order to express this expanding feeling inside of me. It was not a knowing in words but something I felt deep in my soul. Even at that age I had no choice but to express myself in words and follow them where they led me, despite the fact that it would be years before I felt comfortable enough to call myself an artist or own the title of "writer." That kid was hungry, though. He was hungry, hopeful, and believed in his dream. But then things got messy. What happened to that seventeen-year-old kid?

No sooner did I ask the question than I heard a voice within me say, *Who is going to take care of me?*

The epiphany. I looked around, dumbfounded, wondering if what I had just heard came from within or without.

And then I sat with it.

Holy shit…

Beneath the blue sky of Ha Long Bay, the portal opened up and brought me face-to-face with the unconscious question that had been running my life for the past two decades.

Who is going to take care of me?

As a child growing up with elderly parents, I lived under the constant fear that my parents were going to die and I would be alone. To make matters worse, when I was seventeen my family lost the financial security I had always known. I felt vulnerable, and not only was I afraid to express it, but I didn't have the means to bring it to my awareness.

In their advanced years, my parents could barely take care of their needs, never mind mine. Being a sensitive kid, I took this burden on as my own. *Could it be that this soul ache is not mine? Is it just an unconscious thought loop programmed by my father's pain from World War II and my mother's fear, uncertainty, and depression?*

The thought kept playing in my head like a song on repeat. But the truth of the matter was that I was a man, a grown man who could take care of himself. *Who is going to take care of me*, was the thought of a young child, as the massage therapist told me the day I left on my journey.

My presence in Ha Long Bay—the journey I had undertaken, the things I had accomplished while traversing countries and continents—was the proof I needed that I could take care of myself. Like a software program running in the background, this underlying fear had been running my life, and without the ability to express or exorcise it, it turned to anger. When I was unable to express that anger outwardly, it turned inward, manifesting as depression.

As if experiencing a download, I realized that in the face of uncertainty, I had adopted certain coping skills, but they no longer served me. Despite the weight of fear, unworthiness, and other negative thoughts that fought so desperately to anchor me in the past, somehow the pure intention of my seventeen-year-old self transcended those thoughts. Intention had pulled me into my future, into the present moment. I was no longer in transit toward my dream; I was living my dream, the dream of that seventeen-year-old self.

Above the captain's bridge and in the silence of my heart, I celebrated a victory for the seventeen-year-old who dared to dream bigger than his provincial New Jersey life, the kid who dreamed of getting paid to travel the world, to feel the grit and dust of foreign soil on his face, to lie upon the sandy beaches of other continents, to taste the planet's briny oceans, to experience the mystery through the point of his pen. It was a victory for the twenty-something-year-old version of that kid who felt trapped by a mound of debt, which brought with it a paralyzing resignation. It was a victory for the early thirty-something-year-old version of that kid who was too afraid to step away from the false security of an unsatisfying career.

The burden had always been the questions: *What's it all for? Who is going to take care of me? What if I don't meet the woman of my dreams? What if I'm not good enough? Who am I to tell this story? How will I make it on my own? What's the meaning of life? What if my life has no purpose?*

In my imagination, I pulled these harmful questions of uncertainty, insecurity, and distrust from my heart, closed them in the palm of my hand, and threw them off the port side of the vessel. The questions no longer held any purpose in my process of becoming, so I surrendered them to the peaceful bay and said a prayer of gratitude for the propellants they had been. I gave thanks for the shape they had given the current iteration of myself as an adult, a traveler, a human, a seeker, a spirit, an artist, and a writer.

With this new information, and in light of how successful my experiment in surrender and creation had been so far, I was coming to an empowering and terrifying realization: *I am more powerful than I ever imagined, and my ability to create—or lack thereof—has always come from my thoughts.*

The more deeply I surrendered to the mystery, the more I moved from a state of solid to liquid, from force to acceptance, from struggle to surrender, and from resistance to flow. I thought of Minna and how she said it took her most of her life to let go, but once she figured out how, all that she needed appeared.

I realized I was in the midst of transformation. This is what it felt like in the chrysalis. I was beginning to not only believe but also feel in the core of my being that something else was in control of my life, that I was being taken care of and guided. Even though the path or the answers wouldn't necessarily appear overnight, I no longer needed to fear the unknown. And that felt really good.

***

Another night in Hanoi and my one-week vacation in Vietnam was over. The realities of the rigors of my life as the Assistant to the (International) School Photographer were once again upon me. I answered the call to help my friend immortalize adorable children and awkward adolescents in yearbook photos.

In the future, as their yearbooks faded with time, the pages yellowed and the corners rounded with the violence of being boxed up and moved from apartment to apartment, beneath the cryptic writings of, "Have a great summer. I think you're really cool," and, "You were the funniest person in math class," my work, my signature, my thumbprint—my blood, sweat, and tears—would serve as an unspoken testament to their time served in middle school. If it were not for me working tirelessly behind the scenes, their pockmarked faces and uneasy braces would never be remembered.

These kids will not recall me, the Assistant to the (International) School Photographer. No one ever remembers the assistant (and they probably barely remember the photographer), but let the record show that when I was called to serve, I showed up.

The thought gave me a chuckle as my plane touched down in Beijing.

Chapter 17. Beijing and Shanghai

"Your attention please. All after-school outdoor activities will be canceled today due to poor air quality. I repeat, the air quality today is a four. Therefore, all outdoor school activities will be canceled."

This was the announcement that came over the loudspeakers on a Wednesday afternoon at one of the Beijing international schools where we were working. It was by far the most oppressively gray day I had seen since landing in China.

When I first arrived, beyond the green and white logo of Starbucks just outside baggage claim, I was greeted by a clear, blue sky. I had been warned about pollution and the inevitability of the "Beijing cough," but as far as I could see there was no evidence of it.

Yet, every day thereafter the sky lost more of its blue luster while the sun seemed to lose more of its strength. I later learned that my first day in the capital of China coincided with a visit from several foreign dignitaries. Turns out every time heads of state or other important diplomats visit Beijing, three days prior all factories are ordered to shut down. The government then "seeds" the clouds, meaning they fire silver iodide rockets into the clouds to cause precipitation, temporarily washing away the smog and pollution hanging over the capital. What polluting the atmosphere with the silver iodide actually does, only the future will tell. Perhaps one day, whether out of foresight or necessity, mankind will not be so shortsighted.

After several long days of taking yearbook pictures for the children of international dignitaries and executives, we left Beijing to photograph kids in Tianjin, an industrial hub two hours southeast of Beijing. Thirty minutes outside the capital, it felt as if we were on rails, gliding along Beijing's flawless, newly constructed superhighways. An hour later, like ropes along a gangplank, giant bundles of power lines appeared, lining the highway, along with massive apartment complexes that lacked distinguishing features. The thought of living there felt suffocating and claustrophobic.

"You know what those are, right?" John asked.

"Electricity. Power lines," I replied.

"Those power lines are feeding all the factories along this superhighway, and all these crappy, communist-era-looking buildings are where the workers live. You know the cheap shit you get at Walmart? A hell of a lot of it is made right here. That's the ugly cost of development you don't see in the States."

For every mile we drove toward Tianjin, the sky became heavier and more oppressive. It reminded me of a mid-winter fog rolling in off the Puget Sound. One minute there's the sun, the next it's a faint, glowing orb, and the next moment it's gone.

"What's with the crazy fog out here?" I asked.

"That's not fog, man. That's pollution."

"Are you serious?"

"Fuck yeah, I'm serious. We're fucked man. It's like this. Imagine you're sitting in a smoky, windowless dive bar called Heaven's Gates. In the corner God and archangels

Michael, Gabriel, and Raphael are drinking, smoking cigs, and playing poker. There's all these saints mingling and having a good time. Everyone has things to do, but they're waiting on the outcome of the game. But there's just one thing, and this doesn't bode well for us."

"What's that?"

"The currency they're betting is how much time humans have left before we fuck it all up. Tianjin, where we're going, it's the fucking ashtray at this poker game. It's not a pretty place, which is why we're going to be in and out."

The closer we got to Tianjin, the more it felt like we were skiing through a mid-mountain cloud on a balmy day, conditions that cause you to lose your depth perception and spatial awareness. It gave me the impression I was in a post-apocalyptic world, and I imagined purgatory to be similar in its lack of light and definition. At least in Beijing you could see the sun's perfect orb burning through the haze.

I couldn't help but hear JD's voice echoing in my mind: *If our leaders don't get their hands out of their benefactors' wallets, and if we as the human race don't wake up and change our course, we're going to hit a point of no return. If there are no resources to be had, even the rich won't be able to save themselves. The earth can survive without us, but we can't survive without the earth.*

As if answering my thoughts, John said, "I hope our children and grandchildren don't say that the greatest tragedy of human history was that our generation just sat around with our thumbs up our asses while we collectively made the world uninhabitable, but shit, look at you and me. We're not doing much more than recycling. But what do the rich and power brokers care? The few who hold the power know that as long as they can keep us slaving away for the almighty dollar and keep us fighting over religion and ideas while convincing us to consume shit we don't really need, then we'll be too busy to see what's really going on."

"It's hard to wake up when you don't even know you're asleep."

"Exactly. Most people go to work, then they come home and turn on their favorite program. You know why it's a called a program? Because it's literally programming people. The news makes us all pawns, and the game is so well rigged we don't even know it. And then you look at these poor Chinese bastards working for most of the day—fuck, for most of their life—in windowless factories with forced air. They're producing crap the rest of the world uses for ten minutes and then throws away. And all this shit is designed to have a short shelf life—planned obsolescence—so we have to buy the next version, and so on and so on. It's a goddamn fucking game.

"These poor bastards are living in these shitty, overcrowded houses just trying to survive. They're going through hell so their kids can have a better life than they had, but chances are they won't because, again, the system is rigged. And now the American dream is rigged. The thing is, these people have no other options. Man, I can't think of a worse place to be than out of options. On top of it all, they're probably going get some fucked up form of cancer because they're building toxic trinkets for the Western world."

He stopped speaking, let out a big sigh, and looked out his window into the impenetrable gray.

"China's going to have a real fucking health and environmental disaster on their hands in the very near future if they don't get their shit together. When a country as big as China, India, or the United States has a problem, it's a problem for the world. All us industrializing countries, we got to get our shit together because we're reaching a real tipping point."

Two days in Tianjin was enough to give me a cough, a sore throat, and a genuine, anxious concern for the trajectory of the human race.

***

We arrived back in Beijing at 7pm on Friday night. By 8pm, Ben, a teacher at one of the international schools, two of his buddies, and his twenty-three-year-old nephew Sammy picked us up for an evening on the town. Sammy, a skater kid from Southern California, had never been outside the United States, let alone California, and his enthusiasm could barely be contained. It was a big night out for Ben as well, considering he had a wife and kid at home. Not only did he want to show us a good time, he wanted to have a good time, so when we piled into his minivan a cooler of cold beers awaited us.

"So I guess there's no open container law in China?" Sammy asked as he cracked a beer.

"I'm not really sure. I don't worry about it too much. The cops don't really fuck with expats as far as I know."

After a hot-pot dinner and several more beers, we met up with more teachers at an Irish bar. Beers and shots ensued, all serving to warm us up for Chestnut, a Russian nightclub.

Upon entering Chestnut, we were greeted by Russian dwarves who collected our money and escorted us to an escalator. We descended into the bowels of the building. Red velvet curtains lined the walls, accentuating garish gold frames that housed famous imitations of nineteenth-century paintings. When we arrived at the bottom floor, we could feel the bass of the Russian techno music pulsing through the walls.

We walked through the ornate metal doors that opened into an underground space the size of a hotel ballroom, in the middle of which was a parquet dance floor with three poles in the center. All around us, chesty women in tight pants and painted-on faces beamed seductive, inviting smiles while chiseled Russian men in Armani and bad cologne rolled up their sleeves to reveal Rolexes and Rolex knockoffs.

I walked up to the bar where a woman in an extremely form-fitting dress seemed to take an immediate shine to me.

She said, "Your friend over there, he says you like to have fun. Would you like to have some fun tonight?"

The spirits I had been imbibing gave me the confidence of playfulness rather than the intimidation I might have otherwise felt in the presence of such a juggernaut of sexuality.

"Oh, I love fun. Who doesn't love fun? My middle name is fun. What kind of fun do you have in mind? Board games? Twenty questions?"

"What are you doing after this and where are you staying? Let's go back to your hotel room. I want to go home with you tonight."

"Just tonight, or do you think we might have a future together?"

"Yes."

"Yes tonight? Or yes future?"

"Yes," she repeated stoically.

"What am *I* doing tonight? Well, I'll probably just

go home, masturbate, and call it a successful day. How about you?"

She couldn't comprehend this, nor could she decipher sarcasm. Instead, she stared at me blankly. After a pregnant pause, she began stirring her Stolichnaya vodka.

"That does not sound like fun to me."

Realizing I wasn't interested in paying for her companionship, she said abruptly, "Very well then. Good evening," and walked away.

The smell of sweat and cheap perfume became stronger as the dance floor filled and swayed with Russians and expats. Our crew found a table on the edge of the dance floor while John ordered a bottle of vodka. Sammy, who at home earned a living as a parking attendant, bought the group a round of tequila.

"Sammy, you should climb the pole," we urged. As if a little brother eager to please his older siblings, Sammy made a dash for the pole, which from floor to ceiling was nearly twenty feet tall.

Sammy was all in. His approach to the pole was strong, but he quickly realized he was not up for the task. His hands and feet pawed at the pole furiously, like a puppy on ice. On his final attempt, he neared the top but gave up and slid down the pole in slow, concentric circles.

Just then, a Chinese man in leather walked up and motioned with his hands, as if to say, "Step aside, this is how it's done."

The man proceeded to do a handstand into the pole. While upside down, he wrapped his leg around the pole and, using the muscles in his abdomen, pulled himself upright. He then did the same move in reverse, bringing his legs down on either side of Sammy's shoulders. Squeezing his legs together, he startled Sammy by pulling Sammy's face into his crotch. When he released Sammy, laughter and applause ensued, and when Sammy returned to our table, his face was as red as the velvet drapes. We contorted in fits of belly-aching laugher.

It was nearly 4am when Ben told us it was time to go.

***

Next up was Shanghai. With a skyline that might have been designed by someone on LSD, skyscrapers made of shimmering glass, negative spaces, and antennas like praying mantises made it the most modern skyline I'd ever laid eyes on. At night, LED lights turned the buildings into shapeshifters.

We spent nights roaming the city, bargaining with shopkeepers at various markets and passing through the false walls of retail shops. The inner chambers held the latest bootlegged DVD movies and television series from the United States, fake Armani belts, knock-off Rolex and Omega watches, and Monte Blanc pens that barely wrote.

One day, John bought what he thought was a Ben Sherman shirt, only to realize when he got it home the tag actually said—in the same font as the Ben Sherman brand—Bobby Snowmen.

"That's funny," he said over a beer. "It makes me look like even more of a douchebag than I am."

Our best nights were filled with laughter over good meals and drinks in restaurants and rooftop bars, from dive bars to fancy lounges in the French Concession where Frank

Sinatra, Ella Fitzgerald, and Louis Armstrong provided the soundtrack. We'd order a bottle of scotch or vodka, finish it with new friends, then retire to our hotel.

The low point of my time in Shanghai was my own form of Shanghai surprise, which was characterized by sudden, severe abdominal pain followed by violent, unexpected bouts of explosive diarrhea. The surprise is that one minute I was driving down the highway having a leisurely morning, and the next thing I know I'm thrown into a panic, begging the driver to pull over as beads of sweat pour down my brow.

As I motion to the driver that my problem is soon going to be a problem in his car, he swerves across six lanes of the elevated highway that encircle the city and finds the one and only place to pull over. Next, I find myself dropping my pants on the side of the highway as cars and trucks roar past me at seventy miles per hour, the drivers of the passing cars laughing and pointing at the fragile bowels of the Westerner. In the meantime, my supposed friend snaps pictures of me with my pants around my ankles as I simultaneously express embarrassment and relief, and the driver searches for newspaper so I can clean myself up. Surprise!

Despite my Shanghai surprise, the Beijing cough, and the impending doom of the human race, I was feeling great. Through attention and intention I had left some of my mental and emotional baggage at the bottom of Ha Long Bay. For as long I could remember, I had been living in the past or dreaming of the future, always wondering what was next, comparing myself to others, and seeing deficiency in everything I looked at. I always wondered why I wasn't where I thought I would be at "x" point in my life and why things weren't working out the way they were "supposed" to. But those were thoughts of the past. On the other side of the world, far from where my mother brought me into it, life *was* working out, and it was working out quite well.

When the ride of life is smooth, when everything you need comes to you before you can even ask for it, it's something to be grateful for and celebrate. And that's exactly what I was doing. I was traveling with a friend, laughing for hours at a time each day, seeing the world through fresh eyes, learning about new cultures, and experiencing novel things, all the while getting paid to travel.

Despite all the circumstantial obstacles or the ones I created in my mind—my parents' financial ruin, a lack of direction and certainty, permeating depression, crippling doubt, paralyzing fear, and bottomless unworthiness—the dream of the seventeen-year-old had anchored itself in the future like a grappling hook shot from my past. I was living that dream. Whether I was paying attention to it or not, the dream had a power and energy of its own that had always pulled me toward this moment. It was only in the present, being on the road, away from everything familiar, that I was finally learning to see with my eyes open.

It's an old story, the road. At thirteen Jesus hit it. We don't know where he went or with whom he interacted, but when he returned he had a new understanding of himself. As a result, he had a lightness of being, and people took notice. In the twentieth century, Jack Kerouac hit the road, hopping railcars and chronicling his experience in a dizzying, ecstatic, orgiastic journey of frenetic, expressive, and explosive movements. This was my turn.

While no journey is the same, there's a reason why people depart from the road well traveled. In our daily lives, we flitter to and fro on the familiar longitudinal and latitudinal grids of our neighborhoods, commutes, city blocks, and minds, but when we set out on this new road there is but one direction—forward. A forward momentum from the familiar to the foreign.

The act of leaving is an outward expression of sound and movement and an inward process of discovery and healing. Even more than healing, it's an unfolding into the lightness of being.

In the act of travel, lightness of being comes through the kindness of strangers, the serendipity of synchronicities, the surrender of control, and trust in the path. One comes to discover their strength, resilience, and potential, and in doing so begins to understand the limitlessness of their potential.

With every new person I met, I learned more about myself. Each time I told my traveler's tale, I had the opportunity to rewrite it. This rewrite was not a matter of making up events to impress the person across from me; rather, it was about changing my underlying belief system. Whereas I once had a hunch that my negative belief system of doubt and disappointment was holding me back from my true potential, I was finally beginning to see how it operated in my life.

Negative thoughts were the malware hidden in my computer. Not only did it make my computer sluggish and dysfunctional, but it wasn't even my program.

It was time to wipe the computer clean and upgrade my operating system.

Chapter 18. Reunions and Retox

Needless to say, I was more than excited when the plane touched down in Bangkok. After nearly two months of pollution and excessiveness in Beijing—excessiveness that included but was not limited to: heavy, unhealthy foods, copious amounts of booze, late weekend nights, and early weekday mornings—I was feeling empty, overweight, and run-down. Luckily, I swung to the other extreme on the island of Koh Samui, Thailand: a ten-day yoga and detox retreat.

Most people travel to Koh Samui for the beaches and parties, but I was there to get my head clear, lose some weight, and feel healthy again. For ten days I practiced yoga, read books on the beach, took steam showers, ate nothing but vegetable broth, and gave myself a colonic twice a day (you haven't lived until you've given yourself a colonic on an island in Thailand). By the time I was ready to leave the mini health retreat, I was hungry, ten pounds lighter, ready to party, and had a new lady friend.

I was most excited, however, to meet up with one of my best friends, Rich. Several months prior, Rich decided he wanted to travel around Asia, and we agreed that if I were still on the continent, we would meet up and travel together. It just so happened that the timing lined up. We were about to embark on two months of itinerary-less travel.

***

After exiting baggage claim in the airy, light-filled terminal of Bangkok's Suvarnabhumi Airport, I hailed a taxi and was on my way. From Sukumvit Road, we turned left onto Soi 8, where I spotted Rich sitting outside at a corner bar. He was exactly as I had seen him last—with his head buried in his iPad.

"Get your head out of your iPad," I called out as we drove past him.

Thirty minutes later, we were catching up over a beer.

"I can't believe you're here!" I said.

"I know! I can't believe I'm in Asia. I can't believe we're in Asia together! How have you been? What's going on? How was Koh Samui? You look fit and healthy," he said.

"Well, I should be. I just spent ten days doing yoga twice a day, eating nothing but soup, and shoving a tube up my ass to shit out all the poison I put in my body in China for the last month."

"Come again?"

"Colonics. They're the future. It was shitty business, but I feel pretty damn good. Now I'm ready to retox!"

"Cheers!"

"How are you feeling?" I asked.

"Not too bad. I slept some on the plane, so I'm just trying to power through to about midnight."

"Well, that's good to hear because I made some plans for tonight."

"Oh yeah? What's that?"

"I met this sexy woman at the detox place in Koh Samui. She was only there for three days, but we got on pretty well and we've been texting all week. She invited us to an art opening tonight."

"You always make things happen."

"I've gotten even better at it since I've been traveling. Turns out I've figured out a little secret and I'm passing it on to you. Here you go."

I reached into my bag and handed him a gift that I had wrapped in a local newspaper. It just so happened to be an advertisement for pussy ping-pong and ladyboy shows.

"Pussy ping-pong. Fascinating. What is it?" he asked.

"Quit asking questions and open it, dipshit. It's the secret of my success. Open the first page. You're going to be amazed at how powerful this is."

He opened the cover and read my inscription.

Dear Rich,

Every day you're to write down five things you're grateful for and five things you want to create. Literally write, Today I am so grateful for...and Today I intend and create...You're going to be amazed at what comes out of this. So excited to co-create great adventures!

Thomas

"Thanks, man!" he said, giving me a hug. "I can't believe I'm here and we're about to travel all over Asia. I wonder where we'll be in a week!" he said enthusiastically. I could tell he was genuinely excited.

"I have no idea where we'll be in a week, but it will be great. We should head back to the room and get ready to meet Sophia. We're having dinner with her before we go to the opening."

***

Rich and I met Sophia on Soi 23 at a French restaurant called Le Petite Zinc. I had pretty much only seen her in a bikini, but as I suspected, she had great style and looked incredible. After splitting a bottle of wine, the three of us made our way to the gallery opening.

"What day is it?" I asked Sophia.

"I have no idea," she said. "I never know if it's a Tuesday or Saturday. That's why I love living in a Bangkok!"

The "gallery" was actually the art collector's home. It was a narrow, modern, three-story structure full of glass and light from which the owner had cleared out almost all the furniture. In its place, he adorned every space with paintings, pottery, mobiles, photography, sculptures, wood carvings, and more.

Erik had been an entrepreneur who made a small fortune being in the right place at the right time. With that money, he started and sold two companies. After his third company, he bought a motorcycle and drove around Southeast Asia for a year, collecting and investing in art.

Rich could not stop talking about two of the artists in the collection—one from Hoi An and the other from Phnom Penh, Cambodia. "We're hunting down this artist if we go to Phnom Penh," he said.

The rough plan Rich and I cobbled together was to first travel from Bangkok to northern Thailand, but Thailand was experiencing the worst flooding it had seen in more than fifty years. With parts of the train tracks in northern Thailand completely shut down, Erik convinced us that Cambodia was where it was at.

After the event, Sophia organized a small group to go out to dinner. Three bars and several hours later, we landed at Mekanic Supper Club. From the outside it looked like a giant oil drum turned on its side, and on the inside it was two floors and several rooms of lights, lasers, high heels, short skirts, sweat, and eager individuals looking to see and be seen. I was still in beach mode and made the poor decision to wear flip-flops. With an unnecessary air of superiority, the bouncer turned me away. However, since jet lag was finally catching up with Rich, he gave me his shoes and headed back to the hotel in my flip-flops.

Once inside, the deejay played along with a live drummer to produce hypnotic, thunderous, tribal beats that pulsed through the room, causing the patrons on the dance floor to spin like Sufi dancers. A small bag of coke was passed around our group, and Sophia and I spent a good part of the night grinding not only our teeth but also each other. It would be the first night Sophia and I spent together.

"When we were in Koh Samui and I told you I wanted to kiss you, I thought you didn't want me to," I said to her as the morning light came through her window.

"You never ask a woman for a kiss. You have to be a man and take it," she said.

If you're looking for addictions, deviances, and excess, they're never far away in Bangkok. For the next five nights, we charged forward in a similar fashion. Sophia's friends, who ranged from early twenties to early fifties, all had the stamina of recent college graduates, and most nights I ended up staying at Sophia's. Seeing as Rich and I would be spending the next two months together in hotel rooms all over Southeast Asia, he was happy to have the hotel room to himself, and I was happy to share a bed with a beautiful woman.

After five days of retoxing, Rich and I were relieved to make our way to Cambodia, where we planned on relaxing and giving our livers a reprieve.

*** *** ***

I am so grateful for:

1. Sophia showing up in my life.

2. Spending the next two months traveling with one of my best friends.

3. The fun and interesting people I've met through Sophia.

4. The adventures Rich and I will have.

5. For the countless ways this journey has opened up my life and heart.

Today I intend and create:

1. To have spiritual experiences that deepen my understanding of who I am.

2. To have great adventures with Rich that will deepen our friendship.

3. A free plane ticket home for Christmas.

4. To be the magician and sorcerer of my life.

5. To learn to move to the rhythm of my own life.

Chapter 19. Border Crossings and Fallen Angels

As far as we knew, when we woke up on the morning of October 9th, we'd be heading to the train station, but a last-minute decision found us instead heading to the bus depot. The bus was more expensive (almost seven dollars as opposed to a dollar-fifty on the train), but it was air-conditioned and a shorter journey. We figured air conditioning in a bus that took six hours versus a ten-hour train ride with heat and humidity pouring in through open windows was more bang for our buck.

Rich and I boarded the crowded bus late and luckily found two empty seats next to each other. By the second stop the bus was full, and by the third it was standing room only.

We passed the first two hours giggling and battling over double-letter and triple-word scores on Rich's iPad. In the process, we had not been paying much attention to our surroundings. When we finally did look out the window, it appeared we were driving through an ocean. From one horizon to the other, the land surrounding us was completely submersed in water. In some places, the floodwaters covered the roadway, causing our bus to leave a wake in its trail. The horizon was dotted with rooftops peeking out from the water, and people rowed in canoes to the houses of their submerged neighbors.

After a few stops, a nap, and six hours, we neared the Cambodian border. There were only a handful of people left on the bus, including two British men between fifty and sixty years old. I had noticed the skinny, shorter one at the bus depot in Bangkok because he kept reassuring the woman on the other end of the phone that he would only be gone a few days, that he loved her very much, and that when he returned they would spend a night together in a hotel. Five minutes from the border, the larger gentleman began looking through the rubbish that was left on the bus, collecting a bounty of three bananas and two unopened bottles of water.

"You never know what you'll find until you look, eh gent?" he said with an English accent.

"Hard to argue with that logic," I agreed curiously.

In researching how to cross into Cambodia by land, one travel writer called Poipet, Cambodia the armpit of Southeast Asia, and all of the guidebooks and websites recommended not using this border crossing at night. Instead, they advised spending the night on the Thai side of the border and crossing into Cambodia during daylight. When the critical moment arose as to whether or not to stay in Thailand or push on, Rich decided there was plenty of light left in the western sky. Hesitantly, I agreed.

Through careful observation, Rich assumed the English duo knew what they were doing, so he made the executive decision to follow them toward the border crossing. They paused to withdraw money from a bank machine and asked us if we had any U.S. dollars to exchange for their Thai baht. A crisp twenty-dollar bill was required to get a Cambodian visa, and they didn't want to lose money on the exchange. Rich, amiable and still travel-green, agreed, but I was suspicious.

Our new foursome and other fellow bus travelers were paraded along a chain-link fence lined with barbed wire. On the other side of the fence, disheveled Cambodian men offered their guidance and assistance.

"Oh, thank you but we're fine," Rich said through the fence.

"Ignore them," I said. "Come on. We have to keep up with the Brits. Just do what they do."

Several feet in front of us, we heard the gray-haired older man say, "Oh, don't pull that shit with me, you fucks. We live here," at which point he turned around to see Rich and I on his heels, looking like frightened deer in headlights.

"Well, come on boys. You might as well follow us. Don't just stand there with your thumbs up each other's ass," he said, motioning us onward.

The chute through which the nationals and foreigners were usually funneled had been rerouted. The Brits paused, looked around to see if anyone of authority was watching, then slipped through a gated fence. We paused to consider the legal ramifications for the crime we may or may not be committing.

"Well, come on already, lads. Don't just stand there with your dicks in your pants."

We couldn't fit through the fence with our oversized packs on, so we slipped them off and passed them over. The gray-haired man helped me with mine and said, "Jesus fucking Christ, son. You have everything *and* the kitchen sink in here?"

Rich and I exited Thailand and entered Cambodia with a fresh green visa in our passport and one hundred baht lighter, which we paid to the Cambodian border guards as a rite of passage. When we stepped onto Cambodian soil, a hungry crowd converged on us, including the Cambodians that were trailing us when we were on the Thai side of the border. It was as if we were Red Cross workers bringing relief to the starving masses. Everyone was calling for us to come with them for free rides. Alarmingly, they were even more aggressive and animated than the Indian touts I encountered at the New Delhi train stations.

Rich had done a bit of research, so he knew not to take the free rides. We pushed through the mass of men vying for our attention. Like Moses on a mission, our forward momentum parted the crowd. When at last we found an old man with his feet kicked up, sitting peacefully in his tuk-tuk, we hopped in the back and thought we were on our way.

"Could you take us to the nicest hotel in town?" Rich asked ever so politely.

"No hotels. Only guesthouses," he said. But before he could even start the engine, the crowd surrounded us.

The leader of the group, a well-dressed Cambodian man in a striped shirt, black pants, and black shoes, held a walkie-talkie in one hand and with the other shook his finger in the face of our driver. He yelled at him in Khmer, bringing attention to the man's body and fear to his face.

"I sorry. I can no drive you," he said apologetically.

"Come. Come now. You come with me. I take you for free. This way," said the man in the striped shirt, trying to forcefully escort us.

"No, thank you. We appreciate your generosity but we're just going to find a ride on our own," Rich replied.

"No! You come with me. You cannot take this! You must take free ride. Why you pay? This is free! I offer you free ride to your stay. Do not be rude!"

"No, thank you. We just want to pay for the tuk-tuk. We just want to pay for it," Rich said, maintaining an air of politeness and civility that was less than well received.

"I work for the government! I have been doing this for ten years. You don't believe me? Look at my badge!" he screamed, pointing to a lanyard around his neck then pointing back at us. "You want to call my office to prove my credentials?"

"That's fine," Rich replied, maintaining his composure amidst the building maelstrom. "I'm happy for your employment. That's great, really. I believe you. But why are you yelling at us?"

The man regained his composure. "Please. I am sorry for raising my voice. Come with me and I take you politely kindly to your hotel."

Rich held his ground in the Cambodian standoff until I had finally had enough.

"Excuse me. We'll be right back. Rich, come on," I said, grabbing him by his arm.

We made our way back toward the border crossing, and once outside the building I had Rich watch our bags. The Brits had not yet cleared customs, but I could still speak to them through a window.

"Excuse me," I said. "Do you guys think you could help us out? There's some really aggressive people out here trying to force us to take a free ride. You know anything about it?"

"Just a second, boys. And don't worry. You can follow us. You have a place to stay yet?"

"We don't," I replied.

"We'll set you up. I'm Hal," the gray-haired older man said. "And this is Titus."

"But everyone calls me T," he added, hoisting up his pants. We had little choice but to trust the men, so we adopted them as our guardians.

It was nighttime in Poipet, and as soon as we walked back into the street, the desperate Cambodian crowd once again descended upon us like vultures to fresh kill.

"Oh, go fuck yourselves, you bloody cunts!" Hal said commandingly to the air while swatting at them like flies. "I've got a local friend on his way with a motorcycle. I'll have him send two more bikes!" he yelled over the crowd. "It's a goddamn scam. These fucking wankers offer free rides and then take you as far outside of town as possible so you have to use their taxi service, and then they jack the prices on you." Then, turning his attention back to the crowd, he waved his arm and yelled, "Fucking twats!"

Minutes later, four motorcycles pulled up. Rich hopped on one and I on the other. We had no choice but to trust our drivers; the alternative did not seem pleasant. For a moment, I wondered if we would wind up as missing persons on the CBS nightly news.

***

The first thing I sensed upon entering Cambodia through Poipet was a feeling of lawlessness. In stark contrast to the well-manicured lawns, blooming gardens, and sidewalks laid out with consideration on the Thai side, the roads through Poipet were dusty, unpaved, and littered with potholes the size of small bomb craters. On both sides of the street, patrons who sold electronics, cell phones, and other goods during the day began boarding up their rickety wood and aluminum storefronts. In dimly lit doorways, tweaking prostitutes appeared and the regular working folk who knew better than to be out on the streets at night disappeared behind closed doors. There was a tension in the air as if a gunfight might erupt at any moment.

Our two new friends escorted us to a guesthouse and "worked a deal" for us on the room. We wondered if they took a few dollars off the top for themselves, but we accepted it as a safety tax, especially since the total for the room was only four hundred baht (which was about eleven dollars total for both of us). The room was poorly lit, and the walls had most likely not seen a fresh coat of paint since the reign of Pol Pot. We were definitely backpacking, not flashpacking (a slightly more sophisticated brand of backpacking where you have more financial resources and stay at nicer places but where you are still prone to excessive intoxication, foolishness, rabblerousing, poor decision-making, and general tomfoolery).

"Is there anywhere to eat around here?" I asked Titus after thanking him for his assistance.

"I'm going to have a beer downstairs. You boys are welcome to join me if you like. Hal's just having a wash, but we can grab a bite after that."

Titus was short and wiry, and his pockmarked face bore the brunt of what looked like a severe case of teen acne. He cranked his belt tighter incessantly to keep his pants from falling down. Tattoos crisscrossed his forearms and continued up beyond the sleeves of his shirt. Around his neck he wore a chain, and bulky silver rings adorned several of his fingers. Only a short time ago I had imagined he might be trying to scam us, but in this new light his crooked smile and chipped tooth became warm and friendly.

Titus and Hal had met a few months prior as teachers and were making a border run, something you have to do when you're living in Thailand and not an official expat. By leaving the country every three months, even if it's for five minutes, the new stamp in your passport means you are legal in the country for another quarter of a year. In this respect, border runs became a small industry.

"So, what brought you to Thailand?" Rich asked.

"Hal and I, we're teachers. Sort of. We don't actually have working papers. When the schools ask me for my papers, I put it off as long as I can. It usually buys me half a year and then I jet, so I tend to teach for about six months at a time. 'Teach and run' I like to call it. As long as you don't get caught it's a good gig. I did have one buddy get picked up, though, and now he's serving time." Titus paused to light a cigarette. "A Thai prison isn't exactly the type of place you want to do time."

"I can imagine," I added.

"You probably can't," he replied with poignancy. "Anyway, I've been living as an expat for years now and have traveled all over Southeast Asia, but I do love Cambodia. It's got a wild side. One time I was riding through here on my motorcycle in 1994 and got kidnapped. Tied up, an AK-47 to my head, blindfolded. But you see, I'm smart-like, and I knew they were full of shit, and they knew that I knew that they knew that I wasn't worth shit. The same thing happened to me a few months later in a town between Thailand and Burma. My friend who I was traveling with said he'd never travel with me again. You believe that gobshite?"

From the entrance of the guesthouse, Hal appeared, rubbing his wet, gray head of hair. "Don't use the little tube on the sink in the shower, boys. Turns out it's toothpaste and not shampoo. I never would've thought the Cambodians would favor oral care over body hygiene. They're definitely not Brits," he said, smiling through crooked, nicotine-stained teeth.

Rich and I both smiled and nodded awkwardly, not quite knowing how to respond to the outlaws. "Honestly. Go on. Look, smell my hair," he said, bending his neck and pushing his head into my face.

"Your hair certainly has fresh breath," Rich agreed.

"Ha! That's a good one," Titus interjected. It seemed to win us favor with the duo.

Who knew that Rich's naïve currency exchange at the border would prove to be such a valuable play for us.

***

With the night having fully descended upon Poipet, we made our way through the dusty streets with our adopted guardian angels while skinny dogs scurried down alleys and prostitutes courted us from doorways. With opportunity beckoning from every corner, it didn't take us long to discover that our guardian angels were in fact fallen angels.

"I'm going to slip in here and get us some beers," Titus said.

"Here, let us buy the first round," Rich offered, "as a thanks for getting us out of that pinch."

"That's mighty kind of you," Titus said, accepting the money.

Moments later, Titus exited the mart with four cans of Angkor beer and passed one out to each of us. He toasted to health and wealth, and in one long swig polished off most of his beer.

"Ahh, that's damn refreshing on a hot night like this. I love beer. I drink it every day. In fact, it's usually the first thing I have in the morning, but I'm not an alcoholic or anything," he added.

Three skinny Khmer girls looking no more than seventeen drifted absently down the street. Without taking his eyes off the girls, Hal chimed in. "You can have a good bit of three-holed fun in this town for five dollars, lads. You have to go into the brothel for that price, though. But for ten dollars you can take a whore home, and for twenty dollars they'll spend the night with you *and* get you a bit of ice."

"Wow," Rich said, nodding his head in agreement. "That *is* a good deal. So by ice, I doubt you mean mineral ice, right? Because you're not supposed to drink the water here, right?"

"No, um, not quite," said Hal with a hint of embarrassment. "You know, boys. Meth. Crystal."

"Oh right. Duh!" Rich added. "Crystal. Not a lot of sleep on that stuff, huh?" Rich said with a wink. "I don't want to have to worry about you two not getting your beauty sleep, am I right?"

"You don't have to worry about me, boys. I'm married and I love my Thai wife," Titus said, trailing off pensively. "But there is one girl in this town, I tell ya. Oh boy, I don't know what it is about her, but I've got a real sweet tooth for her."

We sat beneath the only light on a mostly abandoned street while a swarm of bugs circled above our heads. No sooner had Titus cracked his third beer than his sugarcane girl came flailing at us from a doorway in high heels she had not yet learned to master.

"Ti-toos! Ti-toos!" she shrieked in unadulterated excitement.

"Hello, darling!" Titus said, warmly leaping to his feet, cinching up his pants, and pulling her in for a hug and a kiss. In a tender tone he spoke a few words to her in Khmer.

To say she was eighteen years old was being generous. She was skinny with big, tragic eyes, and her body twitched, lurched, leaned, and fell into Titus. She was short and slight, and with a bend in her knees she squatted before us, her skirt hiking up to reveal leopard-print underwear. When our eyes met, she studied me with electric curiosity and wide-eyed amazement. In her eyes, I saw a cloud of addiction, but she managed to maintain a bubbly innocence that made you want to hug her or save her.

The young girl remained on the sidewalk with Titus while Rich and I entered the mart for another round of beers and a quick recap. By the time we returned to the street, several of the girl's friends had gathered around. They seemed curious about the commotion.

With that, Titus leaned in and whispered something to Hal. Then he declared, "Well boys, I think I'm going to have to call it a night. I'm going to go get me some cash and take this one home."

Titus disappeared to a nearby ATM with his young lady and returned to bid us good night. We wished the reunited couple well and watched as the skinny fallen saints drifted into the darkness of Poipet's dirty, littered streets.

Bathed in a halo of streetlight, the outline of a street girl and a hustler faded into oblivion.

Later that night, we discovered that our room at the guesthouse shared a paper-thin wall with Titus's. In the early hours of the morning, we would hear the banging of the bed against the wall, followed by utterances in broken English, such as, "Give it me, bad boy!" and "Fook my coochie-coo! Fook it!"

After Titus went on his way, Rich and I stayed on the corner with Hal. Hal possessed a paunch like a well-fed cat. It was accentuated by a white shirt with the logo of a software company that he tucked into his gray sweatpants, which he tucked into white socks, over which he wore white, brandless tennis shoes.

"I'm afraid I'm in a bit of a pickle, boys," Hal said when the mention of appetites surfaced. "I'm embarrassed to say this, but you see, Titus and I trade nights paying for dinner and tonight was his night. But seeing as he just left with the girl, he's left me high and dry. But I should have money in the morning when my check clears." There was something else about stolen money, but due to his thick accent and nonsensical nature, we had trouble following the story.

It quickly became apparent that living as an outlaw teacher with extracurricular hobbies that leaned toward excess and debauchery didn't pay the bills; in fact, they were both living paycheck to paycheck. What was even harder for us to believe was that he couldn't scrape together enough money for dinner, which totaled about a dollar-fifty per person.

"Let us buy you dinner," I said. "We really appreciate your help getting us through the border."

Over a basic dinner of chicken amok, Hal shared his encyclopedic knowledge of film stars and musicians who had died in plane crashes (including the plane types and the year they crashed).

"I've been lucky to live several lives, boys," he began. "I was an army officer stationed in Northern Ireland at the start of my career. In gunfights with the IRA I was shot several times by snipers. Look, right here," he said, untucking the right leg of his sweatpants from his sock, revealing two scars that appeared to be the entry and exit points of a bullet. "It shattered my tibia, and look, I've got another one here. Look, right here," he said, showing us a scar the size of a bullet on both sides of his left hand.

"In another life, I fathered seven children to three different wives. There was also a time when I worked and upheld a respectable living in insurance. You believe that? I can't."

"Teaching is definitely respectable," Rich was quick to add. "What happened to your insurance career?"

"It drove me to drink and it damn near drove me mad. I'm not one for that sedentary life. It's just another manufactured dream to keep the masses in check, like religion, you know? I mean, no offense to you boys if that's the life you live, but it just wasn't for me."

"So what happened? How did you wind up here?"

"Funny story. I was a contestant on *Who Wants to Be a Millionaire*. I won a little more than 10,200 pounds, so I told the family I needed a little 'me' time. A little vacation. And that's what I did. I came to Thailand. Now, unfortunately, for the rest of the story. I blew that money pretty quickly on booze, prostitutes, and gambling. But I tell ya what, I had a good time, and how many people get to say they've done that?"

"What happened to your wife?"

"We were on our way to divorce, so I told her there was no money left and that she was on her own."

"And what about your kids?"

"Eh, for the most part they were already grown and on their own. I still talk to them once or twice a year, and three of them have visited me, but I have to live for me, and they get that. They get me. And now, well now I'm a teacher."

"Someone has to teach today's youth," Rich added. "Better you than some bloody wanker."

Rich and I split the bill, and the three of us made our way through the deserted streets to our guesthouse. We walked Hal to his room. On the handle outside the door hung a "Do Not Disturb" sign and inside his TV crackled as it pushed its auditory limits.

"Come in, come in. Shut the door. Here, I want to give you this," he said, scribbling on a torn-off piece of paper. On it read *halspals12@hotmail.com*. "Here's my email. You know, in case you have any more questions or run into any more trouble."

"Thank you, Hal. That's very kind of you. We really appreciate your help," Rich said.

"Not a problem, gents. I was young and stupid once as well."

Rich and I looked at the TV. Its sound was maxed out, distorting the audio that accompanied a bio about Steve Jobs.

"Ah yes. The TV. Number-one rule of travel, boys, at least in this cesspool of a town. When you leave your guesthouse, always put your 'Do Not Disturb' sign on the door, turn the lights on, and turn the TV up as loud as it goes. Tends to keep the curious away, if you know what I mean."

Rich and I later agreed it was invaluable information for the next time we were staying in a brothel/meth house in Cambodia. We didn't bother mentioning to Hal that we couldn't wait to get out of Poipet and into our four-star hotel in Siem Reap.

When we got back to our hotel room, it was just as dirty as we had remembered. A faint trace of mouse feces in our unsanitary excuse for a bathroom added to the mystique. We started noticing new things, like ants and spiders and tiny bloodstains on the walls and sheets. We were relieved to find nothing was missing.

Rich and I fashioned a piece of furniture between our beds and decided we should watch a movie on my computer that would teach us something about Cambodian culture. Neither of us had seen *The Killing Fields* and knew basically nothing about Cambodian history. A cool 141 minutes later, we were trembling, wondering what the hell we'd gotten ourselves into. Meanwhile, next door, Titus imbibed in the flesh of a Cambodian teenager and the escapism that crystal meth provided.

***

The next morning, after an itchy night's sleep, there was a motorcycle waiting out back for Rich and me. The night before, Titus's motorcycle driver had arranged for us to carpool to Siem Reap with his friend.

As we left our room, Titus was packing his bags with his door ajar.

"Oh, hey mates! Hang on a second," he said, looking haggard and visibly stressed as he cranked his belt a notch tighter. "Uh, I've got a bit of a problem, see?"

"What's that?" Rich said.

"I lost my money card last night. I had it at the crossing, but I think I lost it when I got money out for the whore. And it was my anniversary last night on top of everything. I've got a little money, but we're not sure if Hal's check has cleared. Do you think we could get a lift with you to Siem Reap?"

Rich and I exchanged looks. Rich opened his mouth to respond (hopefully with an excuse as to why that was a bad idea) when Hal appeared.

"Good news, boys!" Hal announced as he walked toward us. "The check cleared. We're in the money!"

And so it was that we parted ways with our outlaw friends and made our way toward Siem Reap. Although we bid our new friends and fallen angels *adieu*, whenever I thought of them I sent those characters of serendipity and adventure my quiet gratitude. In a strange way, I admired the freedom, personal authority, and courage it took to live their lives as they pleased, even though I knew I was romanticizing it. Through my own lens, it looked as if their lives hinted at tragedy, but only they knew the true currency of their own hearts. For all we knew, Titus and Hal could have been the happiest men on the planet. If Kerouac ever got around to telling the story of Sal Paradise and Dean Moriarty's latter years, Titus and Hal could have been them.

"There was nowhere to go but everywhere," Kerouac

said in the voice of Sal. "My fault, my failure, is not in the passions I have, but in my lack of control of them."

Titus and Hal, our holy misfits and mystic guides, didn't appear to have anywhere to go, and what they lacked in direction was certainly doubled in what they lacked in control. At least that much Rich and I had in common with them.

Chapter 20. Best. Birthday. Ever.

The evening after our Poipet debacle, we found ourselves sitting behind sandbags at a bar on Pub Street, Siem Reap's main stretch of bars and restaurants. On the other side of the sandbags, calf-deep water flooded the streets.

For most of the afternoon, we waded through the streets in exploration. Having spent enough time waterlogged, we sat down for our first beer around 4pm. A fierce game of rummy 500 ensued, and several hours later we bought a small bag of pot from a local and made our way back to our four-star hotel. Because it was just before high season, at only thirty-eight dollars a night it was virtually empty.

We sat on our balcony overlooking the pool, drinking beers and doing our best impersonations of Titus and Hal. Rich played deejay and I rolled joints. The only other people we saw in the hotel were three middle-aged Japanese men wearing matching tracksuits, which seemed both odd and appropriate.

The next day we toured a small portion of the temples of Angkor Wat, a 400-square-kilometer area containing the remains of the capital of the Khmer empire, which thrived from the ninth to fifteenth centuries. Around midday, as we walked toward one of the temples, it began to rain, so we ducked underneath the overhang of a temple to smoke a joint and let the storm pass.

As the rain came down harder, Rich looked nervous. I assured him it would blow over, but after a while, Rich abandoned our position for the shelter of our hired tuk-tuk. The rain poured off the temple like a waterfall. I noticed a moat forming around the temple, so I too abandoned my position for the tuk-tuk before the way out became impassable.

Our driver made his way to the next temple on our tour, yelling over the sound of the rain that it was a good place to wait out the storm. As we drove along the slightly elevated road, however, the jungle floor disappeared, leaving a great ocean from which silk-cotton trees and strangler figs grew. Only two weeks prior, a flash flood caught two hundred tourists by surprise, requiring them to be airlifted from one of the historic sites.

In minutes, the water on the road was ankle deep and quickly rising, just like our panic. I glanced at our surroundings to consider our next move. *Perhaps just hug a tree and ascend its trunk as the water rises?*

More tense minutes passed as we watched the water rise steadily and incrementally. While Sookum, our sincere and endearing tuk-tuk driver, promised us the water would recede, the look on his face betrayed nervousness. The sound of the tropical rain pounding on the small vehicle was deafening. All we could do was sit and watch the storm through the plastic tarps that enclosed us.

With four-wheel-drive vehicles ahead of us beginning to turn around, it appeared the road was washed out. Sookum decided to do the same thing, but two turns into our three-point turn, the back wheels of the vehicle sunk into the mud. Rich and I surrendered the illusion that we were going to stay dry and jumped into the knee-deep water that threatened to overtake the carriage.

The two of us pushed and rocked the tuk-tuk as best we could as our flip-flops sunk deeper into the mud. The wheels spun furiously, sending jungle muck and mire into our faces and clothes, but we were successful.

Then, as quickly and ferociously as the storm began, it broke, sending splintered sunbeams through the jungle canopy and down to the jungle floor. Where the waters receded to so quickly we did not know, nor did we care. We leapt into the tuk-tuk, soaking wet and caked in mud. Without saying a word, Sookum drove us to the next site. Like a motorboat gliding along a lake, a wake of water spread out behind us.

***

In mid-October we found ourselves in Phnom Penh, the capital of Cambodia. We visited S-21, the Killing Fields, and a war remnants museum that displayed killing instruments of Cambodia's foreign invasions, civil wars, and genocides.

S-21 was one of the detention centers where tens of thousands of Cambodians were tortured or killed from 1975 to 1979 under Pol Pot's dictatorship. In order to create a race of rice-pickers subservient to the Communist state, Pol Pot's plan was to brainwash the children, arm them, and remove all of the artists and intellectuals in the country.

If the Cambodians who found themselves on the wrong side of the genocide were not killed at S-21, they were loaded into a truck under the guise of relocation and brought to the Killing Fields where they were coldly and brutally murdered, their bodies thrown into mass graves. In total, out of a population of seven to eight million, nearly 1.5

million Cambodians died of starvation, execution, disease, or literally being worked to death. It is an unbelievable story, perhaps even more so due to its recent place in history.

This somber day of reflection happened to fall on Rich's birthday. The only comedic relief of the afternoon was when Rich turned to me with tears in his eyes and said, "Best...birthday...ever."

"You'll always remember where you spent your thirty-third birthday," I added with tears of laughter and sadness filling my eyes.

Later that night, we sought out the art of Keo Titia, the Cambodian artist whose work we had seen at the art opening in Bangkok. We found his work on Soi 78, a block consisting mostly of art galleries. As Rich and I played good cop/bad cop—after-offer, counter-offer, offer, and still no agreement—we told the owner of the gallery we were going to have a drink, discuss our decision, and get some cash, which is how we found O'Leary's Irish Pub.

Like any dimly lit Irish bar anywhere in the world, its walls were painted kelly green and adorned in Irish flags, coats of arms, and other Celtic regalia. But what piqued our interest was seeing two framed T-shirts on the wall, both from Seattle landmarks. In a city of 1.5 million people, we walked into the one bar run by Seattle expats.

Chuck and Frank had both worked in construction in Seattle. When the global economy began falling apart in 2008, Chuck decided he was going to hitchhike across Ireland. However, several of the Cambodian men he worked with suggested he check out their homeland first.

After touring different parts of Cambodia, one afternoon Chuck found himself in Phnom Penh and walked into O'Leary's Irish Pub. He fell in love with the idea of owning an Irish bar in Cambodia. A week later he placed an offer.

Chuck then called up Frank—a bald, hulking fellow—to come help him run the bar. Frank had been laying pipe in Seattle as a construction worker, and since arriving in Phnom Penh had been laying pipe as a bartender with Khmer women. Both of them seemed to love their new lives, and Chuck had even found himself a young Cambodian wife.

"Hey, fellas! It's Rich here's birthday," I decided to announce to the bar. Rich turned bright red at the unwelcome attention.

"Really? It's not every day a Seattleite shows up in my bar to celebrate his birthday!" Chuck said, and with that he poured the first of several shots of Jameson.

***

The next morning we decided it was a good idea to stay away from Jameson for a while, a decision we forgot twelve hours later. But we figured we needed to celebrate our successful negotiations; after all, we both ended up purchasing art at the price we demanded.

In another Irish bar, a Cambodian waitress batted her eyelashes at me. She was not our server, but midway through dinner she took over our table. She flirted with me relentlessly and stroked my ego by laughing at my bad jokes.

"I'm Devi," she said. "What are you two doing after? Do you want to go dancing with me and my sister?"

"I don't see why we wouldn't," I told her.

***

I wasn't sure if it was the warmth of the Jameson or the warmth and attention of Devi, but I felt an immediate connection to her. We danced closely in the club in our own little world. Rich had left around 1:30am, explaining that he was tired. Feeling like a third wheel, her sister had left a short time later.

"Would you like to come back to my place?" Devi asked.

We stumbled home, laughing and dancing through the nearly empty streets of Phnom Penh. When we reached her place, we climbed up a dark stairwell. When we entered her apartment, she secured a padlock on the inside of the door.

"What's that all about?"

"Safety. Just give me a moment. I have to get my sister out of our room."

"Huh?"

"My sister. She and I share a bed."

"Who's in the other room?"

"My mother. I'm going to have my sister go sleep with her."

"What?"

"Don't worry. It's okay. You'll meet her in the morning."

"I'm not meeting your mother in the morning. I should probably go," I said. The only problem was, it was late and I had no idea where I was. For a moment, I saw my future as their prisoner, like Paul Sheldon in Stephen King's *Misery*.

"Yes, you will meet her, and she's going to love you."

It was a railroad-style apartment, the kitchen being closest to the door, followed by two bedrooms and a living room. The top of the wall between the two bedrooms, however, was not closed off, allowing sound to easily travel.

We fooled around for a while, but my mounting anxiety about meeting her mother and possible imprisonment impeded the pleasure of the experience. Devi kept insisting I stay for breakfast to meet her mother, but finally around 4:30am she heeded my pleas and unlocked the padlock. She kindly walked me home since I was so disoriented. Exhausted and ready for sleep, I was relieved that her home was only a few blocks away from my hotel.

With the morning light appearing in the eastern sky, she said, "There's some shoes I really want. What do you think about taking me shopping today?"

"Let me think about it," I said.

For the next month, I received emails in broken English telling me how much she would like to see me again.

Chapter 21. The Motorbike Incident and Escape from Phnom Penh

Things disintegrated quickly. It started with two bottles of wine in our cabana overlooking the Mekong River. Multiple beers and pepper shots later, our party commanded the music while I art directed a photo shoot in which Naomi, our new friend from the Netherlands, was sprawled across the pool table trying to pose with a kitten. It just so happened the name of the bar was also Naomi's.

As the squeamish feline tried to get away, Rich climbed onto the pool table to pin them both down. The picture was epic, but the people whose game of pool we interrupted were not as impressed.

***

We first saw Naomi on Otres Beach in Sihanoukville, Cambodia. I pointed out to Rich that she looked uncomfortable with the person she was sharing a table with, not to mention disinterested. Apparently she had taken on a travel-clinger, a parasitic traveler who latches on and won't let go. Chances are this person is boring, undeniably annoying, or a one-upper (Oh, you've been to the moon? I remember the first time I was on Mars!).

Two days later, Rich and I boarded a ferry for a remote island in southern Cambodia called Koh Rong, an inexpensive, unspoiled island getaway surrounded by turquoise waters, coconut trees, mango groves, and a dense jungle. On the opposite side of the small island, quiet fishing villages remained mostly untouched by Western influence. For miles along its powder-white beaches, the only company to be had was the occasional crab that shuffled about. We heard it was what Koh Samui was like thirty years prior, before developers, backpackers, drunks, and opportunists washed up on its shores.

Unfortunately, the local inhabitants on the other side of Koh Rong who had been going about their way of life for an untold time had no idea what was in store for them in the next decade. A Cambodian billionaire had purchased a 99-year lease on the island and planned to build marinas, a small airstrip, and several five-star resorts. But for the time being, we were in Shangri-La—well, Shangri-La Bungalows to be exact—a series of small, no-frills bungalows carved into the side of a hill in the jungle.

The proprietor of Shangri-La Bungalows was a German man about fifty years old named Franz. It was rare to see him without a joint hanging out of his mouth, and by the end of dinner on the first night he was buying us a round.

"So Franz, how the hell did you wind up in this remote part of Cambodia?" I asked.

He took a drag off his joint, raised an eyebrow, exhaled, and said in his thick German accent, "Well, for one thing, there are no natural disasters. No earthquakes, typhoons, volcanoes...or tsunamis."

Franz had expatriated from his country more than thirty-four years ago. He was not only lucky to call the island his home but also to be alive.

In 2004, he ran a dive shop and a guesthouse in Sri Lanka when the Christmas-morning tsunami came ashore, taking forty-three thousand lives with it. Because of the structure of the reefs surrounding Sri Lanka, there was no warning of the sea receding. One minute Franz was organizing his office and putting away equipment, and the next a wave burst through the scuba shop, pinning him against a wall. Out of instinct, he put his arms out to brace himself, but the strength and weight of the wave pinned him against the back wall, snapping his arms like toothpicks in the process.

After seventeen days in a coma, the final tally of broken bones included both shoulders, both upper arms, both wrists, an elbow, eight fingers, and fourteen ribs (along with two ruptured lungs). After a long, painful journey, he decided to finish his recovery in Cambodia—a beautiful, peaceful place without tsunamis apparently.

On the ferry to Koh Rong that morning, Rich and I decided to use our gratitude-intention journals to co-create. We both penned in our journals, "Today we intend and create to make a new friend for life."

That afternoon we met Ingrid, a German woman who recently gave up her job in Berlin as a technical project manager to teach scuba diving in Southeast Asia. We invited her to dinner at Shangri-La.

When Ingrid arrived at the restaurant that evening, whom did she bring with her but none other than Naomi, the girl we had spotted in Sihanoukville. In almost no time we made the backward leap from Otres Beach in Sihanoukville to Naomi staying at the guesthouse attached to O'Leary's Irish Pub in Phnom Penh. She too had spent time with Chuck and Frank, our new expat Seattle friends.

We also realized that we had been crisscrossing paths with each other throughout Asia for almost a month. One of the only places we didn't intersect was when she drove a motorcycle through northern Vietnam for more than a week, which both Rich and I found to be most impressive. Her humor, wit, and charm (not to mention her cute Dutch accent), immediately won us over, so we adopted her on the spot.

***

The result of handing over the music to us at Naomi's was a raucous, enthusiastic burst of intoxication. Because I won rock-paper-scissors, I started the round-robin playlist with "Sympathy for the Devil" by the Rolling Stones. Rich came in next with "Weird Fishes Arpeggio" by Radiohead, and Naomi chose last, selecting "The Power of Equality" by the Red Hot Chili Peppers.

With each song we helped ourselves to the volume control behind the bar. After the first bottle of wine and during the second one at dinner, I tried to remind everyone that since we each had arrived on our own mopeds, we should really keep our wits about us. My heeds of caution were all but ignored, and by dessert we were doing kampot pepper shots—abusive, alcohol-infused concoctions that used peppercorns from the surrounding world-famous pepper plantations. The results of these shots often brought grown men to their knees, and I was no exception.

"When in Cambodia," Naomi said as we threw back our first and only pepper shot. Fiery pepper coursed through our veins, accompanied by an overlay of freedom and joy.

That afternoon we had driven through the verdant Cambodian countryside on our mopeds, stopping in coastal towns for fresh seafood and cold beers, driving to the top of Bokor National Park, snapping photos to memorialize the day, and eventually making our way to the Vietnam border, where we opted to turn back since it was getting late. Surrounded by lush rice paddies, with the throttle maxed and the wind in our hair, it was hard to imagine a greater outpouring of inner and outer freedom.

And so a day of joy and freedom turned into a night of spirit-filled celebration. Arm in arm we sang and danced, throwing our fists into the air with the enthusiasm of liberated Parisians, fully aware of how lucky we were to be living in, and sharing with each other, this Cambodian night. It was the icing on the cake.

Drunk on alcohol and gratitude, I made my way to the bar to order another round of Angkor beers for us. "Low" by Cracker blasted through the music system, and strings of Christmas lights cast a soft light in the open-air bar. In the corner by the pool table, an old friend and a new friend were having a moment, dancing together like carefree dingledodies. I was in Cambodia on my seventh month of travel, four more than I had imagined, and as I reveled at this fact, a moment of clarity unfolded before me.

In that moment, my senses heightened to record my surroundings. I knew it was a moment I would not forget for the rest of my life. It was the perfect storm of love, friendship, alcohol, music, joy, and freedom, and I thought, *I fucking love my life*. The strange thing is, the words didn't come from me; they came *through* me. My body was just the vessel, the instrument, the antenna through which this frequency and vibration passed. I took it all in and let the experience move through me, pass over me, and pass through the filter of gratitude I was coming to know more intimately.

Last call came and went. As the bartender wiped down the bar, we asked if she would sell us some more beers. She obliged. We stashed beers, along with a bag of ice, underneath the seats of our mopeds.

As we were about to fire up our engines, Rich said, "Shit! I can't find my camera."

"Maybe Naomi has it," I said, turning around to see a single red taillight disappear into smoke, dust, and darkness. I went back into the bar to help him find it but to no avail.

"Nope, it's gone. Damn it."

"We'll come back tomorrow. It will show up."

We returned to our mopeds where Rich started his bike, forgetting it was still in first gear. Once the starter caused ignition, the bike lurched forward into a line of other bikes. I watched in slow motion as Rich lost control of his bike. He tucked up his leg and rolled to the right. In the process, he fell into another moped, which proceeded to knock over another bike, and like a row of cascading dominoes, one by one eight bikes came crashing to the ground.

"Holy shit! Are you okay?" I said, leaping off my bike and running up to his motionless body. "Dude! Are you okay?"

"I think I hurt my foot."

"Is it bad?"

"I don't think so."

"Good. Get the fuck up and let's get out of here." My

concern and empathy were suddenly replaced with sobriety and concentration.

For the two-kilometer ride back to town, I had Rich follow me very slowly, trying my best not to drive off the road from hysterical laughter.

After a kilometer, a light appeared from the darkness on the side of the road. In a flurry of dust, a bike peeled out. It was Naomi, who had been patiently waiting to intercept us. Once again, our inept moped gang was back together.

"What took you so long?" Naomi asked as we walked through the front door of our cabana.

"I either lost my camera or it was stolen."

"What? That's bullshit! Come on. We're going back to town."

"Whoa. *We* are not going anywhere," I said. "You two can go but I got a bag of ice and a bottle of Jameson I've been carrying around. Let's just worry about it tomorrow. We shouldn't be driving anyway."

Naomi, full of piss and vinegar, insisted they go back into town.

When they returned, Rich recounted the story with excitement. "It was great," he started. "We were on a mission. I mean, after we realized we took a wrong turn out of here and drove ten minutes in the wrong direction."

"Well, when you add everything up, that's a fair distance at 3am when you're drunk on a moped in the all-consuming darkness of the Cambodian countryside," I interjected.

Brushing past my comment, Rich continued. "When we reached Naomi's, Naomi went into the bar with her guns a'blazin'."

"Accusations flew around the room like the balls on the pool table at break," Naomi added dramatically. "We left no stone unturned."

They spared no details in recounting the tale, and I wondered if the story was going anywhere.

"The bartender was very patient and accommodating," Rich said. "I think it was actually Naomi the owner, but whoever it was, she helped us move couch cushions, she searched the pockets in the pool table, she looked behind the bar."

"And figuring it was stolen by another drunk," Naomi continued, "Rich was about to leave a note for the thief to at least mail him the memory card."

The excited way these two were talking, it seemed like a you-had-to-be-there type of story.

"It was at that point that Naomi decided to check her bag one more time...and it was at that point...it was at that point that she found my camera in her bag!"

"We apologized profusely and left the bar as quickly as we could," said Naomi.

"But the girl who owned the bar, she was so cool about it. She was like, 'Don't worry. You'd be surprised. This happens about two or three times a week.' I mean, here we had ditched her in the middle of a pool game that she asked us to play, we took over her music, I pretended to be a cat on her pool table, she sold us beer, then we accused her staff of stealing my camera. And she was smiling the entire time."

For the rest of the night, we drank Jameson and beers, smoked cigarettes on our balcony overhanging the Mekong River, and took turns art directing another photo shoot. At some point, Rich passed out.

As the sun began to rise over the Mekong, Naomi and I stepped out onto the balcony off our cabana. With a beer in her hand and a Jameson in mine, we sat in silence on the edge of the balcony, our bodies draped upon a rail while our bare feet dangled over the river's currents. In joyfully intoxicated awe and wonder, we watched the Cambodian night succumb to sunrise.

As if some universal force wanted to reinforce the thought I experienced earlier in the bar, Naomi broke the silence by saying, "I fucking love my life."

I looked at her surprised, then we both burst out laughing.

"You know what, Naomi? I really love my life too."

***

Cambodia may have taken from us our livers' ability to function optimally, but it had given us so much more. In its gracious serendipity, Cambodia gave Rich and me a new friend, and driving through its countryside on our mopeds gave us a sense of invincibility. Traversing from one town to the next gave us a sense of accomplishment. In Angkor Wat, we got a sense of our place in history and evolution. Meeting new people from all over the world gave us a sense of connectedness and community. Deciding what we would do day in and day out gave us a sense of authority and personal freedom. Walking into O'Leary's and meeting owners from Seattle gave us a sense of magic.

And it was for those reasons and more that Cambodia reminded me of why I had set out to travel.

At the heart of travel is discovery. In discovering other cultures and lifestyles, I was discovering my place in the world, and in discovering my place in the world, I was discovering a new understanding of compassion and global connectedness. It didn't matter where I was on the earth, what culture I was a part of, or where I came from; we were all united by the peaks and valleys and the joy and suffering of the human experience. There is only one way to truly transcend that suffering—through the doorway of love.

The human experience is such that we have no choice but to interject meaning into it. This is what Preetika told me on the flight from Newark to New Delhi. I was learning that the hero's search is not something simply to be read and studied; the search is for each of us to live. I didn't necessarily have any new conclusions after Cambodia, but the questions didn't seem to matter as much anymore.

Perhaps most importantly, in falling in love with travel and its provisions, I was falling in love with new aspects of my life that I couldn't have otherwise known. On the road, I had no one to rely on for happiness. If I wanted happiness, it had to come from within. If I wanted new friends, it was all on me. If I wanted to stop feeling lonely or sad, I had to rise above it.

What I was experiencing I call an "earned happiness." I took a chance, and what I needed appeared. In every accomplishment on the road, however great or small, I was learning I was capable. I was expanding my relationship with the generous Source—the life-giving energy—that flows through me and all other living things. I was learning to communicate with it through trust and surrender, which created a feedback loop. The more I trusted and surrendered, the better I felt, and the better I felt, the better the experiences I attracted into my life. My heart relaxed, becoming more open and unburdened.

I was ready.

***   ***   ***

I am so grateful for:

1. The currency of gratitude and intention in my life.
2. To be living the realized dream of that seventeen-year-old kid.
3. Titus and Hal stepping in to guide us through an intense situation.
4. Making a new friend in Naomi.
5. Learning to fall in love with my life through trust and surrender.

Today I intend and create:

1. To be surprised by something I manifest.
2. Direction as to where to go and what to do when Rich goes home.
3. To have more experiences that give me a deeper understanding of myself.
4. Some time to slow down, relax, and get focused.
5. That the story I am searching for continues to reveal itself to me in unexpected ways.

Chapter 22. Getting to Know Your Travel Partner

You think you know someone. You're friends, you have a history, you've traveled together more than once for extended periods of time, and then...and then this person says something so disgusting, so deplorable, so egregious, so unconscionable that you wonder if your friendship can actually survive. Once those words are out there they can't be taken back. This is exactly what happened over a game of rummy 500 at a small bar in Luang Prabang, Laos.

"What are my top three songs? Well, that's easy," Rich said. "Number three is 'You Can't Hurry Love' by the Supremes. Number two is 'Dream On' by Aerosmith, and number one is 'Nothing Compares to You' by Sinead O'Connor."

"Are you kidding me? Tell me you're kidding."

"Why?"

"Why? Why! Because I don't understand how someone with such keen musical sensibilities could come up with such a mundane, pedestrian list of drivel."

"You might also be surprised to know I like Motown."

Sabrina, an attractive German girl we met waiting for our flight from Phnom Penh to Luang Prabang watched the conversation volley between us like two strong-willed tennis players battling it out at Wimbledon.

"I've never once heard you listen to Motown."

"Well, you're not always at my house."

"Okay, on a *very* loose sliding scale, I will give you the Supremes, and that scale would be dated 1966. But Sinead O'Connor? And Aerosmith? Seriously, Aerosmith?"

"You just love hyperbole."

"You guys," Sabrina finally interjected, "I don't even know what the hell you're saying."

"What I'm saying…what I'm saying here is I'm so offended by Rich's shitty list of top three songs—of all time, mind you—that I'm not even sure I can travel with him anymore."

Whenever Rich and I started talking about music, we constantly tried to one-up each other. We could talk for hours about little-known bands, when the bands broke up, what a particular artist went on to do and with whom. We would argue about how much of an impact an artist had on a certain scene or where the artist was now, all the while trying to outdo one another with bold references and obscure influences.

So, when the topic of Rich's top three favorite songs came up, I was horrified. Then I thought, *Perhaps he's trying to play to the sympathy of the beautiful girl across the table. That's it. That makes much more sense.*

***

Apart from the embarrassing statement Rich made at the bar, he was an outstanding travel companion who perfectly complemented my style, which was not having a plan. I was not one for research, scouring websites for hotels, or being locked into an itinerary. I couldn't even commit to what to order for dinner.

"I'll have the chicken...no wait, the pizza...I'm sorry, could I change that? I'll have the pad thai. Three stars. No two stars. Wait, how many stars is your spice scale based on?" By the time our food came, I would be disappointed with my meal and suffer from order envy.

Instead, I often relied on Rich to tell me where to go, where to stay, what time we had to be at the bus depot or train station, and how much I owed for our costs. In short, he was a meticulous researcher and far more adept at simple addition and subtraction. Before we even arrived in a new location, Rich had a mental layout of it in his head. Whether relaxing on a beach or traversing territory, he would read and reread the *Lonely Planet*. And then he'd read it again after doing research on the Internet.

If I even dared to question something, he would reply, "Well, it's not like I haven't read the *Lonely Planet: Laos* cover to cover fourteen times. Here, maybe you can find a better plan." And he'd hand me the book, knowing full well I would hand it right back.

He scoured blogs and websites for tips and tricks, recommendations for places to eat and areas to avoid, and learned about local scams before the locals even had a chance to scam us (the free rides at the Poipet border crossing being a prime example). When I told him about a nice Malaysian man I met in Ho Chi Minh City one afternoon, he immediately replied, "His sister was moving to Seattle to be a nurse, and his mother was sick, right? Yeah. I read about that one." *Damn it. Got me again.*

As time wore on, our roles came more into focus. Rich was the Director of Ways and Means, and I was the Social

Director. The ironic thing was that at home, Rich was one of the most social people I knew, but "traveling Rich" was often shy and reserved. I wondered if he was getting tired of me talking to so many strangers, but I had been on my own for so long that I began conversations without even realizing it.

Even when you have a history with someone, traveling can bring out things you didn't know about the other person. For instance, I had no idea how much Rich loved the challenge of a good knot. He found them gratifying to unravel, whereas my only solution to a knot was scissors.

Another thing I found fascinating was observing him in the water. I first noticed this on the island of Koh Rong. Like a dog in a river, he would stand in the sea for hours, and like a sunflower, his head would be cocked back facing the sun. I'd see his head—eyes covered with Ray Ban sunglasses—and his arms would be unnaturally poised above the water as if he was about to do jazz hands.

My curiosity finally propelled me to ask the purpose of keeping his hands above the waterline, to which he replied, "I don't like the feeling in my fingertips when my hands get wrinkled and pruned. I don't like what the salt water does to them."

Something I envied about Rich was his vehicular narcolepsy. The moment we started moving in a car, a bus, a boat, or a plane, he fell asleep with infant-like precision, and when he slept, he slept as soundly and as long as any teenager. Many mornings, especially in Luang Prabang, I would set my alarm with the most sincere intention of getting up and going for a run, doing yoga, taking a walk, or meditating. Inevitably, however, I would hit snooze on my phone every nine minutes for anywhere from twenty-seven minutes on a good morning to seventy-two minutes on a very bad morning.

All in all, I came to know three persons in one Rich as we traveled, kind of like how I learned about the idea of three persons in one God from a lifetime of Catholic school. Instead of the Father, the Son, and the Holy Spirit, there were Rich, Richard, and Dick.

The Rich most people knew was one of the kindest, most sincere, most generous people in the world. He talked to every beggar who approached us, showering them with sincere attention and kindness, as well as dollars, baht, dong, or whatever currency he had in his pocket. He valiantly supported the local economy his first week in Asia, much like the mafia might do for its neighborhood at Christmas (minus the turkey, of course).

When less fortunate people asked us for food or money, invariably their opening line would be, "Hey friend, where are you from?" to which Rich might reply enthusiastically, "I'm from Seattle! Have you ever been there?"

Rich also tipped everywhere he went, even though in most places in Asia it was not the custom. Beyond the occasional good-hearted musical disagreement, tipping was our main point of contention the entire time we traveled together. It was the only time he ever snapped at me.

"Dude. How many times do I have to tell you? You don't have to tip."

"Look, it's my money and I can do what I want with it. Can you just leave it alone?"

He recalls it differently, and I can assure you he would claim I was being hyperbolic.

Then there was Dick, Rich's alter ego. Dick was someone I referred to as "mischievously aggressive." Dick might appear when copious amounts of alcohol were involved, specifically tequila or brown liquor. The first thing one notices when encountering Dick is that he does not stand for injustice (more specifically, an injustice against him).

If Dick feels he has been insulted or wronged, Dick becomes cutting and sardonic, or he may just say point-blank to someone—in front of an entire table, maybe in Siem Riep, Cambodia—"I'm sorry. I don't want to talk to you. I don't like you, and I don't recognize you at this table."

The third person in one Rich was Richard. Richard was the traveling entity of Rich. During our first few weeks, regular Rich was bright-eyed, good-natured, and naïve. Slowly but surely, however, Richard emerged. Richard was a shrewd negotiator, a quick study, and even more quickly learned how to play the game.

Richard might say to a tuk-tuk driver who was vying for our business, "Look, I'm not in the mood to negotiate, okay? Give me your best price or I walk," to which the driver would throw out a high number. Richard thoroughly understood the law of supply and demand.

"What did I say? Last chance. Take it or leave it, buddy. There are a million other tuk-tuk drivers around here. You want my business or not? It's a simple yes or no. Last chance. Come on. We got places to go and people to see."

The driver would throw out his final price, and Richard would walk. Nine out of ten times we wouldn't get five paces before the tuk-tuk driver broke down and conceded the price. Richard would flash an accomplished smile, and we would have an additional fifty cents to put toward beer, lodging, or more likely than not, homeless people on the street.

"It's not about the money," Richard said time and time again. "It's about the principle. I know when they're trying to rip me off."

By the time we left Laos, I was in awe of Richard's command. As the Director of Ways and Means, it was a natural progression for him to assume the role of chief negotiator, and I had no problem taking a back seat.

Whether he was Rich, Dick, or Richard, his face was always buried in his computer, phone, or iPad, and I would not hesitate to comment on this. It just so happened that whenever he was on one of his electronic devices, he was like a seven-year-old boy immersed in a video game. A hurricane could sweep through the room and he would not notice.

Late one evening after being out most of the night, I was trying to talk to him while his face was plastered to his phone. I took on my own alter drinking ego and said in a slur, "Hey! It pisses me off when I'm talking to you and you're in your computer and you don't answer me. Answer me when I'm talking to you!"

Of course, my timing wasn't very good. This happened the night of his birthday. He was simply checking his birthday wishes from Facebook. He had more than six hundred messages on his wall, and he was responding to each one individually. The quintessential middle child in action.

What he did earn the right to claim, however, was that I had the memory of a goldfish. For instance, I might ask him three to four times in a span of five minutes, "What time is it?"

At one point, he finally took off his watch, handed it to me, and said, "Just take it. Seriously, it's cool. Just take it."

He refused to put it back on, so I had to wear it for the rest of the day.

On the other hand, as each day blended into the next in a haze of alcohol, I was amazed at Rich's ability to recall information. He could recount with Rain Man-like precision the exact dates of where we were, where we stayed, how long we stayed, and what followed.

"We were in Bangkok from the fifth to the tenth. No question. Definitely the fifth to the tenth."

When I called him "Rain Man," his rebuttal was often, "Well if I'm Rain Man, that makes you the character from *Awakenings* prior to his awakening."

One of my favorite facts about him, which I discovered over the course of travel, was that in high school he founded several clubs. The first was S.M.I.L.E—Students Making It A Little Easier. The other was H.E.L.P—Help Every Living Person. Even after a decade of history, I loved that there was always something new to learn about Rich, Richard, and Dick.

Those are the best kinds of friends.

Chapter 23. Out in the Open

All over Southeast Asia you see eighteen to twenty-somethings wearing sleeveless shirts that say, "In the Tube, Vang Vieng."

Vang Vieng is a small town in south-central Laos surrounded by majestic nature. Hidden caves and grottos draw adventurers and naturalists, but what draws the backpackers is the river that runs through it. In the late nineties, a few ambitious backpackers decided it was a great place for outdoor recreation, so they created the small town around river tubing. But what was even a better idea was to get a bunch of young, attractive women in bikinis from all over the world to serve drinks. The result was a scene right out of *MTV Spring Break*. Perhaps more bizarre than *MTV Spring Break* in the middle of Laos was the fact that beyond soccer matches, the only other shows broadcast in every bar and restaurant were reruns of *The Simpsons* and *Friends*.

At the mouth of the river, testosterone-fueled frat boys with chiseled bodies and homoerotic sayings painted on their bodies wrestled each other and shot-gunned beers in a complex dance to attract female attention. Science calls this a mating ritual, but mostly they just struck me as loud, emotive meatheads. By 4pm, when the sun began its descent behind the mountains, most were generally fall-down drunk.

In the tube, people puke. People paint their bodies. And people get hurt. Sometimes people who are hurt get puked on. Sometimes people even get paralyzed from drunken, foolish behavior on the rope swing that swings out over the river. Occasionally, people even get killed.

While most people rent a tube for the day, very few actually make it more than two hundred meters down the river. The reason is because on both sides of the first bend in the river are four bars. Most tubers get waylaid there for a beer, which turns into an afternoon of drinks, which turns into barhopping, and by the end of the fourth bar, tubing down the river seems too great of a task (and too great of a risk). By that point in the day, the sun begins to dip behind the mountains, and it gets cold quickly, especially when wet. Of course, Rich and I weren't aware of this when we went to Vang Vieng. We went there to relax and have a few quiet nights.

The first night we met a group of college dudes from Vancouver, British Columbia, and the party was on for days, late night after late night. They were fun, energetic, entertaining, and constantly trying to one-up the others in moronic contests and fantastic feats of foolishness.

By the third day in town, when we finally did make it to "In the Tube," Rich was exhausted. We were drinking beers on the river in the sun and watching the youngsters do their thing. For most of the day, while I was throwing back beers with the enthusiasm of the twenty-somethings that surrounded me, Rich was drinking half a beer and pouring the rest out when I wasn't looking.

When I finally caught him, I called him out. "Are you kidding me? You're so lame," I said teasingly.

"You know," he replied in his typical dry fashion, "sometimes I wish you'd act your age."

"I am. For today I'm a born-again twenty-three-year-old."

"You're exhausting."

In actuality, his exhaustion was understandable.

The night before was supposed to be a quiet one to reflect our daily intention of slowing down since we had been charging so hard. Per our quiet-night tradition, Rich and I went to dinner. While waiting for our food, we had a couple beers and played a few hands of rummy 500. Our dinner arrived, but our subsequent quiet-night plans were waylaid by the arrival of the Canadians. They had been on the river all day, and as expected, they were as drunk as they were sunburned.

"What? Hell no you're not staying in tonight," said James "Danger" Daniels, the ringleader.

"Here. Have a little of this. It will get you where you need to be."

Uninvited, they sat down to watch us eat dinner and passed around a two-liter mixture of Laos vodka and Pepsi, a concoction that sounded as wretched as it tasted. By the end of the bottle, the transformation was underway. It made Rich believe it would be a good idea to buy another shitty bottle of vodka for the gang. By the end of that bottle, the transformation from Rich to Dick was complete.

When we returned to our room that night, my alter ego also appeared, and that person had what seemed like a brilliant idea.

"Rich, come here. Check this out."

"What?"

"You have to come here. Check this out. Come on. Over here."

"What?"

As Rich drew within striking distance, I threw an entire bottle of water in his face.

"Dude, what the fuck?" he said, shoulders hunched, water dripping down his face and arms.

I found this so funny that I also decided to throw an entire bag of peanuts at him (they were unsalted). He followed my aggression by dumping my clothes out all over the ground. I parried by turning his suitcase over, and he answered by throwing his desk lamp at me, so I cleared off everything on his desk with one swipe of the arm. While my body convulsed from laughter, he retreated into the bathroom.

As a precursor to what followed, it should be known that throughout much of Asia, you're not supposed to flush toilet paper down the toilet because the plumbing can't handle it. Instead, you are supposed to wipe your ass and put the used toilet paper in a wastebasket next to the toilet. The bathroom was so tight that shower water seeped into the basket, creating a wet, nasty, shitty mess. If that weren't enough, the toilet paper in this case was pink, which gets quite a bit darker when it's wet.

Because Dick does not stand for injustice, he fought back by going into the bathroom, grabbing the wastebasket, and hurling it at me, not realizing that I had been following the plumbing rules that govern Asia.

I had the wherewithal to duck, but it did not stop the barrage of wet, pink toilet paper from exploding on the wall behind me. The result looked quite literally like a murder had taken place. Wet globs of pink toilet paper stuck to the wall and soiled my bed, appearing as if someone's brains were splattered all over both.

"What the fuck, Rich! That's shit paper!" I yelled back at him.

"What? You actually do that? I always flush!"

"That's what the fucking signs say all over Asia, you fuckhead!"

My bed was soaked. My clothes were soaked. There was shit and dingleberry-laden toilet paper all over my bed and the wall. There were peanuts everywhere, crushed and whole, all unsalted. There was a broken lamp. There were two bags of wet clothes scattered all over the floor, and one spotless desk surface.

Quickly realizing that in his stance for justice he had actually created an injustice, Dick went to the lobby and purchased another room. He also took the opportunity to inform them once again that their Internet was crap and rarely worked.

Fortunately for our torpid stupor, the new, freshly made-up room was right across the hall. Like thieves under the cover of night, we removed our belongings from the room and walked across the hall. I imagine the patron at the front desk thought one of us was getting lucky, but in fact it would be an unlucky morning for whoever was cleaning our original room. For the first time in both our lives, like rock stars of the seventies, we destroyed a hotel room (although it would be a stretch to call this place a hotel).

With our room completely trashed, the following morning, both nauseous and with splitting headaches, we quietly exited the hotel, leaving the keys locked in the soiled room.

***

With all the fun we were having, time seemed accelerated, and before we knew it our time in Laos was over. After a few trips up the Mekong River to some remote villages, we made our way back from Luang Prabang via an overnight train to the capital Vientiane.

Per usual, our intention was to take it easy, play some cards on the train, and finally get some rest. It always started the same way—with one beer. But one turned into two. Then a chatty British expat sitting next to us, a seasoned veteran whose luggage also doubled as a cooler, saw the opportunity to strike up a conversation. We guessed that seeing our beers he felt a common bond with us. However, we weren't in the mood to learn about his life story, so after one beer we made our way to the train's bar car.

The car was thick with smoke from off-duty Thai police officers getting fall-down drunk on cheap whiskey. Across from us, an angry Anthony Bourdain look-alike gave us dirty looks. The policemen sang karaoke to awful Thai pop music on television monitors, and without even asking if we wanted another round, our waitress brought us drink after drink. Once again, we slowly morphed into our alter egos.

The waitress sat down with us. We bought her a drink, and just like that we all merged with the police officers' party. None of them spoke much English, but who needs language when invested in alcohol and good cheer?

Throughout my travels with Dick, I noticed he loved to say things to people he didn't think spoke English, such as, "Do you have a secret bathroom for shitting?" Dick relies on assumptions.

So the party on the train would make a toast in Thai, and we'd try to repeat what they said. When it was our turn to offer a toast, Dick would say something like, "To fellatio!"

"To fellatio!" they replied.

"To cunnilingus!"

"To cunnilingus!" they echoed.

At one point, Dick pulled out his nipple to the waitress. She chuckled, and when Dick turned to me to get a laugh, she gave him a titty-twister that caused him to shriek in pain. The Thai police officers were on the floor laughing.

The exposed nipple was the litmus test for whether Dick had overtaken Richard, and in fact this was the case. The next move for Dick was to pull his shirt over your head and wrestle you as if you were in a hockey fight. Fortunately we didn't last much longer, so he didn't get to try that with the Thai police officers.

When we returned to our sleeping berths, much like I thought it might be funny to throw a bottle of water at him in a hotel room in Laos, I thought it would be funny to throw the rest of my dessert at him while he was lying down in his sleeping berth. I was sleeping on the berth above him, so I leaned over, pulled back his curtain, and threw a plate of sliced pineapple at his face.

I howled and guffawed from above, but moments later he pulled back the curtain by my feet and returned fire, launching pineapple all over my face and pillow.

"Okay! Okay! You win!" I was too drunk and tired to deal with a counterattack. To make sure the war was over, I ate the pineapple and we laughed ourselves to sleep, much to the chagrin of those sleeping around us.

A few days later, we were on a bus heading to Vientiane. I was hungover and trying not to throw up. All the while I was spinning out in my head, full of the anxiety that accompanies days of imbibing in the depressant that is alcohol.

In my mind, I wondered what I was doing with my life, what I was going to do when I returned home, and what the future held after this liberation. I was inches away from Rich in body but years away in mind, landing at the outcome of living on Medicaid and bagging groceries. Rich was peacefully sleeping with his head against the window, drool rolling down it.

In contrast, I couldn't stop thinking about my future, the constant state of stress and anxiety that comes by living paycheck to paycheck. When I finally got out of my head and expressed this to Rich, he assured me it was just a byproduct of the drinking.

"I just hope grocery stores have good benefits because I don't want to have to live off Medicaid in my later years," I told him.

"Oh, you don't have to worry about that. Medicaid's not going to be around by the time we're old. Republicans will see to that," he added.

At some point I finally dozed off.

When I woke up, Rich was staring off into the distance as he often did, probably pondering something large and heavy.

Still wrestling with my own anxiety, I said, "Let me ask you something, Rich. What do you want in life? Do you want a wife and kids? A family?"

"Well, I'm just really happy on my own right now. I'm just concentrating on working on myself."

"Come on, man. That's bullshit. You always say that crap. I'm your best friend. Level with me. I know about one girl you liked in San Francisco, but besides that, I've never known you to have a girlfriend, yet tons of girls like you.

We had a chance with those sisters in Phnom Penh, and you went home early. What gives?"

"Why are you doing this?"

"Doing what? I'm just asking you a question that you never give an honest answer to."

"You want the honest truth?"

"The truth is always honest, right? That's why I'm asking you."

Rich paused, looked out the window, and took a deep breath. "I sat next to a monk on my flight from New York to Bangkok. He's kind of famous actually. They call him the 'Monk of Wall Street.' He was an investment banker—million-dollar bonuses, cars, vacation homes—he had it all. And then one day...one day he just walked away from it all."

"Why?"

"That's exactly what I asked him. I've been thinking about his answer every day we've been on this trip." Rich paused. "He said he wanted his outside to match his inside."

"What's that mean? Why have you been thinking about it so much?"

"Because I want that for myself. And I can't live like this anymore. I mean, I thought this was my life, and this was how it was going to go down. My father's a well-known conservative politician, and I don't think he could handle this. And I don't know how my friends are going to react. And I don't know how you're going to react."

"Handle what? React to what? What the hell are you talking about?"

Over our ten-year relationship, Rich was never one to express internal distress, but I could always tell when he was under duress. He was just more of a private person and tended to deal with things on his own. However, I had never seen him so visibly perturbed. He was trying to catch his breath, and tears welled up in his eyes.

"I'm gay, okay? I'm gay. You happy?"

The content wasn't so shocking as the fact that he finally said it. All our friends suspected it, but he had become adroit at deflecting relationship inquiries. He would do his best to change the subject, sometimes awkwardly, and as a result he had trained me over the years to stop asking. I figured when the time was right—if he was indeed gay—he would come to it on his own terms.

I smiled, turned toward him, and gave him a hug.

"Yes. I'm happy. I'm really fucking happy. What the hell did you think, I'd disown you as a friend? You're my best friend. I love you, regardless of where you stick your dick."

He began laughing and wiping the tears out of his eyes. "I can't believe I just said that. I never thought I was going to be able to do that. I thought this was just my life and that I was destined to be alone."

"Buddy, no one gives a shit if you're gay or not, and if they do, they're just backward hicks on the wrong side of history. They'll die out in a generation or two and the world will move on. What matters, what everyone who loves you wants, is for you to be happy."

Rich wiped the tears of laughter and pain from his eyes.

"I can't believe how much lighter I feel right now. I've known I was gay since I was in fourth grade."

"Are you serious?"

"Yeah. I used to go to church every Sunday with my parents, and sometimes I would make a deal with God that if I stood on one foot for the entire mass he would take the gay away. I actually used to pray to God to take the gay away. You believe that?" he said, wiping his eyes and blowing his nose.

"Honestly? I can't. I can't imagine living with a secret like that all these years."

"It's been terrible. I just came to terms with that fact that I'd never have a relationship and never fall in love, or if I did, it would have to be a secret."

"That makes me so sad. Well, at least now it's possible. It's going to be a very interesting Christmas in your household."

"Hell no, it's not."

"Hell yes, it is. You have to come out to your parents. You're their son. They love you no matter what."

"I can't."

"You can and you will. You're not the first person to go through this. This isn't something you can just throw out there and take back. This is the beginning of the rest of your life. Nothing is more important than moving into this. The integrity you're showing me right now, this is what you have to show your family, and everyone else for that matter. It's not going to be easy, but nothing without struggle is worth it. I love you, man, and I'm really proud of you."

I hugged him again, and another thought occurred to me. "One more thing," I added. "Should I be insulted you never hit on me?"

"I may have been in the closet, but I'm not stupid. You're straighter than a dog's back leg pissing."

In his coming out of the closet, I knew our friendship would deepen even further. For the next several hours on the bus, we talked about his experience of living in the shadow of his truth and discussed the endless possibilities of his new life. While he was still fearful, in his eyes I saw a new clarity and from his being I felt a new lightness. A new field of possibility was opening before him, one in which he no longer had to hide.

Chapter 24. When thoughts take form, you fly.

Sometime in the middle of October, somewhere in the middle of Cambodia, I wrote in my daily gratitude-intention journal that I wanted to create a free plane ticket home for Christmas. Just for the hell of it, occasionally I wrote something completely outlandish and unattainable.

Each day after I finished my writing exercise, I closed my notebook and did not give it another thought; it was, after all, simply an alchemical experiment in consciousness. The unexpected results, however, were taking me deeper into the mystery. The beauty of it was that I didn't have the desire to understand the mechanism or purpose of the mystery. All I needed to know was that gratitude and intention were the glue that held it together.

***

A few weeks later, Rich and I found ourselves back in Ho Chi Minh City. I didn't want to go for a second time, but my travel options were limited since I had run out of pages in my passport. My original plan was to stay in Phnom Penh an extra day and have pages added at the U.S. embassy, but seeing as Monday was a national holiday and the embassy would be closed, I would have had to spend two extra days in the city.

From Phnom Penh, my plan was to go to 4,000 Islands in southern Laos and then meet Rich somewhere in northern Laos a few days later. After a two-week bender starting in Koh Rong, followed by excess in Kampot, which was proceeded by Halloween in Phnom Penh, both Rich and I were suffering the side effects of post-hangover anxiety. We had been outrunning our hangovers for weeks, but when they finally caught up with us, they hit us hard. The nagging voice and exhausting questions were relentless. "What the fuck am I doing with my life," began to play in a loop in my head. In this wretched state, I couldn't bear the thought of spending more time in Phnom Penh because chances were strong that I would belly up to the bar at O'Leary's.

On the morning of November 1st, while Rich went to the Vietnam War Remnants Museum, I set out for the U.S. embassy to pad my passport for future adventures. Somewhere along the walk, it dawned on me that it was All Souls Day. Growing up Catholic, All Souls Day was a Catholic holy day of obligation, meaning my mother would inevitably drag me to church. On this day you're supposed to remember and pray for those loved ones who have passed before you. Therefore, after getting pages added to my passport at the embassy, I found myself aimlessly meandering the streets of downtown Ho Chi Minh City, missing my parents.

With Rich soon returning to the States, I was feeling a bit lost and uncertain as to what my next move would be. Despite the fact that I was literally living the dream, I found myself longing for the security and stability my parents created in the home of my youth.

It was the first time in a month that I'd had any time to myself, and in the uneasiness of solitude, I quickly got lost in my mind. Acting like a twenty-three-year-old his first summer out of college, my physical body was run-down from weeks of boozing and constantly being on the move. Discombobulated and drifting, I knew I was disconnected from my spiritual life, the part of me in which I had invested so much during the first half of my trip.

After some time of wandering aimlessly about Ho Chi Minh City, feeling lost, lonely, and missing my parents, in the center of the city on a busy traffic circle I came upon Notre Dame Basilica, a Catholic church built by French colonists in 1880. I stood before the church, staring up at the beautiful facade, and after a few moments, something reached out to the wayward, repressed Catholic within.

Dodging taxis and motorbikes, I crossed the street and entered the nave of the church. Around me were statues of the saints and martyrs I had known in my youth—some in agony, some in ecstasy—all in service to an idea that was greater than themselves. Although it was nearly uncomfortable to be still, I knew I needed the silence that the church's four walls could provide, and at the very least, I could momentarily get centered and connected.

Sitting beneath the vaulted ceilings and looking about the basilica, a conversation I had in India with Pranav came to mind: *I don't need to ask for anything when I pray. I have all I need. Shiva knows what I need and desire, so I just say hello and ask how He is doing.*

I followed Pranav's advice. I cleared my mind as best I could and tried to be empty and still. I felt small, unworthy, and disappointed in myself that it had been so long since I paid any attention to the spiritual aspect of my inner life.

Before I left the comfort of the basilica, I had a conversation with my parents, as I often did. I thought that perhaps being in church, a place they frequented in their later years, I might have a more direct line to them.

Hello Mom and Dad. It's been a while since we've chatted. I miss you both all the time, but I really miss you today. I wish I could hear your voices and that you could give me guidance. I'm worried about traveling alone again. It's been so fun to share my experiences with Rich, but now I have two months to fill before I meet up again with John in China. Please give me some sign or direction about where to go and what to do next, because I'm feeling really lost. I just need a place to recharge.

I left the basilica and slowly meandered back to the hotel to meet up with Rich. We were both so run-down and exhausted we couldn't be bothered with any more sightseeing, so we slept for a few hours until dinner.

When I awoke around 7pm and hit refresh on my email, John's name appeared in the "from" field.

Hi Tom - I woke up with a crazy idea this morning. I was thinking about how I would have to pay for you or someone else to fly over to China, so how about instead of a raise, I fly you back to the States, we go see The National, and then I'll fly you back to Bangkok. If that doesn't interest you, we can just meet up in China and you'll take home an extra grand. You've got 24 hours to decide. Come on...Live a little.

"Holy shit! Rich, Rich! Wake up! You have to hear this." I read Rich the email and his reaction of awe was similar to mine.

"What do I do? This is crazy. It's not the plan, though. I was supposed to be somewhere in Thailand in December.

I mean, I did ask my parents for direction in church today, but—"

"Whoa, whoa. What? You asked your parents for direction…at church? Today?"

"Yeah. To be honest, I've been getting a little stressed out about where to go and what to do after you leave because…shit, I've had so much fun traveling with you and getting to share this experience."

"And you asked your parents for direction today?"

"Yeah. And well, at some point in October I also wrote in my gratitude-intention journal that I wanted a free flight home for Christmas, but—"

"Dude. For real? Are you an idiot? I mean, you really couldn't get a louder, clearer sign about where to go next. Not only did you get both of these things, but don't you also think that if your parents were alive they would want you to spend Christmas with your family? I'm not even sure why you're questioning this."

Nonetheless, I took the full twenty-four hours to deliberate, and at the end of those twenty-four hours I had an itinerary. When all the details were worked out, not only was John going to fly me back to Seattle, but he also agreed to fly me to New Jersey to see my family and then from New Jersey back to Bangkok, all in addition to paying for my ticket to The National.

I was not only humbled by John's generosity but by the generosity of whatever this mysterious Source was that continued to surprise me with the unknown and unexpected. It appeared there really was something to the equation of intention + gratitude = blessings and grace.

I felt peace once again as the mystery of creation unfolded before me. Its beauty was that I need not understand its workings; I needed only to actively participate by moving in the direction my heart took me.

***

Once the ticket was booked, I was not only relieved I had an itinerary, but I was excited to go home. I now had a direction to move in, a course to chart, and a reprieve from what had become the exhausting road. Beyond seeing my friends and family, I was looking forward to taking long, hot showers, sleeping in familiar places, having a reliable Internet connection, being able to reliably drink water from the tap, and hearing the voice of my family in person.

A week later, I parted ways with Rich in Bangkok, congratulated him on standing in his truth, and wished him well on his new journey. Once he left, I made my way back to Bangkok, reunited with Sophia, and spent a relaxing week with her on the Thai island of Ko Samet. Then it was finally time for me to go home.

On the night of November 28th, I had a late flight from Bangkok to Seoul, where a twelve-hour layover awaited me. It was nearly 7am when I found a nice quiet nook within Seoul's Incheon International Airport. Before closing my eyes, I opened my computer and browsed Facebook to see what was going on with my friends at home. Confusion overtook me when I saw not one, but multiple Facebook posts about my friend Skip. It was too cruel to be a hoax. I went straight to Skip's Facebook page where I found an outpouring of grief, shock, and condolences.

One of the world's largest and busiest airports was beginning to wake up, and there I sat after a sleepless six-hour flight from Bangkok, shocked and paralyzed. I closed my computer and took a short walk. When I realized how tired I was and that I could no longer keep my eyes open, I found a bench upon which to rest. I lay down on the bench, pulled myself into the fetal position, and looked through the green plastic plants in the planter before me. A salty tear made its way from my eye to the corner of my mouth. Seconds later, I was that person you see in the airport or on the street, crying hysterically.

I was so tired I must have cried myself to sleep.

*** *** ***

I am so grateful for:

1. Manifesting a free flight home for Christmas and getting to see my siblings, nieces, and nephews.

2. All the time I was blessed to spend with Skip, and despite the circumstances, for all of the friends I will be reunited with at his funeral.

3. That I've managed to make money while traveling and still have a large reserve of cash.

4. Being shown direction by my parents.

5. Everything I will learn from this new, unexpected twist in the journey.

Today I intend and create:

1. To have a great visit with my family and grow from the experience.

2. To gain a deeper understanding of myself through this journey.

3. To be divinely guided on the rest of my trip.

4. The courage and strength to be myself and follow my dreams.

5. To gain a better understanding of what this whole journey means and how it fits into my life.

Part III. Mind

For a long time it seemed to me that life was about to begin—real life. But there was always some obstacle in the way, something to be gotten through first, some unfinished business, time still to be served, a debt to be paid. At last it dawned on me that these obstacles were my life. This perspective has helped me to see there is no way to happiness. Happiness is the way.

"Happiness" – Alfred D. Souza

Chapter 25. A Funeral, Family, and a Fix

Over the course of hours and miles logged, travel reveals your best and worst selves. I had found my best. I was expansive, confident, joyful, full of hope and triumph, and perhaps for the first time in my life, I could taste my dreams. I did not yet know the entire plot unfolding before me, but I could feel the story forming in my subconscious.

Beneath my clothes, I also held a secret: I was wearing invisible garments made of serendipity and abundance. My internal world was expanding and colliding into my external world, and the collapsing of particle and wave seemed to be creating magic.

As I stepped off the plane and walked through the terminal of Seattle-Tacoma International Airport, I was ecstatic to see on the walls the familiar images of Coho and King Salmon, Mount Rainier and the Space Needle, and the distinctive artwork of Pacific Northwest indigenous artists. Despite the news I had just received a half day earlier on the other side of the world, I was feeling grateful for not only the secret I held beneath my clothes but that on my shoulders I also carried an invisible backpack of experiences that I could translate into a lifetime of stories. And I still had many miles to travel.

When I cleared baggage claim, John was waiting for me in the arrivals area.

"Dude, I'm so happy to see you!" he said, wrapping his arms around me in a brotherly embrace. Then he stepped back and looked at me in curiosity. "I'm not sure what or who you've been doing, but you have this huge presence about you." He was more fit than the last time I saw him, so I waited for him to tell me how comparatively thin and weak I looked.

"It's never too soon to mock me, huh? Come on, I can take it. Is that all you've got?"

"I'm not kidding. Your energy is huge. You just look so happy."

He was right.

Outwardly, my smile and open heart felt like they were lighting the way before me. Inwardly, I felt like a great lighthouse. During the past six months, I had shepherded incredible people and experiences to my shores, and in the process I had accomplished something larger than what I once thought possible. As a result, a new form was emerging. No one could see it—not even me—yet I could feel it. But how would this new form fit into an old environment?

I remembered Sophia explaining to me what could happen when returning home from extended travels. "It's not necessarily the environment you might shrink to. You may have just outgrown it. When you return home after being away for a long time, you're a new person in an old environment. If you don't stay awake to this, you will just shrink back to your old self." When she said this, we were surrounded by palm trees, drinking rum on the beach, our bodies tan and glistening beneath the tropical sun. In that moment, returning to my old form was unimaginable, so I didn't bother to ask her how to prevent it from happening.

Not long after landing back in Seattle, however, I began to wonder where I fit in. Friends who were single were no longer, and friends who were married were pregnant. Friends who had one baby now had two, and most were living the same lives as when I left—ones of routine, upward mobility, and increasingly padded 401(k)'s.

It didn't matter how riveting my stories were: living in rural India; volunteering for a profoundly brilliant and humble man; the Shanghai skyline from the Bund at night; spending your best friend's thirty-third birthday at a Khmer concentration camp; falling in love a week into my trip; thinking I may get swept away in a flash flood in the jungles of Angkor Wat; or watching the prizefighter Manny Pacquiao in a bout from a small home in Laos. The sensory experiences that were changing my life were simply outside the bounds of even the most creative imaginations.

But it wasn't even about those outward experiences. How could I explain what was happening within me? And so it was that I felt more like I was passing through the lives of my family and friends instead of being a part of them. Their lives had become a pit stop—a place to catch my breath, eat a good meal, and get some restful sleep on a journey of discovery only I truly understood.

If my life was not in Seattle, and if my life was not to be the corporate life I had once known, then who was I? In the womb of the chrysalis where there is room for only one entity, this question enfolded me. Even for the caterpillar transforming into a butterfly, no stage of instar is an easy, comfortable process. I simply had to hold onto the walls and see the process through.

Instar was a state that I knew all too well, and as much as it was a process of life, I always struggled against it. It was the state of living between the past and the future—waiting for high school to end and college to begin, or college to end and real life to begin, or the pain of a relationship to end so I could think about a new one. This state was the present moment. For the longest time I tried to escape it, but now I understood it as a state of becoming; it was only through the present moment that you could achieve your dreams. It was only through the present moment that the future could be created. "If you've got one foot in today and one foot in tomorrow, you're pissing on today," my father once said to me.

While it was great to be home and carefree, the victories of the previous six months were quickly overshadowed with familiar, fearful thoughts: *What am I going to do when this is over? Where am I going to live? How am I going to make a living? Do I even want this American lifestyle anymore?*

Removing myself from the familiar for half a year allowed me to see it in a new light. All I had to do was turn on the television for thirty minutes to realize the American dream might actually be a sham, a blitzkrieg media campaign controlled by a few and built on messaging pillars of fear, greed, competition, and consumption. It was an old model built on the Darwinian paradigm. In actuality, from the cell to the species, it was the survival, health, and cooperation of the community that allowed the human species to flourish. If anything good was going on in the world, you'd certainly never know it through the lens of the American media.

The road holds many secrets, I remember thinking to myself one night on the Mekong River in Laos. Rich and I were staying in a small village, and after he went to bed, I made my way to the edge of the river. Above me stretched the lattice of the Milky Way. *If I can just hold on, trust, and surrender to whatever this thing is with completeness and without fear...*

Yet here I was in Seattle, soon transiting to New Jersey to see my family, and I was contracting faster than a shrinky dink in a hot oven. Home was certainly shaping up to be a test.

While it was nice to plug an electronic device into an outlet with the knowledge that there would be no sparks, and while it was lovely to brush my teeth with tap water, what I brought home was the reminder that my life was scattered throughout the basements of various friends and a storage unit in north Seattle.

Within me resided a dichotomy. On the one hand was the desire to be settled, have a place to call home, have a relationship, and eventually a family. On the other was the desire for freedom—to go as I please, where I please, and to create what I please with whom I please.

Even though it was months away, the thought of having to find a job, a car, and an apartment spread out before me in daunting luminosity. These comforts I once relied on now felt like anchors capable of inducing crippling anxiety. I told myself that my belongings were just stuff, and since I had survived close to six months without them, in the grand scheme of things it was apparent I no longer needed them.

While I loved the idea of home, home had become wherever I could rest my head and take off my backpack. All I needed, at least for the time being, was what I could fit into it.

***

A week after arriving in Seattle, I said goodbye to Skip at Sunset Memorial Park in Bellevue, Washington with many of my Seattle friends whom I had known for close to a decade.

In sunglasses, dark suits, black dresses, and overcoats, at 2:40pm we all gathered around the freshly dug burial site, each of us waiting our turn to throw the customary handful of dirt on Skip's grave. From the top of a sloping, picturesque hill, evergreens and Douglas firs stood tall with us in reverence. I looked beyond the boundary of the cemetery, over the 520 Bridge, and past the border of Lake Washington. In the distance, with the sun casting a spectacular, radiating glow upon it, Seattle awaited our return with one less person from our old group of friends.

At a somber gathering afterward, we laughed and cried with one another as we recounted Skip's life and antics over drinks. We laughed at our favorite stories, like when he put his entire life on eBay (including his ex-girlfriend's used panties) to fund a trip around the world. From the *Seattle Times* to CNN to Fox News, every media outlet picked up the story. Or when he bought the URL of a very prominent fitness trainer. Skip thought it would be funny to post gay porn on the site. It didn't take long for the fitness trainer's lawyer to serve Skip a cease and desist order.

At one point, my friend Rebecca asked me in her blunt yet sincere way, "So, is this trip going to change your life or what?"

In my typical fashion, I made a joke and skated around it, but I knew it already had. Nonetheless, I threw the question deep into the cauldron of my consciousness. It was a question I wanted to explore, knowing full well an honest answer may require weeks, months, perhaps even years to answer accurately. But what else is there to do with our lives if we're not seeking truth and answers?

After spending two weeks in Seattle visiting with friends and further complicating my life with an old girlfriend, I was on the familiar flight from Seattle to Newark to see my family. It had been so long since I had been engaged in Western life that not only did I forget people wore suits to work, I also forgot people worked.

On my flight to Newark, I was full of hope and excitement. I was also as high as the Boeing 757 at cruising altitude, not just on life but on a pot cookie. John drove me to the airport and sent me on my way with an edible, just one of the many perks of being the Assistant to the (International) School Photographer.

After reorganizing all of the files on my computer and journaling for an untold period of time, we descended into the greater metropolitan New York area. Butterflies filled my stomach with excitement. I was excited to share all I had seen and learned with my family.

***

Christmas had always been the best time of the year in our house. When my siblings started going to college and moving out, I was essentially an only child for the better part of the year; my closest sibling was ten years older than me.

During the first week of December, our house transformed into a tinsel-laced wonderland of lights, wreaths, advent calendars, and crest sets. It also meant my siblings were soon coming home. I didn't know it then, but it was one of a dwindling number of times we would all be together, signifying the end of a tightly knit family era.

The home my mother decorated for the holiday was a joyous backdrop to many parties that brought my friends, my older siblings' friends, and all of the stragglers and foreigners who had nowhere to go for the holidays. As a youngster in the security of my parents' household, I never would have imagined that one day I would be that person.

When my parents became elderly and unable to afford the only home I had ever known, they moved to a retirement community at the New Jersey shore and Christmas was never the same. It happened between my junior and senior year of college. No matter how excited I was to see my siblings, going home for the holidays as an adult was never easy.

Home. The loss of it and the proximity to the former idea of it had a way of reminding me I was alone, and that had a way of creating storms in my heart and mind.

Because I lived on the other side of the country, even though we loved each other and couldn't wait to see each other, it seemed like every time I got together with one of my siblings we spent the first few hours, if not days, pacing around each other like wild animals. We'd size each other up, lose our tempers quickly, and test one another's mental and emotional boundaries with pointed words we knew would stick to the other like the tiny hairs of a cactus. In my impetuousness to feel the closeness of my family, I tended to forget that connecting—as well as remembering who we were to each other—took time. Connection in any form is not something that can be forced. Like everything else that moves through seasons, it takes time.

It seemed that as we got older, moved to different places, developed different politics, and tried on different ideas, when the four of us came together it was as if four tornadoes were merging into a superstorm, each spinning uncontrollably to create one giant vortex. It doesn't take a genius to realize that when all of those weather systems got together, crazy shit was going to happen. Throw in a nephew on the autism spectrum, a few strong opinions, opposing politics, two puppies, and me—the discontented younger brother relentlessly on the search—and the already tenuous balance unraveled into chaos.

Every time I journeyed "home," I couldn't help but long for the days of our infamous Christmas parties. It seemed the adhesive that held us together was no longer there. While my immediate family had grown larger through marriages and the blessings of children, that growth brought new demands and stress. Again I was reminded that despite all the experiences I'd had in the previous six months, the one thing I wanted—love and connectedness—alluded me. Beneath my awareness, I clung to my refrain: *I am alone in the world.*

The moment I stepped off the plane at Newark Airport, I was on edge. Instead of being grateful that my sister had come to pick me up, I was annoyed that she was late.

"I've been sitting out here in the cold for forty minutes. How the fuck do you lose your keys all the time? How hard is it to put them in the same place?"

"Are you fucking kidding me, Thomas? Try living in my shoes for a day. My God, you just got off the fucking plane. Can you give me a goddamn break? It's eleven o'clock. I'm usually asleep two hours ago and you know I hate driving at night."

Silence ensued until she reached into the back seat and threw a pizza box on my lap from my favorite pizza parlor, making me feel like an even bigger asshole than I was being. Thus began a circle of negative emotional affirmations: She couldn't manage her life, and I was an unsympathetic, ungrateful, self-absorbed asshole. And then a loving gesture and the circle began again.

I was in a state of growth, which is never easy, but the presence of these familial and authoritative figures retarded the process. I had been undergoing a metamorphosis, systematically shedding layer by layer of my old self. I was trying to break my old habits, trying to break the synaptic and neural connections that held the mold together, but within the confines of my family I regressed into the person I was trying to escape. I stepped into the energy of who I once was, energy that said, *You don't know where you're going. You don't know what you're doing. Disappointment is the most familiar thing in your life. There is never enough money, and all you know is lack. You're going to be stuck in this purgatory of your life with a dream that, like the carrot and the stick, is always just out of reach.* The internal landscape can be such a harsh, arid, unwelcoming place.

Of course this was all illogical fear. I had proven these things not to be true in the past half-year. I had even doubled my money on the road. Sometimes I lacked faith, but everything had been provided for me. Yet, these chattering voices from various parts of my life all said that I *was* lacking faith.

***

On Christmas morning, for no reason at all I woke up at 4am. Not knowing what to do with myself, I checked Facebook, wrote in my gratitude-intention journal, thought about making a fire but didn't, thought about getting stoned but didn't, thought about masturbating and did.

There was a heaviness I felt within me that was all too familiar. I thought I had outgrown it, but perhaps I had just been running from it. The heaviness had to do with wanting to come home and the disappointment of unmet expectations. It was wanting to wake up and see my parents Christmas morning but knowing they wouldn't be there. It was wanting experiences that couldn't be replicated and traditions that couldn't be relived. It was desiring my own family yet being powerless in its creation. It was, as I had come to know it, the veil.

After several days of trying to manufacture moods, connections, and conversations, of trying to force artificial states of family, I said, *Fuck it. These people are nuts. In three days I'm going back to Asia, and I can't wait. What do I care anyway?*

With the exception of working in China, the year ahead of me was a blank slate. The frontrunners included going to Italy to work on writing a book, take a writing course in northern Thailand, or surfing in Bali. All options were better than the bullshit of Connecticut. *Fuck this. I'm outta here.*

***

Family is a lot like a drug; you're always seeking it as a fix. Depending on your health it can be good for you. Depending on your emotional anchors, it can tie you to the past and lock you in place. Family can be a great construct for renaissance, or it can have adverse side effects such as anger and anxiety. It can be addictive, and depending on what you've emotionally ingested that day, there's no telling when it might kick in. But you keep at it for that one time you feel really good. Everything up to that point, up to that fix, however, is just chasing a dragon.

Fortunately for me, I got that fix the last night I was home, and as usual I regretted all of the time I spent pissed off. All of the time I had put in for Christmas vacation, it was all for this one night. It was the night of my sister's birthday. What she asked of her husband was that she have a few hours out with her brothers and sister without husbands, wives, or needy kids.

It only took two hours and two martinis for me to unfold into the reality of who my siblings are, who they were, and who they would be for me in the future. As much as these people annoyed and disappointed me—these people who I thought had become strangers—and as crazy and disorganized as I thought their lives were, and as much as they tried to hold me tighter when I struggled to push away, they loved me and accepted me no matter who I was or who I was being. I needed this crazy tribe. They knew me better than anyone else in the world, and certainly for longer. I didn't want to conform to the younger brother role, but it was who I was and who I would always be. Without parents, I looked to them for advice, support, strength, and courage. They were, whether I liked it or not, a part of my internal compass.

"To Mom and Dad," my brother toasted at the start of our second martini.

This elixir, also responsible for my birth, brought something to the surface I didn't know I needed to exorcise. "You know, I obviously know who Mom was, but fuck, sometimes I have a such hard time *remembering* who she was. I know she was sick and deteriorating for a long time, but in my mind I can't help but think of her as this weak, timid, fearful person."

"The fear was always in her, but it was manageable. I think it leaked into all our lives in its own way, but the disease just exacerbated her fear. We all know she would give her life for any of us or our friends, though," my brother said.

"I know, but it still kills me. The disease clouds my memory and I hate that. I miss her so fucking much. I miss that nurturing strength. I can feel it, but what I see when I look back is this fearful, shrinking woman in both mind and body. You all had healthy Mom much longer than I did, and you got to have an adult relationship with her. There were times when I was traveling through Asia and the self-doubt was so heavy I didn't think I could go on. All I wanted to do was hear her say it was going to be okay."

"Well, she loved you in a special way because no matter what, you were always her baby. She would be very proud of you and what you're doing," one of my sisters added.

"If she let you go," said my brother.

"Yeah, she was always there for me and never missed anything I was involved in, but sometimes I think her love was so smothering that anytime someone gets close to me now I just want to run in the opposite direction."

"I never got that love," my other sister replied. "I went from being the ignored middle child to becoming one of two ignored middle children." In the cruelty and humor of an Irish-Catholic family, we ignored her.

With me at the helm, we piled into a minivan to join the rest of the family at home. As soon as we got close, for old time's sake I pulled out a joint John had given me in Seattle. I fired it up and passed it around the car. This scene of just the four of us had not played out in at least two decades.

After several hacking coughs, we regressed to our earlier years. We made silly jokes that caused timeless giggles to reverberate around the minivan. We laughed at the fact that we never could have imagined we would be getting stoned in a minivan with child seats. Then we wondered, as we had throughout high school and adolescence, if we were too high to go into the house. As we made a slow approach to the house, the answer was a resounding yes.

Upon seeing my nephew running to the window, one of my sisters yelled, "Go, go, go! Keep going!"

"Hit the gas!" my other sister reiterated.

As I hit the pedal to the floor, a unison of laughter bridged the past to the present, and I knew that no matter what our differences in the future would be, laughter would always be the bridge.

We decided to do one more loop around the neighborhood—the long way—and each time we approached the house, the same scene repeated. It happened five more times, and each time another equally excited and confused child appeared in the window.

When we finally had the courage and composition to pull into the driveway and walk into the house, it didn't feel like a celebration. My brothers- and sister-in-law were sitting around sipping wine and listening to Christmas music.

"What the hell you guys," I said. "Christmas is over. This is a birthday celebration!"

Like a well-trained guerilla army, we took action. I disabled their Christmas music, replaced it with my own, and turned it up. One sister stoked the fire and the other distracted the kids. My brother went straight to the bar and started mixing cocktails. In a matter of moments, we had disarmed the enemy and replaced the room's sentimentality with our own propaganda love machine. And then, like the old days in my parents' living room after a dinner party, we pushed the furniture to the perimeter and created a dance floor.

We danced all night to the Rolling Stones and Frank Sinatra, the Grateful Dead and Ella Fitzgerald, the Talking Heads and Elton John. We spilled drinks and laughed so hard they came out of our noses. We danced the kids, twirling them around as if they were Ginger Rogers in the arms of Fred Astaire, and then we held them close like the babies they once were. The collective energy of our best selves elevated the room.

Late in the evening, I took a step back and soaked in the moment. With a full heart, I observed the scene I had imagined and hoped for since I discovered I was unexpectedly heading home for the holidays. Finally, the junkie scored his fix. *Rocket mannnnnnnnn…And I think it's gonna be a long, long time…*

I remembered how good family felt and was reminded how important these people were in my life. The warm, familiar feeling of family flowed through me, and I let it soak into every cell.

Late at night, long after everyone had gone to bed and all that remained of the fire was the glow of burning coals, I wrote in my journal. As if experiencing a download, in a moment of drunken clarity I realized I had an answer to Rebecca's question: *So is this trip going to change your life or what?*

I realized the greatest gift I received starting in India was a profound sense of gratitude—not just the gratitude that exists in words, but gratitude as the foundational structure that exists at the atomic, cellular, and energetic levels. Gratitude had its own frequency and process, albeit an alchemical one, and through it Me (the observer), Me (the ego), and Me (the experiencer) could tap into another realm of information.

All I had to do was listen.

And move into that frequency.

And be.

Chapter 26. A Less Than Joyful Reunion

"I've never met someone who tries so hard to live in the fucking present moment even though they can't!"

I stood in protest, but the strength of the raw emotion felt like I was being blasted by a water cannon, and I wasn't sure how much more I could take.

"Don't pull that shit with me. You're just as guilty as I am. You didn't have to see me."

"What don't you get? I can't say no to you. I'm not strong enough to walk away."

I heard the tears, which always brought me to my knees, but I continued. "That's not true. Stop using that as an excuse."

"You don't get it, and you never will because you don't know how to love. You live in a walled-off kingdom and you won't let anyone in. You know what? Go fuck yourself! And while you're at it, don't ever talk to me again!"

"Then stop emailing me while I'm trav—"

Before I had a chance to end the sentence, a dial tone.

These were the last words I heard over Skype before boarding my flight back to Asia. It had been my intention that we wouldn't be in contact while I traveled—after all, we were broken up. In moments of loneliness, however, we had a tendency to reach out to one another. Is there a lonelier holiday when you're single than Christmas? At least on Valentine's Day you can commiserate with other single friends.

Karen and I had one of those relationships where you love the person deeply, but it probably should have been over after a few months. Three years later, you find yourself having the same arguments and expecting different results. Still, I didn't expect the words to cut so deep.

Relationships. *Good grief,* as Charlie Brown would say. One day you're cruising along, having a good time, going out with your friends in packs like wild dogs and fooling around with whoever will have you. It's good fun and you think nothing of it because you've got time and youth on your side.

The next thing you know, you wake up and you're in your mid-thirties and more than half of your friends are married. It's shit-or-get-off-the-pot time. Not only are you learning to navigate the complexities of relationships, but you're also up against commanding biological clocks while trying to figure out who you are, who you're becoming, and ultimately who you want to be. Would that part of me ever find peace?

You can love someone with every ounce of your being and be willing to lay down your life for them, but if the whisper in your heart tells you the timing is wrong or the relationship cannot sustain you, you have to listen to it. If not, you betray not one but two people.

So, you crush the other person's heart and crush your own in the process. Things get more complicated when you try to leave the relationship and the other person won't have it. The problem is, you're not strong enough to walk away because all you really want in your life is to love, be loved, and to be understood. With each person in the relationship seeking something external for completion, the outward push bounds each of you to emotional addiction, and you both slowly, unconsciously drown in a toxic stew of dysfunction and codependence.

Because of the state of incompleteness from which you operate and the desperation with which you desire to love and be loved, you want to be there for them when they need you, but often you're not. You want to love them the way they need to be loved, but you can't. You want the relationship to be forever, but the reality is temporal. The relationship is close to what you want so you keep forcing it, yet something you can't put your finger on is not present. You want the relationship to work because you love the person and would do anything for them, but sometimes in life, love just isn't enough. I was tired of being alone but falling in love wasn't a timetable I could control.

On ferries, buses, and planes all over Southeast Asia, I often found myself indulging in daydreams about love, yet when I observed others who seemed trapped in unhappy marriages, I felt revulsion. And my freedom, which I valued beyond all else, was a whole other story. Whatever the freedom was that I clung to at that moment, it was stronger than my desire to build something with just one person.

The one and only thing I knew I no longer wanted, however, was to be reckless with the hearts of women.

***

By the time I arrived in Bangkok at 11pm, I had lost an entire day in the air. I knew Sophia was meeting me at the airport, but I hadn't expected her to bring her children—a twenty-year-old daughter whom Sophia was dropping off at the airport to return to university in France and a sixteen-year-old son with whom she lived. Between the conversation with my ex and unexpectedly meeting her kids, I was spun out of sorts. Having had almost no sleep on the flight and looking inward the entire time, I was not feeling social. Still, I tried my best to smile and be cordial.

By the time we arrived at her home it was 2am. I slept in the guest room because her son was staying with her. I found rest for perhaps two hours, yet by 5:30am I lay wide awake in bed, wishing like hell I could fall back asleep but knowing all too well the light and the songbirds outside my window were not about to let that happen. I was left staring at the ceiling fan in dizzying anxiety and jet-lagged confusion.

With the morning light coming in, I was regretting my decision to spend New Year's Eve and the ensuing days with Sophia. I just wanted to be alone. I knew all too well from experience that I was not good company in my current state, a state of being that provided safe harbor for all my fears. When this happened, my mind was not strong enough to control the autonomic pivot inward: *What am I doing here? What am I going to do? Where will I go? Do I have enough money? Am I not capable of love? What if going home to the States cut off the flow of creation I was in? What if I can't handle the loneliness of being on my own?* And so on and so on…and so on.

***

New Year's Eve arrived without so much as a full day of rest. I was Sophia's date at a party of French expats, very few of whom spoke English. They were curious about the younger traveler on her arm, and with her friends' teenage children fluttering about the apartment, for the first time I became aware that Sophia was a decade older than me.

I was still jet-lagged and tried to tell Sophia and her friend I was fine going home and sleeping through New Year's, but against my will we left the party and went to a nightclub. It was damn near impossible to get a cab, so by the time we finally arrived at the club, made our way through security, went up the elevators, and walked into the celebration, the New Year's countdown was on.

We stepped into a sweaty, humid, outdoor club on the sixty-eighth floor of a Bangkok high-rise with nineteen seconds left in 2011. Sequined cutouts of "2012" hung shimmering on the walls while lasers, disco balls, and mood lighting set the scene. Seconds later, everyone yelled, "Happy New Year!"

"Auld Lang Syne" began to play, and the sky erupted with fireworks. As each rocket burst with the unmet expectations of the previous year and the hopes and dreams of the upcoming one, reflections of the starbursts crawled up the glass exterior of the surrounding high-rises.

I tried my best to give Sophia a passionate New Year's kiss, but passion is hard to fake. We stepped back from the kiss and looked at each other for a moment. An unspoken distance arose between us; we recognized that whatever romantic feelings we'd had toward one another were gone for good. To my right, an ostentatious Asian man danced on a catwalk, blatantly shoveling cocaine up his nose. To my left, people on the dance floor celebrated. *What the fuck am I doing here?*

When the man on the other side of me heard my American accent, he engaged me, giving Sophia the opportunity to wander off and find her friends. He was forty-four years old and his face was a mess. He told me he had been a sergeant in Iraq, done three tours, and during the last one his vehicle hit an IED. He was one of two people that survived the blast. But that wasn't the reason his face was a mess; he had gotten in a fight the night before but couldn't remember the particulars. It was a momentous Christmas for him since his seventeen-year-old son was visiting from the States. Not only had they smoked pot together for the first time, but he also got his son his first prostitute.

As the night wore on and the alcohol built a nest in my bloodstream, I realized I was stuck in the vibration of old energy, and like a black hole consuming everything in its field, it was pulling the best part of me down into it. Something had shifted, and I was no longer the carefree person I was before I left Asia to go home for Christmas. Like a grunt in a ground war, on my shoulders I carried the survival gear that held me in my past—old relationships, old notions of family, old pain, and old fears.

An hour later, Sophia and I sat down over a martini.

"So, what's really going on with you?"

"What do you mean?"

"Oh, come on. You know what I mean."

I paused to think it through. "Honestly? I just don't know what I'm doing here. I know I should be celebrating with you and living in the moment, but I just can't right now. I'm tired of being alone, and despite the fact that I'm here with you, I feel so fucking lonely and lost. I'm at the point in my life where I just want to meet someone, and I feel like we're just wasting each other's time."

"Are you kidding me? You think I want to be alone? I don't want to be alone. No one wants to be alone. All my friends who are single are going back to France because the men my age in Bangkok are slimy and gross."

The room had begun to thin out, revealing a floor littered with confetti, streamers, and plastic cups. We were two lonely people who momentarily found solace in the excitement of each other, but the moment had passed.

"I don't know what it is with you, but you're not the same person you were when you left me in November. You were full of adventure and ready for a good time. Even my friends commented."

"I'm just jet-lagged," I tried to insist.

But that wasn't entirely the truth. As I said the words, I fought to push down an unnameable something just below the surface that threatened to fill my eyes with tears. Somehow, something, somewhere inside of me had changed. Or collapsed. Or fallen in on itself. It was hard to identify just what it was, but one thing was certain: I was no longer the intrepid, larger-than-life character I was when we first met beneath palm trees on the island of Koh Samui. I was now a stranger to Sophia…and to myself.

"I don't know what it is. Maybe it was going home and seeing my family. Maybe it was seeing my friends who are 'getting ahead,'" I said, throwing air quotes into the first early morning of 2012. "Maybe it's the realization that I don't know where I fit in anymore."

"But you know the life your friends are living won't make you happy. That's not what you want or who you are. You're a writer and an artist. You belong to the world. This is what you chose, or at the very least where you are now. Just be where you are. Be present to this moment."

"Maybe I took off to travel because I didn't know what else to do with my life. I feel like I'm floating and disconnected from anything that can ground me. I went home to Seattle and felt like a visitor. And then I saw my family, hoping they would be that anchor, but they weren't. Well, maybe for a night, but it became obvious my family was no longer my world either. Then I come to Bangkok. I'm beyond excited to see you, and I realize whatever we had is gone. And I go to this party with you, the people around me don't speak English, have adolescent kids, and I think to myself, 'What the hell am I doing here?'"

"You know what the common denominator is here?"

"What?"

"You."

"I'm all too aware of that. And I'm all too aware that I'm always my worst enemy. This thing—I call it the veil because I don't know how else to explain it—it's haunted me my whole life. It's like it blocks out the light, and when it blocks out the light I can't see my shadow. I've been trying to outrun it because it prevents me from connection. I just...I don't know. Wrapped up in this idea of the veil is a deep pain in my soul, and I just want to fucking be free from it for once in my goddamn life. I want to know what's on the other side of it. Maybe my truth is on the other side, or maybe there's nothing. Maybe this whole life is nothing. Maybe it's a meaningless cosmic joke. Maybe I'll always be this rootless, wandering kid."

"Listen to me," she said grabbing my face between her two hands and pulling me close. "First of all, you're a man. You're not a kid. You have to shake that *merde* out of your head. It's a story and you're a writer. Write a new story. You can't outrun this thing your whole life. At some point, you have to turn around and confront it. My God, I can feel your energy everywhere else but here right now. Your mind is running in a million different directions, but those are just thoughts. They're not real, and you don't have to follow them. Your mind doesn't say who you are. You say who you are."

"Who am I then? Who is the I?"

"Thomas," she said, "you have to stop making your life so difficult. It doesn't have to be so hard. You can't even see what a wonderful life you're living right now. You're free. Not everyone can say that."

Drawing on her maternal instincts, Sophia pulled me into her embrace, and all I could think of as she held me was how much I missed my mom. Once again, tears welled up in my eyes, and once again, like a good, repressed Irish Catholic, I did everything I could to push them down.

It was two hours into New Year's Day 2012, and I shouldn't have had a care in the world. I had nothing pinning me down, no commitments toward anyone or anything, and I was about to begin traveling around Thailand for a month, something that made me the envy of several friends. I knew I had no reason to feel scared, but I did. I had no reason to feel burdened, disconnected, or closed off from Sophia or anyone else, but I was. I just wanted my mom to tell me everything was going to be all right. In the midst of the best time of my life, there I was in Bangkok—a thirty-seven-fucking-year-old grown man who just wanted the comfort and security of his mommy.

"Have you ever listened to what you actually say, Thomas? You're so hard on yourself. Just stop it. There's no reason. This is the best time of your life and you're missing out on it. Come on, let's go out and have fun."

"I don't think I can. I'm tired. I'm just not feeling very festive."

"We either go out for three more hours or go back home and make love for three hours. The choice is yours. I'm not letting you off the hook. Come on, how often do you have a sexy French woman make such a proposal?"

For the next few hours we brushed everything aside and managed to laugh and dance our way into the night. When we returned to her home in the early hours of the morning and climbed into bed, I tried to wrap my body around her, but it felt so forced and unnatural that we both wound up retreating to our own side of the bed. After much tossing and turning, she rolled over and our eyes met in silence. On the pillow she folded her hands beneath her head, which pressed her full breasts together.

"When I first met you on the beach, you were this light. You were happy, joyful, larger than life. I don't know what's going on with you, but I just want you to know I never expected anything. This isn't a relationship and it's never going to be. You live in the States, I live in Bangkok. I'm ten years older than you and you're ten years younger than me. I live in the moment, and I'm grateful for everything that comes to me. I'm grateful for our time together and what you've awakened in me. It's not complicated. I just love being with you in this moment and in every one we have together. That's all. That's it.

"You're laying in this bed next to me, but I have no idea where you are," she continued. "You're so far away. With the exception of my ex-husband, I don't think I've ever felt more distant from the person I'm sharing a bed with. I don't know what happened to you at home, but you're not here anymore. And that's sad." She rolled over, leaving my heart battered and bruised.

Whether it was nurture or nature, my life had a tendency to move in dramatic expressions of expansion and contraction, and this was one of contraction.

I was supposed to be in an expansive state. I was supposed to take everything I had learned from the last eight months of travel and master it for the final leg of my journey. Instead, I was scared, not of the unknown and uncertainty like when I left home for India eight months prior, but of becoming the person I was trying to leave in my past.

When I was with my family for Christmas, I couldn't wait to return to Asia and Sophia, and now that I was in Asia with Sophia, I couldn't wait to be on Koh Lanta, my next stop after Bangkok. I was always living in the past or the future.

Sophia and I didn't click like we had before I went back to the States, but after a few days we finally found our way to friendship. On the morning I left, I asked her if she wanted to take a shower with me. She was working at her computer and barely looked up.

"I don't think so. I don't feel the connection anymore, and for me sex is all about the connection."

"All right then. I'll just shower and be on my way."

I turned to walk upstairs when she said, "Thomas, I never had any expectations. I just really liked being with you and spending time with you."

She was so French like that.

Beyond any other uncomfortable conversations we had, that comment crushed me the most. It made me aware of the time I wasted with her and what could have been if I

had shown up as my true self. I often had this regret at the end of relationships.

"Just remember," she added, "everything right now is a reflection of the things you need to learn."

***   ***   ***

I am so grateful for:

1. The many beautiful spaces through which I have moved, both externally and internally.

2. Having the courage to make new discoveries about myself, even if they are painful to look at.

3. The amazing life I am living and that I'm the only one who can express it because I'm living it.

4. Moving on to the next part of my journey.

5. The experiences I had with Sophia and all she taught me.

Today I intend and create:

1. To meet a cute girl to travel with.

2. Free lodging.

3. To know my truth.

4. The generosity of a stranger.

5. To shed the weight of sadness I currently feel.

Chapter 27. How low can you go?

My destination was situated on a lagoon surrounded by palm trees. A gentle breeze blew off the inlet into the Ba Bar. It took me the better part of the day to reach the island of Koh Lanta, a laborious effort that included a plane, two buses, and a boat.

As I ordered a Chang beer, I realized it had been more than two weeks since I'd had any alone time. I pulled out my notebook and sat in silence, taking in the landscape around and within me. As the bartender placed the beer on the table, "Say Hello, Say Goodbye" from David Gray's album *White Ladder* played through the bar's speakers. The soundtrack coalesced my scattered thoughts, pulling me from my past into the present moment. Finally realizing just where I was, I paused, glanced at my surroundings, took a deep breath, and began writing in my journal.

I was waiting for Ingrid, whom I had met along with Naomi on the island of Koh Rong in Cambodia. Ingrid was working as a scuba instructor on Koh Lanta, and it was because of her invitation that I found myself there. The people I met often had a way of laying out my itinerary.

Ingrid had just begun dating a dive instructor, and since she spent most nights at his place, she generously offered to put me up in her small apartment until I found my own. My intention was to spend at least a month on the island writing several hours a day, exercising, eating healthy, and hopefully meeting a cute girl to shack up with. It didn't take long, however, for me to realize I didn't fit in with the divers. I kept different hours and didn't speak their language of ventilators, pounds per meter of air pressure, or how that correlates to oxygen usage. I had nothing to add to their conversations about nudibranchs, swimming with sharks, or the curious behavior of octopuses. Just as I couldn't understand their need to dive or the peace they found beneath the ocean, they couldn't understand why I needed to write.

After spending a few days with the divers, it became apparent that this wasn't the place for me, so I readied myself to leave. Like the endless rise and fall of the tides in the ocean before me, I thought that maybe I'd always keep moving from place to place, job to job, bed to bed, and woman to woman.

Fortunately for me, Ingrid had two friends, Leo and Martin, who were visiting from Berlin, so I wound up staying on Koh Lanta for almost a week. Most days we rented motorbikes and explored the island, and at night when the divers went to bed at 9pm, Leo, Martin, and I shared travel tales and got good and drunk in softly lit, open-air bars. Despite the way I had been feeling, the combination of the camaraderie, the freedom of driving a moped on the open road, and having nothing to do but follow the yellow line around the island each day started to break up the heaviness within me.

One afternoon, the three of us were having some beers at a beach on the southern tip of the island. Leo and Martin were speaking in English and German as I stared out into the sea. With nothing in particular on my mind, I was aware that

I was holding onto life so tightly that there was no room for magic. In this vice grip, I held all my expectations, and magic can't happen where expectations live.

I also realized that—while I was still practicing my daily gratitude-intention exercise—it had become an uninspired routine. The power behind it was clear intention, and that was something I had also lost sight of. *Create, surrender the how, let it come to me, be amazed.*

At the end of the week, I bid Leo and Martin farewell and suggested that perhaps I meet them in Berlin in a few months. From Koh Lanta I took a ferry to the Krabi peninsula to see how Railay Beach felt, a world-famous rocky inlet of soaring limestone cliffs, hidden caves, protected coves, and sandy-white beaches. I heard it was a good place to kill time.

What I didn't know was that it was also one of the most famous rock-climbing sites in the world. This posed a serious problem: it was full of rock climbers. It took me little to no time to realize I had nothing in common with this hyper-focused group either, and nothing makes you feel more middle-aged than a bunch of young, super-fit people wearing almost nothing. The only things Railay Beach had to offer were rock climbers, hippies, and monkeys, and in the state I was in, I could only tolerate the latter.

The rock climbers were a kinetic lot of people, as obsessed with their sport as the divers on Koh Lanta. I couldn't help but find humor in my ineffectual destination choices. *You're learning what you need to learn right now,* I heard Sophia's voice say.

The next day I walked along Tonsai Beach, feeling intensely lonely. I spotted a cute girl coming toward me who seemed to be wandering as aimlessly as me. Knowing

I was the only person who could take away my loneliness, I introduced myself.

Sarah, a twenty-seven-year-old woman from Florida, was on a break from grad school in Portland, Maine. She too had no time for the frenetic energy of the rock climbers. After a brief exchange, we decided to have a drink together, which turned into several, which turned into drowsiness.

Because her room was located on another beach, she came back to my place where we took a nap together. Although nothing happened, the sexual energy of lying next to a new body prevented either of us from getting any sound sleep. Over dinner that evening, we agreed we were done with the rock climbers, and she suggested an off-the-beaten-path island called Koh Yao Yai.

By 10am the next morning, we were on a high-speed boat to Koh Yao Yai. Armed with almost no information and lacking any reservations, we hired a driver at the ferry dock to help us find accommodations. As luck would have it, the first set of bungalows we found was perfect. With not much else to do, we checked in, found our way to the patio, and ordered beers.

"We made it," I said. "Cheers! To kindred spirits. Thanks for the redirect."

No sooner had we taken a swig than the woman next to us leaned in and said, "Excuse me. Are you from America?"

"We are," I replied.

"Where about?"

"I'm originally from New Jersey but moved from New York City to Seattle more than a decade ago, and Sarah here is from Florida."

"No way!" the man replied. "We live in New York City. I'm from Poland, but I did a high school exchange program in Seattle."

The man and his wife had been driving around the island for the day and decided to stop at the restaurant attached to our bungalow to have lunch. Within a few minutes, we realized we knew mutual people in both Seattle and New York. Kuba and Deanna were on month two of a three-month honeymoon around Asia and the South Pacific.

"We haven't talked to Americans in three weeks," Deanna said.

We exchanged emails and made plans to meet up in Chiang Mai in a few weeks. But later that night, an email awaited us, inviting us to join them the following evening for happy hour at their resort.

Sarah and I shared a bed again that night, this time not so innocently. By the next day, as we casually made our way around the island on a moped, she wrapped her arms tightly around me. Like newly minted lovers in a romance paperback, we couldn't keep our hands off one another, and each time we stopped to take in a scenic overlook or swim in the turquoise waters of the Andaman Sea, we held each other and kissed.

Just before we reached Kuba and Deanna's resort, we drove through another posh resort on the eastern-facing slope of Koh Yao Yai.

"Even if I had the money, I don't think I would want to stay at a place like this. It feels so sterile," I said.

"You're funny."

"What?"

"You're jealous. You so want to stay here."

"Nah."

"Come on, admit it. You're jealous."

"Maybe if I had a wife and kids it would be easier to travel this way, but I would never purposely stay in a place like this." But in a way she was right. As a kid getting stoned and driving around the back roads of Hunterdon, Morris, and Somerset Counties in New Jersey, I would look at all the estates and wonder with envy what people did to live in such places. I was always surrounded by wealth but never a part of it.

The Elixir Resort incited the same silent jealousy and awe. Kuba and Deanna greeted and welcomed us to their side of the island. They insisted on paying for our drinks since we were their guests. By the end of our night together, the tab far exceeded the expense of our night's lodging at our own Twilight Beach Bungalows.

A few days prior, the newlyweds had befriended Abby, the manager of the Elixir Resort. Abby was from Finland and in her early thirties. For the next several hours we drank in the pool and played a Finnish game akin to lawn bowling.

I had recently sold an article about Cambodia to BBC Travel, and Deanna and Kuba brought it up to Abby, who replied, "Thomas, why don't you do an article on us?"

"That would be great," I said, acting cool and collected on the outside. On the inside, I was salivating at the idea of living in the lap of luxury for a couple of days.

After several more cocktails, I picked up the conversation where it had left off. "So, what do you do for marketing here?"

"Marketing? What's that? I don't have time for marketing. There's too many other things to be done and not enough people who can do it."

"Well, if you want to put me up for two days I'd love to write an article on the resort." And that was that.

***

The following morning, Sarah was getting ready to go back to the States.

"I'm going to miss you," I said to her.

"You should come visit me in Portland."

"Maine is a little hard to get to via Thailand."

"Oh you," she said. "You'll miss me for about twenty minutes until you find the next girl."

By 11am a taxi arrived to take Sarah to the ferry, and by noon a car arrived to shuttle me to the resort.

For the first half of the day I was ecstatic. Abby put me up in a beachfront bungalow fifteen meters from the ocean. A cool blast struck my face as I walked into the air-conditioned room, and rose petals greeted me on my 1200-thread-count sheets. The outdoor shower area, which included a hot tub, was larger than any room I had stayed in during the last half-year. If I didn't feel like getting salty in the sea, I had my own plunge pool. It was the perfect romantic setting for a couple, but I'd have to settle for myself.

Since everything was paid for, I contacted the concierge and had them send me a few beers. When room service showed up, I cracked open a beer on my deck and checked Facebook. I saw on my friend's Facebook wall a comment by my ex-girlfriend, the same one who eviscerated me before I returned to Asia. She was moving into *my* friend circle at home, and there was nothing I could do about it. It made me furious.

The next morning, I awoke in a manic low. The anxiety in my chest was palpable, and the irrational fears returned. I felt like I just wanted to go home, yet I knew home wouldn't solve any problems, especially since I no longer had one. There was still one problem with that idea—me.

All around me were ecstatic newlywed couples and happy vacationing families. The instant gratification I felt in Sarah's arms only twenty-four hours prior left in its wake a devastating loneliness, and before me spread out my future as a bachelor. I didn't like what I saw, and I couldn't imagine my life without having someone to share it with.

Growing exhausted from the voice in my head, I Skyped my sister.

"Maybe I should just leave the islands and head north," I said.

"But the problem is, you're still there. Don't run from this. Move through it. Write through it," she told me.

So I tried writing again. I worked on the article about the resort, and when I hit a wall, I attempted to work through what I was feeling. Writing is a lonely process and an even lonelier battle. Day after day you sift through the muck and mire of life, searching for the pearl in the oyster, and the pearl is always born out of agitation.

***

There is no predicting the rhythm of travel. Sometimes you ride a wave of elation and joy. Other times you find yourself wandering aimlessly and you realize the only conversation you've had for days on end has been the one in your head. In this conversation, I intellectualized my travel process, analyzing and critiquing what I was and wasn't doing right and questioning why I was having such a hard time being happy. Everywhere I looked I saw people in love, and it agitated me. I couldn't help but think I'd gladly trade in my passport for the emotion, intimacy, and companionship of a relationship.

For the rest of the day I sat by the water in a hammock beneath palm trees and listened, hoping the meditative lapping of the waves would provide me with some sort of insight. That evening, for the first time in a long time, I got down on my hands and knees. *Release me from myself,* I prayed. *Release me from myself. Take away this loneliness. Show me what's behind the veil.*

Two days turned into four, and each day I worked on my mental and spiritual health. To travel and to be a writer meant I had to embrace uncertainty. I lacked a home, a job, had no idea where I would be in a few days or a year, and had no idea if what I was writing was interesting to anyone but myself.

I also caught up on some overdue reading. In my current selection called *We Wanted to be Writers: Life, Love, and Literature at the Iowa Writers' Workshop,* the writer Marvin Bell said, "Pursuing any art throws one in with outsiders. Keeping at it *makes* one an outsider."

I could relate, but this seemed to be a big understatement.

Chapter 28. The Story of Your Life

I fear few things more than a writer's workshop.

If you've never been to one, they're intensely personal, and sometimes they take you places you weren't ready to go. With your still-beating heart in your hands—the same heart that you just ripped out of your chest—you stand before your peers, naked and vulnerable. Splattered across what was only a few minutes ago an empty page is raw, uncultivated language. And although each participant knows it's raw, uncultivated language, you can't help but judge others and compare yourself to them. Occasionally you find yourself wishing you wrote their words. All the while you hold in your hands the paper upon which is written your carnal sacrifice, and although it's shit, you're the only person in the world who sees a path to salvation through the words.

To top it all off, I was in the process of working through many personal emotions, from my faith to my fears, from the loss of my parents to the pervasive loneliness that was once again taking root, strangling me ever so slowly like the Japanese kudzu or the great strangler fig consuming its host.

Sitting around a table with ten other participants, I worked through all of these elements and emotions in a very public, sometimes very embarrassing, way. However, when I left home nine months prior, I made a pact with myself to have new, enriching experiences, even if they were uncomfortable. My only saving grace was that I knew everyone else in the workshop felt the same way.

In the meantime, every time I logged onto email or Facebook, I had messages waiting for me from the many women I had met while traveling. They hailed from all over the world, but the only one who truly stood out in my mind as someone I wanted to spend more time with was Cassandra. Despite the fact that we barely knew each other, we had kept in touch through long emails and the occasional Skype call. Beyond all the others, my heart felt connected to hers.

"When it happens, it happens," Sophia said to me one night in Bangkok. "One minute you're free and single, sleeping with whomever you want, and the next you're tied down with two kids and a mortgage."

Some of my friends who were married and settled down were living vicariously through me, and occasionally I wondered if some of my actions were a result of living up to their expectations. But all I wanted was one woman. Someone to go to the park with on Sunday afternoons and spend weekends with lying on a beach or hiking through the mountains. Someone to come home to, cook with, wake up next to, and share the beauty I often hid deep in my soul. Someone whom I recognized as an equal and vice versa. Someone with whom I could eventually have a family. I needed someone to make me feel loving, loved, and comfortable with myself.

Perhaps the fact that I was putting that expectation on someone else was part of the problem.

***

"What is the overarching question your book is trying to solve?" asked Judy, the workshop leader and Los Angeles literary agent.

There was that question again. Despite having practiced the craft for years, I never thought of storytelling in this manner. The question was not just about the book, however. For me it hopefully held the answer to what I had been searching for but not yet found. What was the overarching question my life was trying to answer?

What happens when we jump into an idea that's bigger than ourselves?

What's on the other side of fear?

What would happen if I let go of control?

What does it mean to surrender and trust?

Is it possible to create a new life out of the experiences of travel?

What does it mean to live intentionally?

What does faith mean?

What's on the other side of happiness?

Fucking clichés. Of course the real question was, "What's behind the veil," but the answer to that question did not feel accessible through art or the creative process. I had been trying to answer that question for years, and not so much as an inkling of the mystery revealed itself to me.

In a bamboo hut with a thatched ceiling, throughout the week we talked about the different parts of story: characters, settings, points of view, voice, theme, dialogue, belief systems, and temporal frameworks, and each day we were led through meditation exercises that put our characters in different situations. After these exercises, we were instructed to put our pen to paper for a certain amount of time without stopping to think. Most meditation and writing sessions led me to my parents, inevitably sending tears rolling down my cheeks. It seemed my only questions were about them, ones that would forever remain unanswered.

Some of the writers told fantastic tales of fantasy or science fiction. Others wrote mysteries, romance novels, and intensely personal stories of abuse and family tragedy. Some were gay, some were married, some were divorced, and some were expats. Many had traveled long distances to get there, and all of them felt this absurd inner compulsion to be a storyteller, a compulsion that only other raconteurs could understand.

Because my life and writing were so intricately entangled, the workshop was about more than just telling a story. I knew to be a writer I needed to embrace uncertainty—the unknown—and I hadn't been doing a very good job of it as of late.

Like life, there was no clearly defined path in writing—only inquiry, choice, and the discernment that comes from experience. Above all, what life and art have in common is trusting the process and doing the work. While trusting the process was the number-one goal I had been striving for the past year, I still found it to be the most challenging aspect of life.

Importantly, what I took away from the workshop was a need to separate myself from my writing so that I was living my life instead of living the story.

Chapter 29. A Winter's Thaw

After completing the workshop and spending my remaining time in Chiang Mai with Kuba and Deanna, on the morning of February 5th I was on a flight from Bangkok to Beijing. In just a few hours I went from a tropical climate to below freezing in order to don the cap of the Assistant to the (International) School Photographer.

Beijing was experiencing the coldest winter in a decade, but even that knowledge couldn't prepare me for the icy blast I experienced as I stepped off the Air China flight. It was the dead of winter, which also coincided with the tail end of the Chinese New Year, so every night the echoing thunder of fireworks sent concussions of sound waves through the thin, biting, winter air.

It took almost no time to get back into my work routine in China. During the week, we tried our best to bring smiles to the faces of private school children who were unaware of their wealth and privilege. At night I'd bring a book into the bath or just lie in my room in the silence and stillness. Somewhere else in the hotel, John would catch up on illegally bootlegged American television shows.

The first weekend night we had off, I went to Sanlitun, a place where expats and affluent Chinese merged for shopping and inebriation, and I scored a small bag of weed. Every few nights I smoked a joint in the shower, which proved to be just the plant medicine I needed to relax and step back from what had become the intense analytical reality of my mind.

On more than one night I got down on my hands and knees in supplication and asked for direction, for the heavy fog to lift, and for the continual release from myself.

One evening while in prayer, an image came to my mind, something I had not thought about in years. I was a young child. It was a typical weeknight where I would watch TV in my parents' bedroom while my father got ready for bed. With a tattered V-neck undershirt, unraveling boxers, and a medal of the Virgin Mary around his neck, he got down on his knees to pray—for what I always wondered.

A week and a half into my three-week trip through Beijing and Shanghai, I was in my hotel room waiting for our car to arrive while John got ready. I looked out from the seventh-floor window of the Forte Hotel in Shanghai to the Xin Hongqiao Center Park below. "Exile on Main Street" by the Rolling Stones was playing on my computer, and I cracked the window to let the tiny fingers of frigid air paw my face.

I leaned back on the seat beside the window, rolled a Drum, lit it, took a big drag, and released it. From the height of my room, the pedestrians on the street below looked like tiny ants going about their frenetic business. I was in my own little world, singing along to "Sweet Black Angel" when out of nowhere I distinctly heard the voice of my father say, "Stop worrying about the future. Everything is going to be okay. You'll see."

With a breath full of tobacco smoke lining my lungs, I looked around the room wide-eyed. I couldn't tell whether the voice came from within or without, but it was certainly audible. There was no mistaking it.

As I exhaled, the truth of the statement—the same message that my mother had told me in a letter from 1995—sunk into my heart, sending tears flowing down my cheeks. I was crying not only because I missed him terribly but also because I knew that I was holding on too tight. But the harder I tried to let go, the tighter the grip felt.

"I can't live like this anymore," I said out loud as the salty waters met my lips. "How do I let this go?"

Oh I know. I just surrender it, an internal voice replied.

No sooner had I uttered that thought than something violent and electric blew out of my chest with such force that it caused me to lurch backward. As if punched in the sternum, I stutter-stepped to find stability and balance beneath my feet.

It's hard to articulate exactly the physical and emotional response my body had to this thought, but in my mind's eye I can only describe the ejaculate as a black, tarry mass of physical, mental, emotional, and spiritual pain. I could sense that in its formlessness it possessed an interconnectedness that had been strangling my psyche throughout this lifetime—and perhaps others—by the very strands of my own DNA.

The moment it was exorcised from my body, I felt an immediate lightness of being. I see this image in my mind of a bird coated in black tar on oil-slicked shores. The bird is using all its might to spread its wings, struggling for the very breath of survival. But on the beach, there is a barrel of magic elixir. When the bird is baptized in the elixir, it is freed of the residue that held it prisoner. When it rises from the water, its feathers and beauty are restored to its natural state.

As if cutting the tethers of a moored helium balloon, my momentary weightlessness left me in astonishment. In the release I had no words, only heightened awareness. Rapt in the extrasensory perception, I got the feeling that perhaps I had not only uprooted pieces of my own past that no longer served me but also pieces of my family's past, stardust that had neither been created nor destroyed but had known many forms and sorrows throughout time.

I knew right then and there, with the winter air lashing my face like a cat's claws, that a monumental shift had occurred, monumental in the way that the spring thaw loosens an ice blockade, heralding not just flow but the dawning of a new season. What exactly the shift was, I did not know, but what I was certain of was that this great shift was beyond words. Though winter was not yet over, the promise of spring was on its way. By the time I met up with John, not only did I feel lighter, but my entire being embodied the lightness.

"You look fresh today. You must have had a good night's sleep," John said to me as we climbed into the taxi.

"I had an interesting morning," I said, looking out the window and taking a deep breath.

The same way you would not know looking down from high above the earth that an earthquake had occurred beneath terra firma, John could not have grasped the tectonic shift I felt that morning. Whatever the future held, I felt assured that I was going to get there one way or another. I just needed to get out of my own way.

In that moment, I stopped worrying about where to go and what to do, and for the first time in a long time I felt calm, loved, connected, centered, and grateful. This giving and compassionate force that called to me and propelled me forward must be the opposite of what was hidden behind the veil.

I was finally awakening to the signposts, serendipity, and synchronicity that had accompanied me on my journey. They not only served to let me know that I was heading in the right direction but also affirmed that as a creator, I had a say in my future. I wanted to be of service on my trip, and I wound up volunteering for a man who had won the equivalent of two Nobel Prizes. I wanted to create free housing for myself, and I had done so in India with JD, in Bangkok with Sophia, in Vietnam and China with John, and in Thailand with Ingrid and Abby. I wanted to create rich experiences of friendship and joy, and they came to me in abundance. About the only thing I hadn't been successful in creating was falling in love.

Four weeks passed by in camera flashes and forced smiles, and every day I felt better and better. China packed my wallet with dollars and my waistline with pounds. Despite the excess weight, I was feeling great on the morning I left Shanghai for the Philippines. I felt truly hopeful. I thought maybe, just maybe, the woman of my dreams was somewhere in that country, somewhere on one of those islands. If I was lucky and blessed enough, I might just run into her. I kept telling people I met along the way that if I fell in love with someone who lived in another country, I would be willing to move there. Deep down, however, I wanted to go home to Seattle.

But I had to be open to chance.

*** *** ***

I am so grateful for:

1. The relief I experienced in hearing my father's voice.
2. The possibilities that have spread out before me.

3. For being fortunate enough to fund a writer's workshop while traveling for nine months.

4. For the quiet nights in Beijing and Shanghai that I got to just read my book in the bathtub after a day of making money.

5. For all the other interesting writers I met at the writer's workshop.

Today I intend and create:

1. To surrender negative feelings and older energies of loneliness, sadness, unworthiness, self-doubt, fear, and anxiety.

2. To not be discouraged by what I wrote at the workshop and to continue searching for the question and the answer.

3. For a sign that I am on the right path and for a sign about where to travel after the Philippines.

4. To be able to someday write the book and express the feelings I've had in my heart since I was seventeen.

5. To have obscene amounts of fun in the Philippines and meet awesome people who I can be friends with for life.

Chapter 30. Moral Hangovers in the Philippines

When I came out of the darkness, looked down, and saw two Filipino prostitutes glaring up at me like starving hyenas, I knew it was time to leave Boracay.

***

From Shanghai, it was a bit of a slog to get to Boracay, an island in the Philippines about 275 miles south of Manila. The slog was mostly due to a failed attempt to get drunk enough to sleep on my red-eye flight.

For all intents and purposes, it should have been a success. The night began on the right track and with the right intention when I met up with two expat-teacher friends at a school benefit. Unfortunately, I made two clinical errors that night, the first being that when you only have two and a half hours to get good and drunk on free booze, it's no time to pace yourself.

My flight was at 12:30am, and seeing as I was more than ready to get out of the Beijing winter and into summer weather in the Philippines, I played it safe and said goodbye to my friends at 9:45pm. I hailed a taxi, and by 10:30pm I was at the airport.

It was an exceptionally busy night at the airport. I was feeling good and loose, relaxed enough to not get frazzled by the pushy Chinese and Filipino passengers aggressively elbowing their way to the check-in counter. The alcohol made me feel magnanimous. I thought, *I'm going to show them courtesy and let whoever wants to go in front of me go. We're all heading to the same place, and pushing and shoving isn't going to make these lines go faster. Perhaps they might even learn some patience from me.*

With only a handful of people left behind me, I approached the counter to get my boarding pass, which is where I encountered my second critical error of the evening: When flying into the Philippines as a foreigner, you can't enter the country without an exit ticket.

"But I don't know where I'm going in the Philippines," I argued.

"I'm sorry, sir. These are the rules. You need to purchase an exit ticket."

"But I don't even know where I'll be exiting from or where I'll be heading to!" I pleaded.

"All flights fly through Manila, sir."

"But it's 11:30pm, and my flight's in an hour and it's almost boarding."

"I'm sorry, sir. The cheapest ticket is to Singapore. You can buy it a few counters down."

I ran from one counter to the next, wondering if they were just sending the American tourist on a wild snipe hunt. When I did finally secure a flight to Singapore, I returned to the ticketing counter with sweat pouring down my brow. I checked in, ran to security—where no one seemed to care that I might miss my flight—and from there on to my gate as the doors were closing. I was the last person to board.

By the time I sat in my seat, I was exhausted, sweating profusely, and the hormones of stress I had been running on had consumed my buzz. Overtired, sober, and packed into crowded seats, I spent the rest of the flight in a twilight daze, tossing and turning with little respite until the wheels finally touched down in Manila at 4am. Exhausted, I fell into a deep sleep in the terminal, nearly missing my connecting flight to Kalibo, the closest airport to Boracay.

After catching a ride at the airport, by 8am I had checked into my guesthouse, took a quick walk along the beach, then returned to my room, only to fall asleep until late afternoon.

The same BBC Travel editor who bought my piece on Cambodia expressed an interest in me writing some stories about the Philippines. I pitched him a few ideas, and he agreed to review the pieces when I was finished. Through another friend I met at the writing class in Chiang Mai, I got in touch with a Filipino travel agent. Together we created an action-packed itinerary of places to visit, foods to try, and things to do while visiting the Philippines.

Because I had just spent a month of early mornings in China with kids, I was ready for some adult fun. The plan was to pad the first four days of my three-week visa in the Philippines sipping cocktails beside the white-sand beaches of Boracay. How could I not? After all, it was ranked one of the top beaches in the world, not to mention its ample party scene. My articles could wait a few days, but a small note in my journal could not: *I could easily see myself spending the entire three weeks here.*

***

Boracay is a 6x1-kilometer island paradise with water as pure and clear as you might imagine heaven's oceans to be. Just a few meters off the beach, palm trees shaded a pedestrian path that ran almost the entire length of the island. On the south side was one of the whitest beaches in the world, creatively and aptly named White Sand Beach, and on the north side of the island, a steady wind made it one of the premier kite surfing destinations in Asia. On the east end of the island, called Station 1, were posh resorts that attracted celebrities, and on the west end there was Station 3, where backpackers like myself found shelter in cheap guesthouses. In the middle, as you may have guessed, was Station 2, a place where all the above comingled over stiff drinks and all-night parties.

It was a scene that brought together people of all nationalities and economic latitudes in a mash of beer, rum, shots, ecstasy, MDMA, sex, cocaine, prostitutes and pimps, and the ensuing debauchery. It would not be far-fetched to be drinking on the beach with a Kiwi backpacker on one side of you and a Silicon Valley tycoon on the other. The day before I arrived, Bono was spotted walking along the beach, as was Jude Law (which was mostly what the women wanted to talk about).

I had met a nice couple from Belgium on the last leg of my flight, and we agreed to meet for a late dinner that evening. While waiting for them at the restaurant on the beach, I picked up a card that was resting on my table. On one side it read, "Follow your bliss." I turned it over, and the other side read, "Anything is possible." It was 11:11pm.

After I started my gratitude-intention journal, I often took notice of the time. Real or imagined, more often than not when I looked at my watch, the time would occur in doubles or triples, like 10:10 or 4:44, or a run, such as 12:34. Whether it was coincidence or not, I took it as a sign that I was right where I was supposed to be.

It didn't happen all the time. For instance, I noticed it wouldn't happen for long stretches when I was worried about the future or trying to control the outcome of my trip. Yet the minute I let go and fell into the flow, the synchronicities would return. It had been weeks, maybe even two months, since I had experienced this. The fact that I literally picked up a very clear message about bliss and possibility on my table—and the fact that it occurred at 11:11pm—well, that was just what I needed to settle my overactive mind.

Every day on the island I met and bounced off new people, but by the third day I had a crew. There was Ricardo, a mid-forties Cuban-American man living in Australia, and there was Nick, a tall, jovial Irish fellow who was nearing the end of his contract as a nurse in Dubai. While an American might describe something as "awesome," Nick would say, "It's deadly-like." This and other Irish colloquialisms immediately won me over.

And then there was Francesca, an easygoing, fun-loving, hard-drinking girl from Melbourne. I remember eyeing her on the beach my first day. She seemed intimidating, so I couldn't find the nerve to introduce myself. I also couldn't find an appropriate inroad to open a conversation. The couple of times I mustered up enough courage to approach her, she would get up and go for a swim or walk up to the bar to order another drink.

On the third day, I saw her at the beach and I finally asked her for the time, or something equally inane. As it turned out, she was warm and inviting. When I first saw Francesca, I may have had unholy thoughts about her, but after hanging out innocently for a few days, we forged a familial bond. She and Ricardo took up with one another, and I was glad we just remained friends.

Rounding out the group was Francesca's friend and coworker from home named Jack, a jovial and wiry guy from an extremely conservative Christian family. In my experience, it always seemed to be the kids from repressed, conservative families who tended to be the wildest when the sun went down.

Once we all coalesced, I fell into a routine with the crew: wake up hungover, have a breakfast of fresh fruit at the guesthouse while flirting with the cute Filipino waitresses, stumble to the beach to read, swim, nap, and/or be social, alternating between the sun, the water, and the shade of palm trees.

Andrew Bird, one of my favorite musicians, had just put out a new release called *Break It Yourself*, so in between my sloth-like activities I'd go for long walks and listen to the moody album. Introspective from the outset, it quickly became an obsession that closely mirrored my own mindscape. The album conveyed in music a longing and searching I recognized deep in my soul. I disappeared from the crew for hours at a time, walking alone on the beach and listening to the album on repeat, all the while wondering what would become of my life.

To not feel like a total alcoholic, each day I would wait for someone else to order the first drink of the day. No matter what time of day it was, it only took one person to order a beer or rum concoction for happy hour to officially be underway. A few drinks in, and after the sun had set the horizon's strata ablaze in layers of gold, fuchsia, and magenta, we'd each grab a beer or two to take back to our rooms while we showered and primped for the evening's festivities. We each operated on our own timetable, so when I felt so inclined I meandered over to Charlie's, the bar/restaurant that served as our rendezvous point.

After getting good and loosened up at Charlie's, we'd find some food to soak up our drinks. As each bar and restaurant slowly filled up, the music emanating from them became louder and louder. This happened like clockwork, day in and day out.

Post-eating, however, it was all about improvisation, letting the "yes/and" lead us to the most appropriate watering hole. And from there, well it tended to get fuzzy around 2am when the club scene kicked in. Some nights it was just booze. Other nights, people in our group found speedier substances, which inevitably turned night into day.

It was no stretch of the imagination to believe the Roman god Bacchus vacationed on Boracay. Every night was filled with drunken, sweaty dancing and rabblerousing. I tried my best to be on good behavior, but in a party scene like the one in Boracay, it was too easy to take someone home. When I did, more often than not it left me feeling empty rather than fulfilled. Sex without intimacy was merely a Band-Aid for a much deeper wound. What I really wanted, and what I believed everyone wanted beneath the endless layers of self, ego, and battle scars of the human drama, was love and connection.

Day four came and went with no plans to leave the island. On the beach in the afternoon I'd make the proclamation that I was leaving in two days. Two days would come and go and still no plans. My BBC article ideas were getting more and more remote.

Each day I woke up feeling foggy and anxious, and each night I went to bed cheerful and feeling blessed. This was the trapping of alcohol. By day seven, it was clear I was not leaving the island anytime soon. I also clearly saw the negative correlation between my drinking, my behavior, and my well-being. It happened in an instant one evening while I was waiting in line for the bathroom.

"What are you looking for?" a beautiful, exotic Israeli woman said to me as we stood side by side waiting for the bathroom.

"Love," I replied, trying to employ wit and charm with just a hint of truth.

"Would you settle for lust?" It was not the answer I expected, and just like that, this woman reduced my willpower to ashes.

The depravity all came to a climax, both literally and figuratively, on the night of a full moon party. Ricardo was sharing a posh, two-bedroom apartment on the other side of the island with his friend from back home, Mabel. Although I had no idea how old she was, it was clear she was older than all of us.

When I joined everyone at the beach that night, the moon was on the rise and the party was well underway. Mabel disappeared from our crew at one point, and later on we all returned to Ricardo and Mabel's apartment to gain some reprieve from the thunderous bass and smoke a joint. As we entered the apartment, Mabel shamelessly walked out of her room completely naked with a man who I guessed was thirty years her junior. She laughed, waved her hand, and chuckled, making a comment that was hard to distinguish in her native Australian tongue.

We returned to the party a few hours into the lunar celebration, and not long afterward I ran into the man I saw in Mabel's apartment. Shots were going around, something I normally didn't imbibe in, but when in Boracay...

"Man, if I knew she was game I would have at least asked her if I could jerk off on her!" I yelled jocularly over the music. I was trying to meet him on some level of bravado and machismo.

The youngster smiled and swayed. He refashioned his flat-brimmed baseball cap emblazoned with a surfing logo, took a pull off his beer, high-fived me, and pulled the cigarette from his mouth. "You want to? I'm telling you, man. She's wild and she's game. The lady's insatiable."

"Sure! Why not," I replied, not thinking much more of it.

He walked to the bar, grabbed me a beer, toasted to the wild times to come, and disappeared. A short while later, he came back and said, "She's down for it. She's waiting for you."

"Great!" I said, again not taking him seriously.

The party continued as sweaty bodies swayed and bounced across the sandy beach to dubstep. Arms flew in the air fueled by alcohol and ecstasy, while eyes bathed in moonlight reflected the purple, pink, and blue stage lights.

Once more the man returned. "Yo, man," he yelled over the crowd. "She says it's now or never. She wants to get back to the party. You in or not?"

"Okay, I'm in," I heard the booze say.

I followed him to the apartment. He let me in and returned to the party, leaving me alone. When I opened the door to the bedroom, she was completely naked on the bed, legs spread and massaging herself.

In one fluid motion (at least that's how I imagine it in my memory) my shorts dropped to the ground and my shirt sailed across the floor. I climbed on top of her, and with one hand I played with my business and with the other I played with hers.

"Cum for Mommy," I thought I heard her say.

It was confirmed moments later when she said, "You like that, do you? You gonna cum for Mommy? You gonna cum for Mommy? Mommy wants you to give her a big load of cum, and if you don't, Mommy's gonna have to punish you. That's right. Mommy's gonna punish you. And you don't want that, do you? Mmm…right here…and here. Yes, that's a good boy. Cum for Mommy."

I paused in a drunken moment of clarity and caught myself thinking, *Well, this is pretty fucking weird.* But then I looked at what was in front of me and got back to business. When it was all over, she insisted I take pictures of what she called my "Jackson Pollock" upon her canvas. *This is definitely weird,* I thought, but not wanting to disappoint "Mommy," I did as I was told.

I came and went, and when I returned to the party, the young man gave me a high five and handed me a drink.

"Here, man, drink this. You earned it." Sweaty and thirsty, I downed the beer.

It didn't take long before I started to feel dizzy and wobbly. The last thing I remember thinking was, *I don't feel right. Could that fucker have spiked my drink? I need to get out of here…*

And with that, the night went black.

When I came out of the blackness, I looked up and saw a filament glowing inside a single bulb that hung from an electrical wire. Everything was blurry, and I felt wobbly and weary. I tried to get my bearings, but it was like peering through the lens of an out-of-focus camera. When things became clearer, I looked down to see my pants around my ankles and two prostitutes about to go down on me. I had no idea how much time had passed or where I was.

The room in which I found myself with the unlikely duo was not much bigger than a broom closet. Upon a rickety wooden frame, a soiled, dust-colored mattress ran the length of the back wall. As my haze lifted, I remember panic setting in. I could have been in a crack house in Baltimore for all I knew. The only thing I could think was, *Where am I, how did I get here, and how the fuck do I get out of here?*

"Whoa," I said, pulling up my pants. "No, no, that's okay. Actually, that's not okay. No thanks. Sorry, there's been a mistake."

"What you doing, mister?"

"I don't want that—or this. There's been a misunderstanding and I'm, I'm just going to go now."

"You pay us first." When she stood up, her head blocked the light hanging from the wire behind her. I vaguely remember thinking it looked like a halo, and then I also thought, *That's a strong jawline,* which only served to double my panic.

"Sorry, I'm leaving."

"No you not! You pay. You pay us now!"

"Sorry, this isn't happening tonight."

As I tried to open the door, one of them launched across the room and slammed it shut, nearly catching my fingers in it. The gesture commanded my attention.

"Look, nothing happened and I'm not paying. I just want to go. Please."

"You going to pay us now or you going to be in trouble. I call police."

"Great. Let's get the police."

"You looking for big trouble mister, you going to get big trouble," she said, jabbing her finger up under my chin.

I slapped her finger away, and the two of them closed in on me. I felt the primordial hormones of stress kick in, the same ones that incite the instinct of fight or flight.

"Look, I'm starting to getting really fucking pissed, and if you don't let me go, something bad is going to happen."

"It going to happen to you, mister!" the other one yelled.

As I made one final effort to open the door, the one with the strong jawline launched at me and grabbed my arm while the other one pinned the door shut. The rest of the scene happened in slow motion. It was as if I could see everything as it happened from outside my body.

***

I see myself become bigger, like a puffer fish.

I see the adrenalin rushing to my neck. I see my biceps fully flexed as I lock my arm underneath the arm of the strong-jawed one to my right and launch her into the back wall.

I see the prostitute to my left lunging at me, locking her hands in a grip around my neck. I bring both of my arms up between hers and push outward to break her grip, and then I bring my right elbow across her face, sending her into the back wall. She grabs my shirt as she falls back, ripping it and taking a small amount of flesh with her.

I try to open the door, but the first prostitute lunges across the room, throwing all her weight against it.

Again, I forcibly remove her from the door.

Out of the corner of my eye, I see the one who just met my elbow reach under the bed and grab a small blade. Hoping for the element of surprise, she comes at me fast and out of control, but I manage to step aside. The blade nicks my left tricep. Her momentum carries her past me, so I grab her by the hair and swing her around.

At the same time, the other one is coming at me and their heads collide. It sounds like two coconuts bouncing off each other, and they collapse in a heap on the floor. I run out the door, down a long, dimly lit hallway, and out into an alleyway. It seems like a maze and I have no idea how I got here or which way the beach is. If I can find the beach, I can find my way home.

A smaller Filipino man is walking up the alley, perhaps having just gotten off work at a bar. I run up to him and grab him by the lapels. In a panic I yell, "How do I get to the beach? Which way is the fucking beach!"

He looks terrified and makes hand signals as if to say, *Please don't hurt me!*

My shirt is torn, and judging from the blood running down my arm, I realize the nick is perhaps a bit deeper than I first thought. My instincts kick in and I run in the direction that feels right. I'm either going to hit the beach or the main road.

I find myself on the main road and flag down a motorcycle taxi.

"To Station 3!"

"Yes sir." The ride seems to take longer than normal.

"Station 3, right? You better not be fucking with me, man! I have *not* had a good night!" I yell over the high pitch of the whirring motor.

"Relax, brother. It's all good," he yells back. "I get you home. You're on Boracay, man. No need to be agro." He gets me to an area I recognize and I can finally breathe with relief. I apologize profusely and tip him heavily, telling him I was just assaulted.

"That arm doesn't look good. You want me to call the police, brother?" My shirt and pants are covered in blood.

I tell him it's not necessary, that I just need sleep.

I make my way to my guesthouse and the morning groundskeepers look on in shock. In my bathroom I try my best to clean my cut, and I wrap my arm in a towel. I look at the clock and it's 5:39am. I fall into a deep sleep.

***

I woke up the next morning feeling physical pain, emotional exhaustion, moral bankruptcy, and spiritual sickness. I was nauseous and run-down. There had been a few mornings on the islands when it was hard to get out of bed, but this one had them all beat.

In a state of restless anxiety, I lay in bed, mentally running through the events of the previous twenty-four hours. It began the morning of the full moon party when I woke up next to the daughter of a mayor from one of the biggest cities in Israel. Both stinking drunk and smelling of boozy-sweat, we decided to shower to cleanse us from the night.

Although it might seem highly illogical, not to mention ill-advised, many showers in Asia are heated by an electric box located in the shower. By pulling a cord, the water heats up (or at least that's how it's supposed to work). Had I been in more of my right mind, I might have noticed that the box appeared to be in a state of disrepair, but no matter.

No sooner did I turn on the cord to heat the water than I heard a pop. The box exploded, causing a small fire in the unit and on the curtain while two live electrical wires danced like unmanned fire hoses. Without thinking, I pushed her out of the shower, punched the box off the wall, and turned the water off, knowing well that water and electricity don't mix. I ripped the curtain down and we stomped out the fire with our towels. When the excitement ended, we stood there naked, looking at each other in a silence that said more than words ever could.

So, in a matter of twenty-four hours, I had almost gotten electrocuted in a shower with the daughter of a high-profile Israeli politician, masturbated on Mommy, fought two Filipino prostitutes off me, and managed to get cut in a knife fight where I failed to bring one. To make matters worse, I had no idea what the prostitutes looked like or if they had a pimp, but chances were more than likely they were going to remember me.

On the bright side, I got a room upgrade and a functional shower. On the downside, with basically only one thoroughfare along the beach, I might have been a marked man. It was time to leave Boracay.

After an incredibly hungover day full of regret, loathing, and shame, I booked a flight out for the following morning. The only thing that made me feel better was that I heard several people had been drugged the previous night. Whether I had been or not, that was my story—and I was sticking to it.

I was a long way from the monastic and inspired life I was living in India. Beyond the story, all I really wanted out of my journey was to fall in love, but instead I was lonelier than ever and making every bad decision possible. I had been operating for days on old, unconscious programs that led me nowhere good, trying my best to outrun the hangover and loathing I was now experiencing, the culmination of which was pushing me further and further from the stillness and clarity I so desperately sought.

I could blame no one but myself, however, and in the self-reflection of my recent actions, one thing was becoming clear: I was starting to hear the homeward call. I missed my friends, I missed a place to go home to every night, and however meager they were, I missed having my possessions around me.

As foreign of a concept as it might have sounded to me a year prior, I was starting to miss the familiarity of routine.

Chapter 31. Curfews and the Sagada Social Club

Besides being known for spelunking, hiking, white-water river rafting, its proximity to 1000-year-old rice terraces, and a 9pm curfew, the *Lonely Planet: Philippines* also mentions that Sagada is known for its medicinal-grade marijuana.

The plant medicine for the mind and soul was just what I needed, not to mention that the curfew offered an inspired reason to get a good night's sleep. After my two weeks on the small island of excess and debauchery, I was ready for a break from the action.

To get to Sagada from Boracay, I had to take a plane to Manila where I waited four hours for a bus to take me six hours north, where I spent a six-hour night at a friend of a friend's place, only to wake up at 5am to catch another 6.5-hour bus ride to my final destination. Due to the Philippines' tenuous infrastructure, the final leg took an extra two hours. After hours of slowly climbing mountain switchbacks, there it was—Sagada—nestled in a valley between two mountains like some mythical destination.

The bus let me off at a fork in the road at the edge of town. I could see why Sagada had not been deemed a city; it consisted of no more than a tiny main street that meandered down a hill. It was barely wide enough for two cars plus parking on either side. I had no trouble finding the guesthouse that my friend had set up for me, and after a brief walk through town, the sounds of Bob Marley pulled me into a Rastafarian-themed bar.

"Hey, man. How goes it? Can I get you a beer? Some smoke?" the welcoming barman asked.

"I'd like all of those, please." I sat down and told the barman the abbreviated version of my traveler's tale. Then I bought two thumbs of hash, even though I knew it was far more than I would need. What can I say? I'm a sucker for a deal.

By the time I made my way back to my guesthouse, I had almost no energy left. I fell into bed for a quick nap, bookending nearly twenty-six hours of travel.

Night came early in the mountains, and when I awoke from my nap, like a sky over Golgotha, the waning light of the day created a holy drama in the western heavens. What was supposed to be a brief nap lasted four and a half hours. I needed a few moments to orient myself and to realize I was no longer on Boracay. I missed my new friends, but I was grateful to be off the tiny tropical island. In a groggy haze, I walked to the other side of the room, pulled out my travel speaker, and hit random on a playlist. The lo-fi sound coming through the speakers of Lou Reed's "Coney Island Baby" matched my lo-fi mood.

When you're all alone and lonely in the midnight hour,
And you find that your soul has been up for sale,
And you begin to think all the things that you've done,
And you begin to hate just about everything...

I couldn't imagine a more perfect soundtrack to match my contemplative mood, so I turned off shuffle and turned on repeat. The song created space within me, and for the first time in a while I felt like I could get a full breath. While physiologically it served to provide oxygen to my brain, it also seemed to facilitate expansion. I grabbed my pack of Drum, broke up some hash, rolled a spliff, and kicked my feet up on the railing of the balcony to take in the epic sunset that was unfolding.

> Remember that the city is a funny place,
> Something like a circus or a sewer...

Somewhere in the distance, the echo of barking dogs rose up from the mountain valley. Below me, a group of Israeli travelers were sitting around a fire pit playing guitar, laughing, and singing songs in Hebrew while passing around a jug of something. Sagada was the polar opposite of Boracay and exactly what I needed.

> The glory of love might see you through,
> The glory of love,
> The glory of love...

I finished my spliff, extinguished the remaining roach on the railing, and felt more relaxed than I had in some time. With not much light remaining in the western sky, I went back inside and began unpacking, separating my soiled clothes from the few clean ones I had remaining. I placed my gear on some shelves and my clean clothes in dresser drawers. These were simple acts that gave me domestic pleasure, like something someone with a home might do.

When I felt settled enough, I grabbed a book and my journal and made my way into town to appease my appetite.

After dinner, I returned to my room, placed earplugs in my ears, covered my eyes with an eye mask, and took a sleeping pill. Like a choir singing in unison, every cell in my body rang out in joy at the good news—the promise of unbroken rest. On Boracay I had forgotten the importance of sleep, so my goal was to make up for lost time.

The next morning I was startled awake by pounding at my door. Shocked again to discover I wasn't on an island, I put on some clothes and answered the door.

"What is up buddy!" my friend Kyle from Boracay said enthusiastically in his Hebrew accent.

"What are you doing here? What time is it?"

"It's 11am. I went surfing in San Juan but it wasn't very good. When I heard about Sagada, I thought, I have to check this place out. Then when I checked into the guesthouse this morning I saw your name on the registry and I was like, no fucking way, man! Thomas! This is so nuts!" Kyle was also part of the full moon party on Boracay, and he too found himself in a bit of trouble that fateful night.

"Wow…okay, awesome. Let me get myself together and I'll meet you in town for breakfast. Pick a place and shoot me a text. I'll meet you there in about thirty minutes."

By the time I met up with Kyle, a veil of clouds moved into the valley, covering everything in a delicate Seattle mist. With our choices of activities limited due to inclement weather, we opted for spelunking.

Since it was the Philippines, there was neither safety gear nor any preparation for the world beneath the surface. We were simply handed a headlamp, told to follow the guide's lead, and watch our heads.

To enter the cave, we first had to climb through a hole that was not much bigger than my body. It required that I remove my backpack, and in my mind I kept hearing, *I can't do this, I can't do this,* but I forged on past the claustrophobia. *If I've made it this far for this long on my own, I can certainly do this. Lots of people have done this before me,* I told myself.

After one minute of scooting through small openings beneath the Cordillera Mountains, the tunnel opened up into an underground vaulted cathedral that appeared to be carved and sculpted by the very hand of God. Light from our headlamps bounced off stalactites and stalagmites that were millions of years in the making. It reflected off the ceiling of the cave in pools of water so still that it was nearly impossible to distinguish where the limestone ended and the pools began. Once I acclimated to the beauty and grandeur, I began rappelling down ledges, climbing up knotted ropes, and scaling rock walls. Not one to be a thrill seeker, the feeling of adventure overcame the fear, and I stopped thinking about the fact that one wrong slip in the wrong place and I could be gone for good.

***

The beauty of travel is such that you can randomly find yourself having dinner with a group of Canadians, Dutch, Danes, Japanese, Israelis, and Peruvians, all of which were the nationalities that comprised our Sagada Social Club. The extent of our club consisted of socializing, exploration, and eating meals together, and although each night they tried to get me to go to "after-hours" parties, I always passed. I simply couldn't wait to go home, crawl into bed, and just read or catch up with friends on Skype.

There is an elegance of design to travel, if you let it happen. In this respect, it felt like things were once again beginning to loosen up within me. The first ice break of my long winter occurred in a hotel room in Beijing, and now it felt as if the great thaw of spring was almost over. What the thaw was beginning to uncover, something that was frozen in the winter's ice, was the fact that my thoughts might actually be affecting the cause as opposed to the Newtonian cause-effect world in which I had always based my reality.

Having ended my cycle of staying out late and getting up late, I had newly found leisure time to look back over the last year. It was beyond obvious that when I became conscious of my thoughts and directed them with intention, they became creations. Even the small act of starting to write in my journal more regularly had a grounding and directional effect.

Whether I was conscious of it or not, my thoughts had been the guiding principle throughout my whole life. When I looked at the world through sadness, fear, and heartbreak, sadness, fear, and heartbreak were reflected to me. The world was a mirror, and the experiment was becoming clearer; each thought carried with it a charge. Thoughts were electric, and the feelings and emotions behind the thoughts were magnetic. Whether the thought was positive or negative, the feeling behind the charged thought pulled into my life correlating experiences that reflected that feeling and emotion.

Living comfortably in the Philippines more than a year after creating the thought that I was going to find a way to travel was a testament to my creation. I left Seattle ten months prior with six thousand dollars in my checking account. I now had ten thousand dollars in my bank account, paid off a credit card along the way, and even managed to put some money into savings. How would this new paradigm fit into my life at home? It was too early to ponder these questions.

On March 17th, I split off from the social club for a day on my own. I only realized it was March 17th because the previous evening at dinner a large Norwegian man with a fair complexion bought us a round in honor of St. Patrick's Day. I woke up that morning and went for a long hike up the mountain behind my guesthouse. It was a warm day, and on the open expanses of the trail the sun punished me. Once in the shade of the forest, the temperature brought a chill to my body. The higher up the mountain I climbed, the more gratitude and accomplishment I felt welling up inside of me.

For the past few days, because I could feel my heart and soul opening up, I felt I needed to give myself space and silence to nurture the new feelings of gratitude. A day of solo hiking to the top of a mountain felt like the right way to do it. When I finally did reach the top of the mountain, "Like a Rolling Stone" by Bob Dylan began to play in my earphones.

How does it feel?
To be on your own,
With no direction home,
A complete unknown,
Like a rolling stone.

At least for today, it felt damn good. It felt victorious.

I found a grassy clearing, took off my shirt, rolled a Drum with a tiny hint of hash, lit it up, and lay in the grass, contentedly watching the clouds transform from formlessness to geometric shapes, to animals, back again to shapes, and back again to formlessness. Wanting a deeper connection to the moment, I sat up and closed my eyes in meditation.

In the meditation, I felt a scene from a friend's birthday party in Seattle several years prior. It was a few days after New Year's, and we were all going around the table talking about our resolutions. I was just coming off a rough breakup and at the same time coming to terms with the fact that my mother's health and awareness were never coming back.

As we went around the table, friends shared that they wanted to lose weight, get a new job, start a new business, or find a new relationship. When it came around to me, I said, "I want a quiet mind and a peaceful heart."

"Aww! That's so sweet," I remember someone saying. But what they didn't realize was that I was barely hanging on.

With the madness of Boracay behind me and the ability to think clearly without the numbing haze of alcohol, I could see that I had been delivered to this mountaintop through a combination of thoughts and grace, by the benevolent organizing energy of the universe that keeps our cells in order and our hearts beating. While I knew a quiet mind and peaceful heart would always be a work in progress, what I wanted next in my life, beyond love and family, was to move through my life with ease, flow, and harmony.

When I came off the mountaintop and returned to town later in the afternoon, I took a right off the main thoroughfare and walked down a street I had not yet explored. At the end of it I found a Catholic basilica, and like a lighthouse guiding a ship to shore, I was pulled into the stillness of the church. The mountaintop had given me an inward direction, but now I needed an outward one.

I tried to empty my mind and be still. At the front of the church in a circle of chairs sat men and women. From the cadence of their prayers, I recognized the rosary in

Tagalog. In the stillness of the afternoon, with sunbeams streaming through stained glass, I asked my parents to give me direction. At the moment, my best option was a free villa in an Italian hill town in Tuscany. It was a friend of a friend's place and certainly not a bad option. My plan was to end up there for three months to write. However, I needed an itinerary to connect me to April in Italy. I meandered back to my guesthouse in a state of gratitude, contentment, and certainty that a path would reveal itself, well aware that it might take some time to come to light.

When I returned to my room, I opened my email to contact my friend in Italy, only to be surprised by a message from Cassandra. We had been talking for most of the year on email and Skype, but it had been at least a month since we connected. I had no idea what was happening in her life. As fate would have it, she was heading to Chennai, India for a wedding and was curious to know if I wanted to rendezvous with her somewhere between Chennai and the Philippines.

An hour later, we were face-to-face on Skype. I was surprised at how familiar it felt to see her eyes, how soothing it was to hear her voice, and how quickly we picked up where we left off.

"The Philippines are incredible. Why don't we meet here on an island?" I suggested.

"I don't think I have enough time to make it work. I don't want to waste days traveling when we could be spending them together."

After discussing several more options, we landed on Sri Lanka. Above all else, she wanted to spend a week at an Ashtanga yoga retreat learning from a highly touted instructor. I would go to the yoga retreat with her the first week if she agreed to travel the island with me the following week. It was settled. We would meet at a retreat in Tangalle, Sri Lanka at Rocky Point Beach.

By the time I went to bed that night, I had booked a flight from Manila to Sri Lanka where we would spend two weeks together. Once I hit purchase on the computer, I could barely contain my excitement. I then purchased an exit ticket from Sri Lanka to Berlin. I had never been to Germany, and since one of my best friends lived there, as did my new friends Leo and Martin, it seemed like a no-brainer. Why wouldn't I add a German stamp to my passport on my way to Italy? The plan was to stay in Berlin until I was ready to move on and then book a flight to Rome where I would spend the last three months of my trip living my dream as an expat writer in Tuscany.

While the decision marked the beginning of the end of my journey, the prospect of seeing Cassandra seemed like the perfect bookend to what had been both the best and most challenging year of my life. I would arrive in Colombo, Sri Lanka on March 30th and fly from Colombo to Berlin early on the morning on April 12th, exactly one year to the day I left home in search of my story. Whereas during different points of my trip I dropped to my knees in supplication, when I went to bed that night I dropped to my knees in gratitude.

The following day, I went with the Sagada Social Club to visit the famous 2,000-year-old Banaue rice terraces carved into the side of a mountain by the indigenous people. The way to travel locally in the Philippines is in jeepneys, discarded American Jeeps left behind after World War II. Think a stretch Hummer, except a Jeep circa 1942 that is beat-up, restored, and decked out with spray paint, trinkets, blinking lights, loud music, statues of the Virgin Mary, and/ or some combo of all of the above.

Generally tourists ride inside the cabin and the locals ride on top with their bundles of rice, tools, or chickens, but after my first ride on the top of a jeepney, there was no going back. I was hooked. The northern Philippines had some of the most spectacular scenery I'd seen in my year of travel, and by riding on the top of the jeepney, there was no window frame to separate me from the experience.

As we climbed higher into the mountains, hugging cliffs and rounding blind corners, rice terraces that had provided a way of life for hundreds to thousands of years spread out below us in descending rectangles of order and ingenuity. As we passed through small villages, barking dogs, clucking roosters, laughing children, and men hammering hammers provided a soundtrack while mountain pine filled my soul with future memories. I put my iPod on shuffle and sat back.

A live version of "Scarlet Begonias" segued into "Fire on the Mountain" by the Grateful Dead. All fans of the Grateful Dead know the thing about their music is that it has a way of pulling you into the present moment, which then becomes a doorway to infinite moments. The album that transported me through time was *Cornell 5/8/77*, named for the date it was recorded at Cornell University. There were few albums I listened to more in high school as I drove around the back roads of New Jersey in my red 1980 Volvo station wagon, smoking pot while trying to get lost with Harry, my dog and copilot.

Looking back through time from my current vantage, I was humbled how grace, good fortune, time, and dreams delivered me that afternoon to the roof of a jeepney in the Cordillera Mountains in the Philippines. The music served as one of many quantum strings that connected the past to the present moment. The experience I was in the middle of living was everything the younger version of me had dreamed of—adventure, freedom, joy, independence, and expansion. These feelings would now live in my biology, and under the right conditions, would give birth to future stories.

With the wind in my face, my head bopping to the bass and percussion, my body groovin' to the rhythm, and my heart dancing to the melody that came through Jerry Garcia's guitar, tears of joy rolled down my cheeks. I felt victorious.

With an expanded heart, in the rapturous joy of the moment, it dawned on me that the mystery was not only consuming me but also initiating me. In surrendering my old life to the possibility of a new one, if for no other reason than there was no going back, my soul had no choice but to open to the possibilities before me. Every time I surrendered what no longer served me, I molted another layer of the sadness and fear that had consumed my thoughts and run my life for so long. In the absence of sadness and fear, love consumed me, and more tears of joy ran down my cheeks.

Wrapped in the comforting blanket of these emotions, there was nothing more to do but bask in gratitude and let the warm, healing mountain air wash over me.

Chapter 32. Anticipation

I had what felt like five long days left in the Philippines before leaving for Sri Lanka. Cobbling together an itinerary based on recommendations, I made my way from Sagada to El Nido, a small, picturesque village on the island of Palawan. As usual in the Philippines, it was a long, arduous journey. Because several long bus trips bookended my flight to Palawan, I planned on spending the night in its capital, Puerto Princesa. In Puerto Princesa, however, a pushy taxi driver insisted I would be fine to keep going and ushered me to a bus company. Not one to argue, I agreed to make the journey in one day.

The bus turned out to be a small Toyota van. It was myself and another man about my age, and I was damned if he was going to get the front seat. This was a clinical error for my nervous system, for out of all of the harrowing car rides I had taken in the past year, this topped them all.

During the four-hour ride, we drove through several blinding downpours, which did not seem to faze the driver, nor did the fact that the tires were so bald we could see the radials poking through. Around several corners, it felt as if we were up on two wheels. I was almost certain, being so close to the windshield, I would meet the end of my road in a violent explosion of glass and metal, ending my life wrapped around a tree or guardrail. The only positive thing about the white-knuckle drive was that the other passenger and myself had something to bond over.

Sam was from Toronto, Canada and owned a small travel company that catered to twenty-something tourists who liked to party. He was on a research trip to see if Palawan might be a destination he'd like to add to his roster of locations. For the past several years he'd been living all over Asia but called Bali his home. With a taste for Asian women, I got the feeling he nailed anything that wasn't hammered down. He too was coming off a bender in Boracay, and sharing our need for quiet time we decided to split the cost of a room while we traveled together. With the exception of one afternoon where we accidentally split a bottle of rum on a small boat tour—and proceeded to scare a polite Japanese family—we kept it on the down-low. I knew if we were in a big city or party place like Boracay, however, together we would do some damage.

"I've got an idea," Sam said one afternoon. "I could use some help with an upcoming tour of the Thai islands. Why don't you meet me in Thailand and I'll pay you to help me out for a month? You just have to be friendly, chat up the tourists, party with them, and maybe sleep with a Canadian chick here and there. I'll cover your travel costs and lodging."

The tempting proposition tore me up inside. Had this happened at the beginning of my trip or at the beginning of the year, it would have been an easy decision, but I was still feeling physically exhausted and morally bankrupt from my time on Boracay. I figured it would be a long time before I could drink in such a fashion again. Instead, a quiet life of writing in Italy awaited me, and I couldn't have been more excited about it. What I was even more excited about, however, was seeing Cassandra, and every time the conversation between Sam and I hit a lull, my mind wandered to thoughts of her.

After spending three days with Sam, he moved on to his next scouting location, and having two more days to kill, I headed two hours north to a small beach town called Sabang, where it proceeded to rain for most of two long days. I spent my days wandering the beaches in anxious curiosity, making my way through the moody, introspective weather, wondering what it would be like to see Cassandra after a year, whether or not she was still unhappy in her marriage, and so on. If she weren't, what would that mean for us?

Having spent little money in China and having the final paycheck from my work there land in my bank account, I had twelve thousand dollars in the bank when I left the Philippines—double what I had left home with almost a year prior. And it all began with a written thought and intention in my gratitude-intention journal several months before my journey began. I simply wrote over and over that I wanted to create a windfall of money. *Yes*, I found myself thinking. *I think my savings probably constitutes a windfall.*

From Sabang I caught a bus to Puerto Princesa where I caught a flight to Manila. From Manila I bid farewell to the wonderful Philippines and flew to Kuala Lumpur where for some reason the airport was closed for the night. So, along with many other travelers, I spent the night trying to sleep on the sidewalk outside the airport.

By 6am I was on a flight from Kuala Lumpur to Colombo. As the plane banked on its final approach to Colombo, with the early morning sun basking turquoise waters and coconut groves in crystalline light, I could hardly contain my excitement.

Once I got situated and passed through customs, I hired a car to travel three of the six hours it took to get to Tangalle, my final destination. Galle was the halfway point and that day England was playing Sri Lanka in cricket, a sport both countries took very seriously.

The town was crawling with tourists and cricket fans. As dusk gave way to night, I wanted to find a comfortable place in the midst of some action to observe and write, but with all the commotion of the match, it was damn near impossible to find a table on the beach. After walking up and down the beach several times, I finally asked a woman if she would mind if I shared her table.

Pam was an attractive, forty-five-year-old nurse in the British army. Holding the rank of second lieutenant, she was on leave from Afghanistan. We had dinner together and shared our stories while British men got blackout drunk around us.

"Fucking bloody Brits," she said several times. "I can't get away from these twats. With the way they're carrying on, I bet these hooligans work on oil rigs. I bet they were all in Iraq, or Afghanistan too."

Pam was staying at a fancy hotel two doors down and had the top apartment. We were both planning on just eating and having an early night, but three hours later the drunken Brits she was referring to befriended us. Pam was right; the men were ex-special forces who served in Afghanistan and now worked as hired guns protecting oil tankers and container ships off the coast of Africa. The man who held the highest rank amongst them brought his cronies in line once he found out Pam's rank. For the rest of the night they bought us drinks and kept the other drunkards at bay.

"These guys," she said, leaning into me late in the evening, "they're fun to drink with, but you wouldn't want to be on their bad side. When they were in the Gulf, they were essentially hired assassins, and I'll bet some of them have done some things you and I couldn't imagine."

The next day, I made my way to Tangalle. I arrived at the guesthouse where Cassandra and I would meet, and a rainbow greeted me. It was a result of water, reflection, refraction, and the dispersion of light, but to me it just felt like a good omen.

Cassandra was flying in from Chennai, India that evening and then had a six-hour bus ride to Tangalle. Time passed very slowly that day. I did my best to fill it with walking, writing, reading, and lounging.

Cassandra expected that she would arrive at the bungalow around 12:30am, so I tried my best to stay awake. I watched the clock religiously and checked it at regular ten-minute intervals until I fell asleep. She finally arrived at 2am. We hugged and kissed, staring at each other in amazement that we were finally in each other's presence. The whole thing was preposterous—after all, we had only spent a total of five days together almost exactly a year ago.

Nonetheless, she took a shower, toweled off, and crawled into bed.

***   ***   ***

I am so grateful for:

1. The opportunity to spend this time with Cassandra and to be able to travel with someone I care about.

2. The fact that we stayed in touch the entire year and how serendipitously the whole thing came together.

3. All of the beautiful places I've traveled to and seen this year.

4. Growth and all the old parts of the self that I've molted.

5. My quiet time in church, the feeling of connection

to something greater than me, and for remembering how to slow down, bring the volume down, and be still.

Today I intend and create:

1. To have an incredible time with Cassandra.
2. For us to share countless smiles and laughter.
3. Adventure.
4. Trust in my new path.
5. Romance and surprise.

Chapter 33. Getting Reacquainted

It took a long time to get out of bed our first morning together. We were tired from a late night, much of which was spent in each other's embrace. Even though our bodies were tired, our minds were electric with possibilities. All morning we dozed in and out of sleep, listening to the songbirds while kissing, spooning, adjusting, re-spooning, dozing, cupping, caressing, and so on. As morning unfolded, the sun crept higher into the sky. When it finally rose above the jungle foliage surrounding our bungalow, sunbeams splintered into our rooms, not only through the windows but also through tiny holes in our thatched roof.

"That's kind of weird, don't you think?" I said, pointing to the roof.

"It's ambiance," she replied.

At one point midmorning, I noticed Cassandra's wedding ring but said nothing. My heart cringed and my body tensed. *She probably didn't have time to take it off*, I reasoned. As I looked over her shoulder at the ring, she rolled toward me. "I guess we should take a shower and find some breakfast, huh? I haven't eaten since yesterday afternoon."

"I stopped by the yoga place yesterday. The food looks delicious, and I think it's all vegetarian. You want to go there?"

"Sounds great. I don't really care what we do. I'm just so happy to be with you. I can't believe I'm here," she said.

She kissed me, rolled out of bed, and made her way to the bathroom. I lingered in bed a moment longer, admiring the tan lines that wrapped around her curves.

After lunch we made our way to a postcard-perfect beach, holding hands as we walked along the pristine sands. "I have to tell you, I don't think I'm going to like Ashtanga yoga," I said. "I'm open to it, and I'll try it, but I think I'm going to get bored doing the same poses every time."

"You don't have to do it, but you might surprise yourself," she replied.

We went for a long walk that afternoon, sharing stories of where our lives had taken us in the past year—the landscapes, mindscapes, and soulscapes we had traversed both externally and internally. By the time we made our way back to the rocky dirt road that led to our bungalow, ominous clouds moved in on us. With our bungalow a few thousand feet away, we got caught in a gentle drizzle that quickly escalated to a tropical downpour. By the time we returned to our room, we were giggling at how wonderful it was to be in our rain-soaked clothes and how good the warm rain felt. Not even the fact that rain was coming through our roof and making puddles on our floor prevented us from the giddiness we felt in each other's presence.

We put on dry clothes, and when the rain did let up we scouted out a new guesthouse a hundred feet up the dirt road. When we told the owners of our leaky bungalow that we were moving, it caused an uproar; he accused his neighbor of poaching us. By the time we gathered our belongings and made our way to the new guesthouse, the owner politely informed us that we could no longer stay.

"I so sorry but that man is crazy and has done very bad things. He thinks I steal guests and has threatened to kill me. I can't take the chance with my family. I sorry." Although it was going to cost us more money than we wanted to spend, we were left with little choice but to stay at the yoga retreat.

***

The whole point of the yoga retreat was so Cassandra could deepen her practice. I was no stranger to yoga, just Ashtanga yoga. Rather than sleep in and be the only person at the retreat that wasn't practicing, I opted to give it a chance. Each morning I bitched and moaned when the alarm went off at 5:30am, but after a few days of practice and observing how quickly it was sculpting my body and centering my mind and energy, I was motivated. The motivation turned into a personal challenge as each day I tried to move deeper into postures. By deepening my stretches, my practice became a physical meditation.

Immediately Cassandra and I picked up where we had left off in Dharamsala, acting as if we were a couple. We stole kisses in public, made eyes at each other across the dinner table when we were with friends, shared jokes with a simple look, or just gazed at each other in the middle of a crowded bus. It was hard to imagine things going any better. There was just one thing—the ring on her finger.

"Are you going to wear your ring the whole time you're here? Can you take it off while you're with me?"

"I'm not taking off my wedding ring," she said abruptly. Her matter-of-fact tone startled me, giving me the feeling that perhaps what we were doing meant different things to us.

"It's just that people are going to ask questions and I'm not very good at lying," I said, trying to justify my stance.

"Well, it's not for you to worry about. It's my problem and I'll deal with it. We're friends, we met traveling a year ago, and if the line of questioning goes beyond that I'll address it. End of conversation."

***

Since it was toward the end of the season, there were only ten inhabitants at the yoga retreat. One morning after practice, a small group of us cut through the jungle to a neighboring beach (only later did we discover that more people die per year from snakebites in Sri Lanka than anywhere else in the world).

After playing in the ocean for some time, George, a Brit about my age, led us back to our abode through the jungle. George had dropped out of a high-pressure job in London six months prior and had been practicing at the yoga retreat ever since. Holding open two barbed wires of a fence for us while we ducked underneath, he noticed Cassandra's ring.

"Is that a wedding ring?"

I pretended not to hear.

"Yes, it is," she replied.

"Oh? I didn't realize. Are you two married?"

"No," she said, passing through the fence, bringing another conversation to a halt.

The people staying at the retreat generally shared meals together, so over lunch that afternoon I heard George say to Cassandra, "I'm sorry for taking you off guard today."

"It's complicated."

"I understand," he said. "I have one of those situations as well, which is partly why I left London." It was never mentioned again.

The more time Cassandra and I spent together, the more smitten we became. One morning I found a giant heart-shaped leaf, so I placed it in our bathroom and filled it with plumeria flowers. When I returned from yoga before her, I would line the room—from our pillows to the bathroom to the shower—with the delicate and fragrant flowers that had fallen off the trees.

On another afternoon, while we were in town eating lunch with our group, I scribbled her a note on a napkin. On the way home on a crowded bus I handed it to her. I watched in joy as her face lit up when she read the words: "I can't wait until I can kiss you again. I love sharing this experience with you."

She agreed. Every day she would express how happy she was, making me feel both excited and out of sorts, like a seventh grader in love for the first time. We were enjoying our routine of yoga in the morning and lounging on the beach in the afternoon, so much so that we decided to cancel our plans to travel around Sri Lanka.

A week into our time together, however, I was having anxiety about what we were doing. I was trying to keep it fun and light, but whether I liked it or not I was falling in love. The conflicting emotions were having an adverse effect on me in bed.

"What's going on?" she asked.

"I'm just in my head tonight."

"What do you mean?"

"It means exactly what I said."

She paused and sat up. "I know what you're thinking."

"Do you?"

"Let's just be in the moment."

"I am in the moment."

"Clearly you're not."

"I've been trying to be in the moment, but every time I see that wedding ring on your finger, I keep wondering what we're doing."

"We're having an amazing time."

"Are we?"

"Look, just don't go there. It's too much for me right now, okay?"

I quickly learned she possessed an uncanny talent for shutting down unwanted conversations.

An uneasy silence fell between us, and in the darkness of the night I felt like a puppy that had just been reprimanded. I was aggravated that she shut me down so abruptly and disappointed in myself that I couldn't control my emotions, take the situation for what it was, and just be in the present moment. My analytical mind would have none of that, however. *Why the fuck did I have to travel to the other side of the world only to fall in love with a married woman?*

We both lay on our backs in what felt like an impenetrable silence. After some time brooding in the darkness, I tucked my puppy tail between my legs, rolled over, and kissed her on forehead. "Well then…I guess this is a great exercise in being in the moment. Good night."

"*We* can't be right now," she quickly shot back. "I have to go home to sort my life out and you're going to Germany. Then you're going to Italy for three months to work on your book, remember?"

"I do. Thanks for the reminder."

I didn't sleep much that night. The conclusion I finally came up with, at least the one that let me rest, was that at the very least we were catalysts placed in each other's lives to move in a direction, whatever direction that might be. For Cassandra, I could only guess it was to see what was on the other side of a relationship that had grown stale. For me, perhaps it was time to let go, open up my heart, and take a risk. At the very least, our time together could serve as an exercise in removing the bubble wrap that for years had protected my heart.

When I awoke the following morning for my practice, I was crestfallen, physically exhausted, and emotionally disappointed. I wanted to go deeper into the poses, but I struggled.

I was frustrated.

It was too hot.

The person to the left of me was breathing heavy.

The person behind me was sighing.

Someone farted, although that was somewhat comical.

And just a row ahead of me to my right was Cassandra, her toned body accentuated by her sporty yoga outfit. The object of my affection was within arm's reach and yet so far away. If this was how I appeared to women in my past, I was certainly paying my karmic debt.

Over the course of the previous year, Cassandra and I had Skyped in great depth about her faltering relationship with her husband, but face-to-face in Sri Lanka, I couldn't even mention his name. Life was complicated, and the hard truth—one that seemed to show its face time and time again in my life—was that sometimes love wasn't enough.

***

On Easter Sunday we set up camp on the beach. I was reading the book *Unbroken* and she was sunning. Occasionally we'd look over at each other and smile or hold hands—all the things that people in love do. She had a shirt over her face and I couldn't help but look at her brown, baking body, following the beads of sweat that rolled down her chest and stomach, forming a pool of sweat in her belly button. I was engrossed in both her and the book, but as I reached the last page, I was overwhelmed with emotion. It wasn't so much Cassandra and our unrequited love; it was the story of Louis Zamperini's life, a downed World War II pilot who went through hell, lived to tell about it, and forgave his persecutors.

Not wanting to disturb Cassandra and not feeling like sharing what I was feeling, I went for a walk, eventually finding a rock outcropping to sit on. Outwardly, I was surrounded by sand and palm trees as the crashing waves of the Laccadive Sea threw spray and mist into the air.

Inwardly, images of Easters past played before me like a carousel slide projector—Easter egg hunts, cousins playing basketball before dinner, the men drinking liquor and chatting, the women doing the same while prepping dinner. Anytime I read about God, love, forgiveness, or matters of the heart, something familiar overtook me and brought me to tears, and considering the book was a WWII story, I couldn't help but think of my father. He was a man of few words, but they were always wise. I wished I could ask him what I was supposed to do in this situation with Cassandra. It had been eight years since he passed away. Still, when I tried to reflect on who he was and feel his being, the pain could be as raw as that first week he was gone.

Unbeknownst to Cassandra, that night I had arranged a romantic dinner on a secluded beach. I made an excuse that afternoon to go into town alone where I purchased candles and a bag of ice. Since I arrived in Sri Lanka, I had hidden in my possession a bottle of rosé and a bottle of champagne that I purchased in Colombo. While she napped, I brought the rosé, the candles, and the ice down to the beach and gave them to the man who would be making our dinner.

When evening finally came, I insisted we take a walk to the beach to watch the sunset. We made our way through the jungle, and when we reached the beach, we were completely alone (except for our friend who was preparing us dinner, of course). In the tiny beach cabana, a candlelit dinner awaited us.

"Guess what?" I said. "This nice gentleman is making us an Easter feast. How do lobster, prawns, and rosé sound?"

"Oh my God," she said, folding her hands over her mouth when she saw the table, tears forming in her eyes. "Thomas, I don't know what to say."

"How about bon appétit?"

We ate like royalty, and when dinner was over, the man packed up and left. I then spread out a blanket and candles on the beach where we enfolded our bodies into each other beneath a nearly full moon.

"You know what?" I said. "From the moment I started thinking about this trip and through all the planning, with everywhere I've traveled and everything I've done, this is all I ever wanted—to be on a beach underneath the moon, waves crashing around me, with someone I love in my arms. I love you. I don't know what's going to happen, but I've fallen in love with you. It's freaking me out, but I'm just going to be present to it."

"Thomas, I love you too. I didn't intend for this to be so complicated, but it's more complicated than I ever could have imagined. I didn't want to face it, but I fell in love with you a year ago. It's why I had to come see you." With a heavy sigh, she fell deeper into me.

We went back to our room and talked into the early hours of the morning, sharing our past and our hopes for the future. I told her how it took me five years to get over the first love of my life and how when it came to matters of the heart, I didn't always know how to negotiate my feelings. While I intellectually understood how to love someone, I didn't know how to live it. I could leap into the unknown by purchasing a one-way ticket to India and traveling alone around Southeast Asia for a year, yet there was a part of me that was so fragile and vulnerable that I had no idea how to give my heart away.

As I told her the story, I became aware that these were not the thoughts and feelings of a man but the wounds of a boy. Whenever I grew close to someone, the wounds formed a moat between that person and me. I rationally and intellectually understood how ridiculous it was that these thoughts and feelings from so long ago had been the driving force of my life up until now, but our bodies have a memory of their own—memory encoded in feelings. Sometimes the memories in our bodies are stronger than our will. And sometimes, until we bring them to light, those memories are the unconscious programs that run our lives. And sometimes, those memories become scar tissue.

And sometimes, part of adulthood is healing the wounds of childhood.

Chapter 34. The Anatomy of Consciousness

On the rare moments when my mind wasn't consumed with Cassandra, I was thinking about the writing workshop in Chiang Mai; specifically, I was still trying to figure out the central question to the book.

One afternoon, Cassandra invited me to a lecture given by Manuel, our yoga teacher from Mexico City.

"What's it about?" I asked her.

"It's called 'The Anatomy of Consciousness.' Just come."

Ten of us gathered in the space where we ate our meals. Above us was a thatched roof and around us three sides of the room were open to the air. Coconut and banana trees surrounded us, and through the leaves of the trees we could see the ocean. The sound of the waves and wild birds provided a steady soundtrack while the briny scent of the sea wafted up the hill. It enmeshed with the omnipresent scent of plumeria, which bathed the property in tranquility.

When we were settled, Manuel handed us each a stapled printout. He was tall, tan, lean, handsome, and bearded, and when I looked down at the title card of the lecture, it read:

The Anatomy of Consciousness Lecture Will

Answer Three Questions:

- What if our intentions and feelings really do create and impact the world in which we live?
- What if our perceptions, rather than our DNA, give rise to our genetic expression?
- What if the human heart is the most advanced technology on earth?

Holy shit, I thought. *There it is.*

These were the questions at the heart of my personal experiment over the last year, the answers to which could only be known through experiential discovery. *Holy shit.*

I had been trying to prove to myself that the intentions and feelings of my internal world actually had power and influence on my external world, beginning with the imagination. Thought and intention were the outward-bound signals, synchronicity and serendipity were the inbound feedback, and gratitude ahead of the event fueled the whole process.

Since late January when I took the writing workshop, I had been asking for the answer to the central question of my book, running over words, ideas, and combinations of words and ideas to try to figure out the right phrasing, the right expression, and here it was literally spelled out and placed right in front of me.

Whatever this expression of creation was that gave me life, whatever the organizing intelligence of the universe was that held 70 trillion cells together to work in unison for one goal, my life—whether the source was named God, the universe, energy, singularity, the unified field, Source, Allah, Buddha, Krishna, Shiva, or Christ—it had always been my desire to know it.

"There is a field that we are connected to," Manuel began, "and what we put into that field is important. Nature creates by bringing the past to the present, but the divinity of mankind—what makes us transcend the rest of the animals—is that we have the power to choose from the future what we want to bring into the present. This is the quantum field where all possibilities exist." I recognized in his statement the power of my gratitude-intention journal.

"We can reinvent ourselves through the way we think, act, and feel. Our perceptions trigger different expressions in our DNA. We don't have to define ourselves entirely by what we are made of or where we came from. Our mind is the master of our epigenetic code and perception is the wild card. Scientists thought there were one hundred fifty thousand genes that operate our being. There are actually only about twenty-two thousand. Where were the others then? What was controlling our predisposition to disease and other genetic expression? Our perceptions. It comes down to what is driving our biology. Is it stress and fear, or is it love and joy? And which of these two options do you think vibrates at a higher frequency? I can tell you, if it's the latter you are going to be a healthier, happier, more fruitful person.

"It's not a bad idea to ask yourself, how much of who I am is expressed through fear? After all, our thoughts are at the core of our uniqueness and our humanity. We write our genetic code thought by thought. You can think of the quantum field as the Internet. All information is stored there. Our brain is the individual computer, but all information is not on the computer. The computer accesses information through the Internet. The computer, or the body, is just the hardware. The brain is this super-transducer that is pulling information down from the server, the quantum field, and translating it into consciousness. The body is just the vehicle for consciousness. The body is a just a vessel where we temporarily house our consciousness so we can learn, grow, and experience. The ultimate expression of health is community, from the cellular level to organized human beings. Nourishment isn't just food. It's self-love. It's community. It's society."

It seemed easy in the classroom, but for most of my life I wasn't even aware of the inherited fear I had been putting into the universe.

"We do not come into life as fearful beings," he continued. "We come into the world as joy and unshaped consciousness. The fears we have within us are learned behaviors. Therefore, they can be unlearned. Each and every one of us has to find the strength and courage to let go of our old selves and the old feelings that do not support self-love. Self-loathing, fear, addictions—whether we realize it or not, they hold us prisoner. And what is on the other side of the prison bars and shackles? Freedom. Everything.

"My friends, we are alchemists. Our feelings have the power to create and impact the world in which we live. When you are who you are without apology, you step into your truth. Where can we find the truth? Increase the space between your thoughts, because that is the place where we find stillness. That's where you find truth."

***

Between teaching yoga, volunteering in town with children, and catching up with the many friends he had from his years of teaching in Sri Lanka, we didn't see much of Manuel. He had been sharing his story piecemeal, but one afternoon while Cassandra and I were sunbathing, he came down to the beach and joined us.

"Where are you from?" I asked him.

"I split my time between Sri Lanka and Mexico City. I've been here for about two months. I was supposed to arrive a month ago, but my girlfriend broke up with me. I thought there's really no reason for me to be in Mexico City right now, so I came a month early."

"I'm sorry to hear that," Cassandra replied.

"Thank you. It was actually quite devastating because it was so unexpected and I thought we were on our way to marriage. I decided that I was only going to feel bad for three days. For three days I mourned, barely got out of bed, and barely ate. But on the third day, when I decided my mourning was over, I got out of bed to answer the phone. Much to my surprise, someone saw me playing on YouTube and called me to audition for a band in London—I'm a percussionist. So I left home a few days later and auditioned in England. I've got a few more weeks here and then I go back to England to start preparing for a tour. One door closes and another opens if you let it."

After a few moments, he added, "It doesn't mean the breakup wasn't still painful, but our futures weren't in alignment. The journey started taking us in different directions."

Magical things seemed to be happening for all of us at the retreat. Everyone was on an inward journey in one way or another. The small property on the edge of a cliff seemed to be a catalyst, turning the yoga studio overlooking the Indian Ocean into a transformation factory.

"What's your secret, Manuel? You seem like you have this palpable inner light."

"I don't think there's one truth, but what I've learned in my forty-two years is that you have to look at life as an objective observer. The key is to not have attachment."

This was what I needed to hear and how I needed to look at my situation with Cassandra. I had no control over the situation with her. Even if there was no future, we had love in the moment. I could force and fret and try to predict the future, or I could surrender and realize it was all part of the journey. If the relationship with her showed up in my life, then it must have appeared to teach us both something. There were no guarantees in life, and loving someone certainly wasn't one of them. Love was a living, breathing, evolving intangible.

"Besides the negative thoughts I've been trying to shed, I haven't been attached to much in the last year," I told him. "When I left home a year ago, I never could have guessed I'd be here with all of you practicing yoga in Sri Lanka. I didn't have a plan. The only one I had was to go to Dharamsala."

"That's fantastic. In my experience, stagnancy breeds misery. You know, if I had another secret—and it's more for me—it's that when people ask me how I'm doing, I say, 'Things are unfolding at an exponentially fabulous rate.' Whether they are or not, I think the words—the lifeblood of ideas—put that in motion. Words and thoughts are energetic, and they do make a difference. Plus, nobody really cares if you're feeling shitty."

"I like that," Cassandra said.

"Well, you're both on the path and moving forward. Seems like you're aware that you just need to guide your path with intention and then let things happen. When things start to feel like they are out of my control, I remind myself that I am of Source and from Source, so I have to believe I am supported by Source. Plus, you're in the unknown, and that's a good thing."

"The day I left home, almost one year to the date, I sat next to an Indian woman on my flight from Newark to Delhi. She said almost the same thing."

"That's not a coincidence. I have to run, but I just wanted to say that there are a lot of interesting people coming and going, so thanks to both of you for showing up and being yourselves."

***

That night I awoke startled from a dream, only to look over to see Cassandra staring at me in the moonlight. I could feel the heaviness emanating from her.

"What's up? Everything okay?" I asked.

"I'm," she said, pausing, "I'm having serious anxiety about leaving you."

"What are you thinking about?"

"I don't want to talk about it."

"You always say that. Do you have any idea how tiring that is?" And with that, instead of engaging with a corresponding emotion, I rolled over and went back to sleep.

I was trying, as Manuel had suggested, to view our relationship objectively. No one was forcing us to stay on the island with each other. We were there because we both wanted to be there, together, and despite the physical distance we experienced for the past year, something kept us connected at the heart. What I needed to do was keep feelings and emotions from getting tangled in possible outcomes. I could view the relationship any way I chose, and choice would give me power and strength. The lesson for me was that when you jump into an idea that's bigger than yourself, when you create the intention from the heart and bring it into being through language and thought, you are supported by functionalities of the universe that you don't understand—and you don't need to. So I chose to let go of my fear of loving Cassandra, and instead I chose to love her as fully as I could in the moment. It was the turning point of the rest of our time together.

When I let go of the fear and the uncertainty of our future together, she seemed to naturally follow suit, and our interactions changed. Our connection deepened. We both found new ways to release and express our sexual energy, and every moment I spent with her I was falling more deeply in love. I finally stopped resisting it and surrendered. Me (the observer) overruled Me (the ego).

On our last night together, while she showered and checked email, I went down to the beach to set up a table with two glasses. I used a ziplock bag as an ice bucket to keep the champagne chilled that I had picked up in Colombo. A thunderstorm had just passed through and electricity still lingered in the air. To the west, out over the ocean, heat lightning lit up the clouds hovering over the sea. Straight ahead of us, a shimmering white carpet of moonbeams met us at the water's edge.

I brought Cassandra down to the beach and once there, blindfolded her. I led her to the table, and when she opened her eyes and saw the candles and the champagne, she cried.

"Thomas," she said.

We drank the bottle and took selfies of us laughing, hugging, and kissing, both knowing the photos would only serve as personal mementos since our relationship was a secret. We talked about our lives—mostly what we wanted out of them—and reminisced about what an extraordinary time we'd had with each other while carefully avoiding the topic of a future or that in twenty-four hours we would be leaving one another.

By the time the moon climbed well above sea level, we slipped out of our clothes and into the warm, gentle surf. As far as I was concerned, in that moment there was no one else in the world. I remember thinking, *If it all ended in this moment, I could die a happy man.*

*** *** ***

I am so grateful for:

1. Our romantic candlelight dinner on Easter.

2. Going to the Anatomy of Consciousness lecture and the insights it provided.

3. The transformation I've experienced over the last year.

4. The new understanding of gratitude I've come to know.

5. The new adventures that await me as the beauty of my life unfolds.

Today I intend and create:

1. To trust that whatever is happening is happening for a reason and serving my story.

2. To be an instrument of peace.

3. To maintain an elevated state of happiness, openness, and gratitude.

4. To always be working toward being a better person.

5. That my words will be read far and wide.

Chapter 35. A Tsunami of Goodbyes

On the morning of April 12th, exactly one year to the day since I left home, I was flying to Berlin while Cassandra was flying onward to Chennai to meet up with her husband and family for a wedding. Despite that minor detail, I was feeling calm and relaxed, like I was on the brink of something. In fact, I was on the verge of completing something I thought was never possible.

For the past year, I had been cooking a stew. Into the cauldron I poured all of the raw ingredients of myself, both good and bad. They were creating something new, and the pot was now on simmer.

***

Colombo was six hours away, and since my flight was at 4:30am and Cassandra's was at 3:30am, our plan was to return to Colombo a day early so we could drop our bags off at a cheap hotel, explore the city, find a nice place to eat, and perhaps even get a shower in before leaving the country.

Following our final yoga practice and breakfast, we said goodbye to our friends and jumped on a small bus that would take us three hours to Matara, where we could catch another bus for the final three hours of the journey to Colombo. Despite the convivial joy we felt at being in each other's company, beneath the surface was something neither of us wanted to think about—saying goodbye.

We found seats next to each other on the twenty-seater bus, and we held hands the entire time, stole kisses, and we each took one earbud so we could listen to the same music. For almost the entire trip we paralleled the clear, turquoise waters of Sri Lanka's coast, beyond which a single line on the horizon separated the cloudless sky from the sea. It was a beautiful day for a ride along the coast.

We made our connecting bus in Matara with plenty of time to spare, and by 2:10pm we were back on the road.

Ten minutes into the second leg of our journey, I saw out of the corner of my eye a man running alongside the road, waving his hands frantically. The bus swerved into the emergency lane and abruptly came to a halt. The driver opened the doors, and the excited man yelled into the bus, which caused all the passengers to leap from their seats and run toward the front. Cassandra and I remained motionless, wondering if we were about to get raided.

Without knowing what was going on, we felt a wave of panicked energy sweep through the bus. People reached for their cell phones and began yelling into them. Others ran out of the bus. I noticed more and more people spilling out onto the street from the nearby buildings.

"Something big is going on," I said.

When the bus began to move, the woman beside us realized we were the only people not privy to the information that had just been shared.

"Do you understand what just happened?" she asked.

"We have no idea," I replied.

"There was just an 8.9 earthquake in Sumatra, and there's a tsunami heading our way."

Cassandra and I looked at each, our jaws dropping in slack.

What? Holy Shit. No way. This type of thing can't happen. I'm just a tourist on my way home. My life is just beginning. How are we going to get out of here?

In seconds, a lifetime of thoughts raced through my head. My heart pounded and raced, a lump formed in my throat, and I felt as if I had just been punched in the stomach. I quickly scanned the tin-can death trap we were in, and I mentally devised a brilliant plan for what we would do when the wave hit the bus. I looked for things we could hold onto and windows I could kick out, and I scanned the roof to see if there were escape hatches in the ceiling (as if we would survive a massive wall of water smashing into us at five hundred miles per hour, not to mention how when hit with the wave, we would all be thrown around like dice in a Yahtzee shaker, and should the bus be thrown into a tree at that speed, it would wrap around the tree like tin foil).

By the time the bus pulled back onto the street, traffic had been reduced to a slow creep.

"What do we do? What's going to happen? Should we get out? Where do we go?" Cassandra asked the woman in a panic.

"The wave is supposed to hit land around 4:20pm. We're taking immediate evasive action and heading inland."

"Will we be able to get to the airport from there?"

"Oh no. You'll be spending at least the night. Maybe you will get there tomorrow, maybe not for days. It depends on the severity. This is very serious. We're near the epicenter of where the 2004 Christmas-morning tsunami hit Sri Lanka. Forty thousand people were killed. But the good news is we have advanced warning this time and should be able to get inland."

"Should?"

"Yes. As long as traffic starts moving."

In no less than five minutes, the road, which was no less than fifty meters from the coast, was gridlocked. Adding to the chaos, motorcycles and tuk-tuks swerved in and out of lanes while cars laid on their horns. Thousands of people appeared out of nowhere, moving as swiftly as they could along the side of the road with crying children in their arms, suitcases trailing behind them, and whatever else they could carry.

Cassandra and I remained speechless. We tried to call our friends at the yoga retreat to warn them, but all of the cell phone signals were jammed. Some riders on the bus got out and began running inland while an anxious, eerie silence fell over the bus. The driver kept a radio station playing, and every few minutes an emergency bulletin came across the airwaves in Sinhalese, causing all of us to lean in.

"What's going on? What happened? What's happening?" Cassandra asked the English-speaking woman beside me.

"They are just saying to remain calm and orderly and to evacuate all low-lying areas. There is now the possibility of a second wave as well."

A year to the day. A fucking year to the day. The best year of my life, and this is how it ends? While I panicked internally, I assured Cassandra that everything was going to be fine, that traffic would give way, and that we would be inland in no time. My main concern was to keep her calm.

"Well, at least we have each other. Imagine if either of us were on our own."

"Are you sure it's going to be all right, Thomas?"

"I'm positive. You have my word. I won't let anything happen to you. We've got an hour and forty minutes. We'll be inland by then. Worse comes to worst, we have another night to spend with each other that we didn't plan on and a story that we'll both never forget." I smiled at Cassandra, pulled her into me, and kissed her on her forehead as she wrapped her arms around my waist.

A few minutes later, an unexpected calm fell over me. A voice in my head seemed to speak *to* me rather than originate from my being: *There's nothing I can do but surrender. If it's my time, it's my time. At least I accomplished what I set out for—love and adventure.* Even more unexpected than the calm was the gratitude I found in that moment. Not only had I fallen in love with the beautiful woman sitting beside me, perhaps more miraculously I had fallen in love with my own life.

From my calm centeredness I decided to snap two pictures of Cassandra and me on the bus. Despite the circumstances, we looked happy, but more so we looked like two people in love, and I found comfort in that. If it was our time, it was my hope that if someone found our camera they'd see that we died with each other and that we both had smiles on our faces.

Outside the bus, people's faces were quite different. They wore the scars of the memories and uncertainties of a not-too-distant past. Meanwhile, I kept an eye on my watch and we both kept an eye on the sea. With every tick of the minute hand perhaps the final chapter of our lives drew closer.

An hour later we hadn't moved much more than one hundred meters. I was beginning to think we should start walking with the rest of the Sri Lankans, but not long afterward traffic finally broke and we made our way inland.

By 3:30 we were out of the tidal zone, and by 3:45pm we were moving freely along the interior of the coast. One by one, people disembarked from the bus until it was just Cassandra, the driver, a ticket collector, a Sri Lankan businessman, and me.

"You both stay on the bus," the businessman said. "The driver will take you to a hotel."

Finally, the tightness in our chests began to loosen up and we could laugh at the absurdity of the situation. While there was no telling where the immediate future would take us, at least we had each other, and most importantly, we were safe.

As 4:20pm came and went with no wave, we were the only people left on the bus. The island was still on high alert for the possibility of a second wave, and it could hit at any time within the next two to three hours. Neither of us could believe what we just went through. Still buzzing from the adrenalin, I wrote notes in my pocket notebook and Cassandra looked out the window in a trance.

"Holy shit, Thomas! Look!" she yelled, her finger tapping the glass of the bus window.

"What?" I said in alarm, expecting to see a wave surging toward us.

"We're back in Matara!"

"What?" I shot out of my seat. "Are you sure?"

"Yes, yes! I just saw the sign."

"What the...are they fucking stupid? Goddamn it! What the fuck are you doing?" My energy amped from one to ten in an instant, and I began yelling furiously at the driver as he tried to calm me down with hand gestures. Sure enough, we took a left turn onto a main thoroughfare, and straight ahead of us I could see the blue waters of the Indian Ocean.

The bus pulled over and opened the doors.

"What's going on? What is this?"

"Hotel. Hotel," the driver said.

"What? This isn't a hotel. This is someone's house."

"You stay here, man," another man said, speaking into the bus doors.

"The water is right there! We're not staying here."

My raised voice drew the interest of onlookers.

"No. We don't want to stay here. This is ridiculous. Does anyone here speak English?"

"I do, sir," a man said as a crowd gathered around the bus.

"Can you please tell the driver we want to stay at a hotel where they speak English?"

"Yes, but you safe here. Away from wave."

"Listen, man," I said, taking a deep breath. My heart was racing and my blood was boiling.

"Thank you," Cassandra interjected in a calming tone, "but we just want to go to a hotel where they speak English."

We got back on the bus, and after driving for a kilometer or two from what I thought was the opposite direction from the water, we turned left and there in front of us, once again, was the ocean—and once again we were driving toward it.

"What the fuck is wrong with them? What the hell is this guy thinking?"

Driving toward the water, my imagination was getting the better of me, and I wondered how quickly it would take a 500-mile-per-hour wave to hit the shore once we spotted it on the horizon. I watched the waters intently to see if they were receding. My entire body was again on high alert.

I continued to bark at the ticket collector, who spoke no English. Finally, we turned up a hill and made a slow climb to the top where he dropped us off at a guesthouse called the Italian House.

"This is a good sign," Cassandra said. "You're going to Italy, this is the Italian House. That's a good sign." Much like me, she was always looking for meaning, inserting narrative into every situation.

Two younger Sri Lankan men in their mid-twenties greeted us and brought us up to the third story where we dropped off our bags.

"Would you like to sit on the roof?" they asked.

"That would be great," I said.

They could feel our frazzled energy and did their best to calm us by bringing chairs and ice water with lemon. Meanwhile, we paced anxiously, looking out to the ocean.

"Do you have anything harder to drink?" Cassandra asked.

"All we have is warm beer."

"We'll take them," I said.

Cassandra and I spent the next two hours decompressing on the roof, drinking warm beer, and smoking cigarettes. In the distance, we could see the ocean, and every so often we broke out into hysterical fits of nervous laughter.

Each time we started to relax, an air raid siren sounded from the city center, followed by announcements from loudspeakers placed throughout the small town. As soon as the alarms sounded, our smiles disappeared as we raced to the roof's edge, scanning the coastline for receding waters. It was a stunning sunset, as beautiful as any I'd seen in Greece, Zanzibar, Cambodia, or Thailand. It was hard to believe that in such a placid scene, perhaps just beyond the horizon, lurked a wave of destruction the likes of which neither of us could comprehend.

We watched the sun fade out of the western sky, our view of the water partially obfuscated by the tops of trees. Across the street from us, Sri Lankans laid offerings at a Buddhist temple while evening prayers arose from a mosque in another part of town. In the distance, at random intervals, heat lightning and starbursts from fireworks lit the dusk sky. It was the Sri Lankan New Year, and the threat of the natural disaster had disrupted many of the celebrations.

The Sri Lankan boys fed us pasta and regaled us with stories about their experiences in the last tsunami, how homes and lives were destroyed, friends lost, but also how people came together and formed new bonds and relationships. By 10pm the tsunami warning was officially called off.

With more than enough time to spare, we hired their cousin to drive us the remaining three hours to the airport. Exhausted from the adrenalin rush we had been riding the whole day, we held hands and closed our eyes for a restless sleep.

We survived the tsunami with a bit of luck, and now there was just one more nudge from the universe we needed. Cassandra's flight had been a full day later than mine, but she was attempting to fly standby so she could get out at the same time as me. A few days prior she was thinking about changing her ticket, but I told her to keep her money because there was no way a 3:30am flight to Chennai would be sold out. I forgot India had 1.2 billion people.

After I checked in, I saw Cassandra sitting with her bags, trying not to cry.

"I'm the fifth person on the standby list. It's not looking good."

"You'll get on. Don't worry, you'll get on," I felt my father's faith say.

She was visibly upset and we were both exhausted. I felt terrible about leaving her alone on an island in the middle of the Indian Ocean. It was my old programming around lack and finances that dissuaded her from changing her ticket to flying standby.

Cassandra spent the next ninety minutes waiting at the ticket counter while I watched our bags. Every twenty minutes I walked over to see if there had been any status updates, but she dejectedly shook her head. She fought with all her might to hold back the tears, fighting equally as hard to keep her body upright from exhaustion.

We had been running on emotions all day, if not for the past several days, all of which were magnified by the lingering notion that we would be leaving each other shortly. The unknown future loomed before us like the blanketing darkness of night. But one thing was certain: This was not the goodbye either of us had imagined.

All I could do was wait helplessly as I watched people board their flights to Bahrain, Abu Dhabi, Mumbai, and parts unknown. One by one, passengers on the standby list were notified that they had made their flight. I couldn't bear the thought of leaving Cassandra all alone at the airport in Colombo, Sri Lanka in the earliest hours of the morning, so I considered skipping my flight and spending another day with her, even if we were stranded all day at the airport.

When it looked as if all was lost, fifteen minutes before the gate to her flight was closing, her body came to life. She jumped up and down, reached across to hug the attendant, and grabbed her boarding pass from the counter.

"Good luck, ma'am!" he shouted.

"I'm on! We have to hurry. Come on!"

We ran toward security and waited for what seemed like an insufferable amount of time. Once we cleared security, we continued to the gate. There were three people ahead of her in the boarding line.

"Oh my God. I can't believe I made it. Thank you, Thomas! Thank you for everything."

"You made it—we made it."

"Not exactly how I imagined this would end," she said.

"We deserve a better ending."

"It's not an ending. Just a goodbye, for now."

"A tsunami of goodbyes. This day has been a tsunami of goodbyes," I said. "This is perhaps the longest day I've ever had." I was smiling on the inside, but the corners of my mouth couldn't quite make their way upward.

"Can you believe that just happened?" she asked.

"I think this one's going to take a bit of time to process. I thought we'd have a nice dinner in Colombo, have a few drinks, make out on the waterfront, get a shower in, I'd get to grope you here and there in public."

She laughed and pulled my hand to her breast where I couldn't help but cop a feel. Then she brought my hand to her heart. "Maybe it's easier this way. We didn't have time to think about saying goodbye."

She looked up at me with her beautiful brown eyes. I remembered the first time I saw them in the Moon Temple coffee shop in Dharamsala a year prior.

"Ma'am, we're closing the gate. Please," the gate attendant said.

"Okay. Okay, I'm coming."

"You have to go. We didn't come this far for you to miss your flight." I pulled her close and kissed her, our lips rapt in embrace. "Email me when you get there so I know you're safe."

"I will," she said. "And email me from Berlin!" She put her hands to my face and looked me in the eye. "*Auf wiedersehen*. I love you, Thomas. You have no idea how much."

"I love you too. Now go!"

She kissed me, handed her ticket to the Jet Air agent, and disappeared through a hallway. She emerged behind a glass partition leading to the gangplank where she put her hand to her lips and blew me a kiss, once again mouthing, "I love you."

"I love you too," I said aloud. I walked beside her on the other side of the glass until she disappeared. Then I continued to stare at the jet for a few minutes, hoping I would see her face emerge in a window. But she was gone.

Exhausted, empty, and not knowing exactly what to feel, I turned to walk toward my gate. It was early in the morning. All around me life was happening. People were coming and going from here to there, in transit from pasts to futures, moving through new doors and closing old ones behind them. I was simply on cruise control, too overwhelmed to process any of it, yet completely aware of the monumental, cinematic moment that had just occurred.

The only thing I could think of as I walked through an unusually busy airport for so early in the morning was the image of Cassandra behind me in yoga that morning. She was holding her downward dog pose as tears streamed down her face. I knew what she was thinking; I was feeling the same thing.

After yoga, we showered together. She didn't share all of what was going on in her mind, but as we held each other beneath the stream of water, she said, "Thomas, you have no idea what you mean to me. I love you and miss you already. I don't know how I'm going to deal with this. I know I'm about to have a really hard time." Nothing more needed to be said.

I knew I was going to miss her terribly, but I also knew she was going to have a much harder time than me. I was free, unencumbered, and unattached, and she was returning to a structure that might no longer serve her. She would have to deconstruct that structure if we were ever going to be together, and a lot could happen in that time.

Less than twenty-four hours later, a new reality set in. Cassandra was anxiously on her way to India to meet up with her husband, and as far as I knew, I was on my way to Italy via Berlin to live the life I had always imagined. Because I was living in possibility, however, anything could happen. If the road took me in a new and interesting direction, I had to be open to it.

When I finally got settled in my seat aboard the Etihad flight bound for Berlin, I wondered if our lives would ever cross again.

Regardless, I was on my way to a new beginning.

EPILOGUE: SUNRISE

I'm alone in the front row of a small theater. Before me, from both sides of the stage, a curtain is drawn. I walk up to the stage and stand before it, but seeing as I have been here many times before, I know it's more than just a curtain. It's a veil, and I am terrified of whatever is behind it. I don't know if it's a thing, an energy, or a monster, but the thought of it has haunted me for as long as I can remember.

My instincts tell me it's dark and ominous. I want to scream, but I know it will only be audible to me. I want to run, but there's nowhere to hide. I'm terrified to discover what's behind the curtain, yet I'm drawn to it. But I'm going to do it this time. I need to know what's on the other side because whatever it is, it holds me prisoner.

Slowly I move toward the curtain. With every inch of ground I gain my heart races. I wonder if it's going to burst out of my chest. My stomach is in knots and I feel nauseous. But I climb up onto the stage anyway. I take a deep breath and reach out to touch it...

For the first time in my life, I touch the veil. Fearing it will disappear before I have a chance to see what's behind it, without hesitation I tear it down.

Before me is a pedestal, the kind upon which you might find the bust of a Roman emperor from classical antiquity, only upon this pedestal is...a mirror. I'm stunned.

That's it? A mirror? All my life I've waited to find out what this terrible thing is behind the veil, and it's a fucking mirror?

The letdown is deflating. I look around. No one. Nothing. With nowhere to go and nothing to do, I fix my eyes on the person staring back at me. The longer I gaze into his eyes, the more compassion I have for him.

I stare and fall into a trance-like state, and then…then something strange begins to occur. The two-dimensional mirror gains three-dimensional depth. Deep within it, from a center I cannot see, geometric shapes stream toward me—cubes, tetrahedrons, octahedrons, dodecahedrons, and icosahedrons.

With no former experience of such things, I sense I'm on the cusp of a mystical experience. *If I can just let go and move more deeply toward whatever is the source of this information…*

The image staring back at me begins to morph backward through time. I see myself at various stages of my life. I'm thirty-three and I take off to Africa to travel alone for the first time. I'm twenty-seven and I've just moved to Seattle from New York City after getting passed up for two jobs in the World Trade Center. I'm twenty-three and I'm traveling through Greece after college with my girlfriend. I'm eighteen. It's the summer before college and I'm filled with anticipation and wonder. I'm fifteen and trying to figure out how to make it through high school. I'm eleven and I experience my first broken heart. I'm seven and my mother is telling me I'll be repeating second grade. I'm three and I float in a pool for the first time. And then I am a newborn, coming into the world. I am crying because I am separate from whence I came.

When I see this newborn, I instinctually move toward him because I want to hold him, protect him, and tell him everything will be all right. It's just life. Out of the corner of my eye, in another plane of the mirror, I catch the reflection of my current form. My attention draws me toward this reflection.

A vortex appears in the center, and I feel myself being drawn into it. Without warning, the mirror shatters inward, pulling me into its field.

Into the vacuum the implosion absorbs me. In an instant, all of the matter of the universe and all of the energy of the quantum passes through the eye of a needle, and I am the eye. I feel as if I am gaining momentum, approaching what must be the speed of light. I sail through streams of light and frequency that I imagine to be layers of consciousness. Although I am moving at the speed of light, all around me hundreds of millions of fractals and mirrored fragments float like particles through space.

They feel like me. Perhaps they are my cells.

The deeper inward I am drawn, the more the particles begin to coalesce. I am ushered into a void where I sense time is not linear but is instead one eternal moment full of infinite possibilities stacked upon itself. The particles take shape as angled mirrors, and I realize I'm moving through a kaleidoscope. I see myself from new angles and dimensions, and in those dimensions I feel my connection to every living plant, animal, and being. The angles of the glass endlessly reflect off each other, and infinite possibilities reflect back to me. I'm enraptured in sound, and I recognize it as my mother's favorite song, "Clair de Lune" by Debussy.

For the first time in my life, I understand what it truly feels like to be fearless and infinite, to conquer death. I'm moving through a virtual reality, and just beyond the images of infinite possibilities I see a supporting cast of loved ones.

I recognize them as angels, guides, friends, and family—people who have been with me for many lifetimes in even more dimensions. They have been there in the background and foreground, surrounding me and propping me up for as long as there has been consciousness, always providing me with opportunities to experience, expand, and ascend.

I see how some of the most painful losses of my life served to uplift me and bring me closer to my light. Then I sense what has been holding me back my entire life. Like a boat towing a buoy through water, I have been tethered by fear: fear of my limits and fear of my boundlessness; fear of failure and fear of success; fear of my humanity and fear of my divinity; fear of living and fear of dying; paralyzing fear that at times kept me from moving in the direction of my dreams, suspending me in anxious states of disconnectedness, doubt, and despair. I sense how none of the obstacles that separated me from the dream came from outside of me; rather, they all came from within. It was not what was behind the veil that terrified me. It was not the uncertainty of tomorrow—it was my free will.

The choice was mine, and always had been mine, to choose how I wanted to live, what I wanted to do, who I wanted to be, how I wanted to feel, and what I wanted to think. It was all my choice and had always been my choice. I just had to will it into being by knowing that it existed as a possibility, and I was connected to that possibility through consciousness.

The information continued to download faster than the speed of thought, and in this telepathic communication comprised of light, frequency, and energy, in this heightened awareness I knew I was not suffering the pains of the world alone. *Pain is a common bond of the human experience. It is all part of a grand design. The pain is a vehicle that delivers us to our freedom if we can just see it with awakened eyes.*

There was power in this realization and even more power in its acceptance. Pain existed for healing, and healing existed for wholeness, just as the darkness existed to show us the light. It was a delivery mechanism for the evolution of consciousness, that thing we can't grasp or touch but can only name. Consciousness—the executive control system of the mind. Consciousness—the mechanism that allows self to reflect upon self. Consciousness—the field of information we are all connected to.

Transformation was not only the constant in the last year of my life, but it was also the constant in all of life and existence because transformation is change from one state to another. With every breath of expansion and contraction the universe has uttered, whether a nanosecond or 100 million light years, no moment has ever been the same. Nothing stays the same. The molecules and atoms around us are constantly being rearranged and reorganized through a field of time and space. Our job is to tune into those patterns and vibrations because they are full of information and possibilities, all of which are governed by our thoughts, observations, attention, and intentions. I understood this as the doorway to awakening.

And the telepathic download continued...

It's in the awakening we learn to trust life's expansions and contractions, its ebbs and flows, its darkness and light. It's in the awakening we learn that life is about the love and relationships we create—the moons and stars of our lives— those earmarked individuals we've been blessed with who help us stand when we've fallen from grace. It's about the beautiful and the ugly, the ecstasy of joy and the crippling effects of despair, about the drama and comfort that is family, and the dharma of our path. It's about the joys of birth and the sorrows of death, and the gradual decay and renewal of all things through which life cycles. The awakening is about remembering who we are.

Life is about learning how to slow down to the pace and rhythm of our *own* life and about having the faith to surrender to *our* life's design. It's about coming in line with the vibrations of our *own* tuning fork. It's about the mental, physical, spiritual, and emotional maintenance that is required for us to live successful lives. It's about learning how to love and forgive others and perhaps more importantly, forgive oneself. It's about how our thoughts are seeds that can serve us or deter us and about owning and tending to those seeds; after all, in the fruit of the enclosed land exists all possibility.

It's about not being afraid to lose yourself in the chaos of disorder while finding stillness in the order of the chaos. It's about asking the hard questions and being still so you can hear the answers. It's about service to your fellow human beings and leaving the world a better place than when you entered it. It's about putting in the hard work to follow your vision while trusting and surrendering the "how" of how it will all come to fruition.

This epic we call life is about all the elements of existence that when viewed through the kaleidoscope of the human mind can seem overwhelming and disparate, yet despite it all you must find a way to retain the flame within you—that flicker of hope that fuels possibility. Possibility waits for the right conditions to grow from a flame to a conflagration or from an acorn to a great oak. Move into ideas that are bigger than yourself, surrender the how, and become the conflagration. Why? Because the mystery conspires to support us when we're living in our truth, and the world more than ever needs truth...

As quickly as it all happened, I was back standing before the mirror. The veil was gone and I had a feeling it was gone forever. Instead, I saw myself for the first time—my naked, vulnerable, sensitive, whole, connected, and complete self, the one whose vision of the world was so beautiful and terrible that he thought if he truly stood in it the world would destroy him. The one who from time to time found himself lingering within the notion that it would be so much easier to die than to suffer the pains of this terrestrial existence. And yet in the past year I had not only felt but also welcomed the world into my heart. I stood in the world as a man, a sentient being, and I was still alive to tell about it.

***

"Ladies and gentlemen, we're on our final approach to Berlin. Please put your tray tables and seats in the upright position."

I awoke from one dream into another and looked out the window of the plane. Light was making its way into the eastern sky as "Clair de Lune" played in my Beats by Dre headphones.

With arms outstretched, I reached toward the ceiling. Then I leaned forward to stretch my spine when something shiny caught my eye. It was a 2005 buffalo quarter in mint condition, buffalo side facing up. I found it a little strange that I hadn't noticed it before, not to mention I hadn't seen any American currency in months. Nonetheless, I picked up the quarter, put it in my pocket, and looked out the window of the plane.

And I smiled.

I smiled because it took me thirty-seven years—one of which was spent traveling throughout Southeast Asia—to finally see what was behind the veil. It was not monstrous and consuming as I had always believed. It was beautiful and holy, and it had always been there, patiently waiting for me to love it.

It was my life.

Questions for Discussion and Reflection

What do you think happens between sunset and sunrise?

1. Imagination...Exploration

Thomas sensed that the only way to free himself from his soul ache was through self-exploration. Therefore, he sets out on a journey to discover himself and actualize the dreams he harbored since he was seventeen years old. Along the way, writing becomes an essential outlet of self-expression and way of being.

- What are your past, current, and future dreams?

- What actions and intentions need to come into alignment to make your dreams possible?

- How do you best express yourself?

- Are there thoughts, conscious or unconscious, that hold you back from the greatest expression of yourself?

- What kind of journeys have you undertaken (or would like to undertake) in the name of self-exploration?

2. Fear...Mystery

For a long time, Thomas lived a life based on learned behaviors and inherited fears, and through his year of travel, he was constantly confronted by them. While he experiences waves of other emotions, fear dominates until he finds his ability to conquer it. This culminates in his final attempt—and ultimate success—in discovering what lies behind the "the veil," the mysterious force that has haunted his life.

- From where are you living your life? Your heart? Your fears? Anxiety? Love? Compassion? Competition? Insecurity? From where would you like to live?
- How does fear manifest itself in your life?
- What's on the other side of fear?
- What kind of veils do we have in our own lives?
- Does society put up veils for us? If so, what's behind them, and why are they created?

3. Freedom...Gratitude

For Thomas, buying a one-way ticket to India and having the power to wake up and decide which way the wind would take him that day was freedom. The simple exercise of keeping a gratitude-intention journal shapes his reality while he travels and becomes a tool to help keep that freedom alive.

- What is your definition of freedom?
- How would you live your life differently if you had no limitations?
- Does freedom come with responsibility?
- Do you think gratitude has the power to shape our reality?
- No matter how big or small, what is one action you could take today (and repeat daily) to change your life? To change the world?

4. Change…Wholeness

Throughout his journey, Thomas realizes his unconscious thoughts, behaviors, and patterns have prevented him from growing and evolving. Therefore, he begins to bridge the gap between the internal world of his thoughts and the external world through which he moves in order to achieve a mindful, peaceful existence.

- Do you have habits, conscious or unconscious, that prevent you from changing and evolving?

- Do your mind and body act as one, or is one guiding the other?

- Is it possible to create things (e.g., events, jobs, synchronicities, serendipities, relationships) in life just from your thoughts and imagination?

- Which is more important—the internal world or the external world?

- In which "world" do you place more of your trust?

Acknowledgments

First and foremost, I'd like to thank whatever the generous, organizing energy of the universe (whether you want to call it God, the unified field, source energy, etc.) is for giving me this opportunity to live, learn, love, fuck up, grow, expand, and express.

To Phil and Sasha Downer, who are actually incredible uppers, for providing friendship, generosity, and a roof over my head when I needed it most. To my nephew Jack Shields, an incredible musician with a bright future, for taking on the challenges of writing the music to the book trailer, creating a soundtrack to the book, and reading an early draft. To Devin Kumar for filming the trailer and putting it together, Phil Vandervort for recording the voice-over, and my amigo David Llama for putting the finishing touches on it.

To Joe Dispenza for giving me an incredible, life-changing opportunity, for recognizing me for my talents, for teaching me new ways of being, and for being my friend and mentor. To Joe Whalen, my first mentor and idol—I wish you could have stuck around to read this. To MC Mehta for your wisdom and generosity of spirit, as well as teaching me so much about life and the environment. To Lucia Fernandez for your patience, devotion, heart, and teaching me so much about love. To B.J. Shannon, for playing a role and always being there. To Shaun Herron and Jesse Long, first for your friendships and second for funding different parts of my trip (directly or indirectly). To Mark Fairborn for years of friendship and for telling me to stay in Berlin. To Susan Dupre for pushing me in the direction of self-publishing, and to Sue Lundquist for putting me in touch with Lisa Umina. Lisa, thank you for being my publisher and guide and for introducing me to my editor, Jodie Greenberg, who trimmed the fat, provided thoughtful and insightful edits, and made this a much stronger book.

To Rosie McGowan for your support and being the first to read a rough version of the book. To my sisters Noel and Therese for reading a draft and giving me the perfect combo of heart and head. To Hillari Hamilton for being crazy and always listening, as well as being a healer and a light in the world. To Linda Hampton for your friendship, coaching, and being my 'Guardian Angel of San Miguel.' To Christopher Schelling, who didn't have to write me back when I sent him a query letter. Because of your kind words, I kept going and changed direction. To Matt Brown for providing encouraging words after reading a draft, in addition to not only designing the cover but knocking it out of the park. To Letty Cal for taking the great picture on the back cover of the book. To Mark Dion, whose Neukom Vivarium installation in the Seattle Art Museum's sculpture garden inspired the title. To Kim Malek and Kathleen Healy for being my West Coast sisters, as well as for the countless times you've made me double over in laughter. To all my friends, both near and far, who have been there for me and believed in me more than I've believed in myself.

Finally, I'd also like to thank my family—John, Therese, Noel, Carrie, John L., Chris S., Jack, Caleigh, Molly, Liam, Owen, Greta, and Wylie—who has shaped me, molded me, supported me, loved me, housed me, and held me up when I could barely stand on my own. And to my parents for giving me the seeds of faith and allowing me the space to grow it myself.

CPSIA information can be obtained
at www.ICGtesting.com
Printed in the USA
FSHW022323041118
53433FS